Edouard Kayihura

and

Kerry Zukus

PRAISE FOR
INSIDE THE HOTEL RWANDA

"This book offers a window into the real-life experience of those who hid in the Hotel des Mille Collines during the 100 days of the genocide. For those who have learned of this story only through the famous movie *Hotel Rwanda*, the story of Edouard Kayihura is a privileged opportunity to put reality to the Hollywood dramatization."

—LIEUTENANT-GENERAL ROMÉO DALLAIRE (RETIRED)
Force Commander of the United Nations peacekeeping force for Rwanda between 1993 and 1994, founder of The Roméo Dallaire Child Soldiers Initiative, Senior Fellow at the Montreal Institute for Genocide and Human Rights Studies, and Co-Director of the Will to Intervene Project

"Truth and reality should never come as a surprise to anybody, especially to those caught up with them. Sooner or later they will always come out. I would like to thank the authors of the book *Inside the Hotel Rwanda: The Surprising True Story...and Why It Matters Today* for providing an honest account of the daily challenges experienced inside the Hotel Mille Collines during the Genocide Against the Tutsi. It stands apart from the tales of those who have abused, manipulated, and diverted public attention and opinion from what has been endured."

—BERNARD MAKUZA,
Vice President of the Rwandan Senate, former Rwandan Prime Minister, and Rwanda's former ambassador to Germany and Burundi

"Historical truth is a slippery thing—even more so when the mass media is involved. The story of 'Hotel Rwanda' is complex and fascinating. This book adds new depth to our understanding of the Rwandan genocide and the episode that has become its best known symbol."

—STEPHEN KINZER,
award-winning foreign correspondent; author of A Thousand Hills: Rwanda's Rebirth and the Man Who Dreamed It; *and teacher of journalism, Brown University*

"Everyone who saw the movie *Hotel Rwanda* MUST read this book in which true survivors tell their story. While the movie indisputably raised awareness of genocide against Rwandan Tutsi, its distortion of facts created one of the most virulent platforms championing trivialization of that tragedy through theories of double genocide and related tactics."

—EGIDE KARURANGA,
PhD, professor at the Laval University School of Business in Quebec; President of Rwandan Diaspora of Canada, and genocide survivor from the Hotel Mille Collines

"I will never forget the eight days my family and I spent in hiding at Hotel des Milles Collines. I was only 13 at the time, but I remember like it was yesterday. Twenty years later, it's important that we continue to acknowledge and commemorate the events that took place during those 100 days through stories such as those captured in *Inside the Hotel Rwanda*. Also important is that we give thanks to HE President Paul Kagame whose leadership has inspired us all, and has helped turn the country around to become the success story it is today. The 1994 genocide is an important part of Rwanda's history and will shape the country for many years to come."

—Ashish J. Thakkar,
Africa's youngest billionaire, Founder of Mara Group and Mara Foundation, a nonprofit social enterprise that focuses on emerging African entrepreneurs

"*Inside the Hotel Rwanda* reveals the real story of the events at the Hotel Mille Collines during the genocide in Rwanda. It exposes the untruths and inaccuracies of the Hollywood depiction of the exploits of Paul Rusesabagina. It lays bare how Rusesabagina has been able to fuel his own dangerous political ambitions as a result of the twisted facts of the film. *Inside the Hotel Rwanda* is important for finally setting the record straight, and doing so authoritatively from the perspective of a survivor of the events. It is this heroic effort, and the continuing achievements of the survivors of the genocide to triumph over adversity, that we should truly applaud."

—David Russell,
former Director of Survivors Fund (SURF) and Founder of The Social Enterprise

"*Inside the Hotel Rwanda: The Surprising True Story...and Why It Matters Today* is a gripping first-person testimony of life inside the famous hotel that served as a sanctuary for over 1,000 souls during the 1994 Rwandan genocide. Author Edouard Kayihura is a genocide survivor who sought refuge in the hotel during a time when extremist Hutu militias, government troops, and civilian death squads brutally slaughtered over one million people. The author artfully blends his personal memoir with a *cri de coeur* for the future of his nation. Kayihura presents an investigative and thought-provoking case against the skewed Hollywood version of life inside 'Hotel Rwanda.' Beyond a personal account, this work attempts to debunk some myths surrounding life inside the hotel and uncover the truth. Along the way, the author strives to set the record straight regarding past and present-day politics in Rwanda. Kayihura tackles the dangers of genocide denial and elevates the role of everyday citizens and UN peacekeepers—not just those created by Hollywood—in saving lives during that turbulent period. *Inside the Hotel Rwanda* aims to depose genocide revisionism by showing that it is up to the everyday citizen to commit to never again be a bystander to such atrocities. It provides a beacon of light for those seeking to eradicate genocide around the world."

—MELANIE TOMSONS,
Executive Director and CCO of Never Again International-Canada

"For more than a decade, the film *Hotel Rwanda* has come to define a particular story and understanding of Rwanda. In this heartfelt work, Kayihura provides a moving tale from within that hotel and seeks to set the record straight on the events there and since. For all craving authenticity about that horrific time, this is essential reading."

—JOSH RUXIN,
PhD, Truman Scholar, Fulbright Scholar, Marshall Scholar, and author of A Thousand Hills to Heaven: Love, Hope and a Restaurant in Rwanda

"I thank the author for this genuine and true recount of the daily fears and threats, hopes and despairs, joys and sufferings experienced by refugees in the Hotel des Milles Collines. Edouard is presenting with humility and a heart-breaking accuracy the reality of what happened in the hotel, unlike those who abused, misused, manipulated, and diverted the world opinion with a far-fetched story for their own interests, fame, and self-aggrandizing agenda. To those, I say, just as Einstein said so pertinently well: 'Everybody is a genius. But if you judge a fish by its ability to climb a tree, it will spend its whole life thinking it's stupid.' To Edouard, you deserve due recognition in general, and particularly from those who were at the Hotel des Milles Collines for this tribute paid to their courage, endurance, and resilience despite the test of tribulations."

—WELLARS GASAMAGERA,
Director General of Rwanda Management Institute and former Rwandan Senator

"Edouard Kayihura's memoir about the actual events inside the famed 'Hotel Rwanda' serves as multifaceted rejoinder to the mythology that emerged from Hollywood's fictionalized version of the 1994 genocide. Kayihura, a survivor who took refuge in the hotel, skewers the self-proclaimed 'real-life hero' who supposedly saved thousands from slaughter. The actual heroic acts are countless, but they were not performed by the inspiration for Don Cheadle's character, Paul Rusesabagina. Instead, among those fighting against the genocidal extremists were UN peacekeepers like Lt. Gen. Roméo Dallaire, French ambassador Bernard Kouchner, and selfless citizens like Victor Munyarugerero and a refugee named Maria. Kayihura helps dispel the romanticized savior image spawned by *Hotel Rwanda* and inflated by Rusesabagina's publicity machine. We see how a taxi driver turned celebrity came to fancy himself a rival of the actual saviors of the Tutsi: the Rwandan Patriotic Army and then-General Kagame. This important book demonstrates the dangers of seduction by media-generated history lessons and the resulting damage done to the sacred memory of the victims of the genocide. If you want to become a better-informed global citizen and go beyond glossy feel-good images, read Kayihura's account of how twisting a story can spiral into a maelstrom of deception and divisiveness."

—GERISE HERNDON,
PhD, Director of Gender Studies and English professor at Nebraska Wesleyan University

"This is a serious and well-written reappraisal of the events at 'Hotel Rwanda' in 1994. Kayihura's survivor account demonstrates the gulf between media portrayals and reality, and shows how myth-making has done nothing to resolve the polarity of perceptions of the genocide."

—DAVID WHITEHOUSE,
a journalist in Paris, editor with Bloomberg, and author of In Search of Rwanda's Génocidaires: French Justice and the Lost Decades

"A chilling account by a Rwandan who was targeted by name and narrowly escaped death during Rwanda's time of genocide, his desperate flight seeking safety into the real 'Hotel Rwanda,' and his first-hand report on who really kept him and the other refugees in the hotel from being slaughtered."

—JOHN QUIGLEY,
LL.B. Harvard University, President's Club Professor Emeritus of Law at Moritz College of Law, Ohio State University

"Edouard Kayihura and Kerry Zukus's extraordinary first-hand account of the Hutu genocide of the Tutsi in Rwanda describes the violence of the genocide the struggles of the survivors, and both the community-building efforts and the corruption encountered by those who sought shelter in 'Hotel Rwanda.' The book dismantles and challenges some of the heroic accounts in the film on the topic and instead exposes some of the dark episodes in which some people profiteered from the misery of others, some betrayed others, and some risked their lives for others. Like *The Diary of Anne Frank*, this book provides a glimpse into the day-to-day life of people combating the insanity of genocide. The hotel became a safe zone for the Tutsi, the Hutus who did not want to participate in the genocide, the Hutus who needed a place to stay while they planned their departure from the country, and the UN peacekeepers. Interaction among these groups was complex, and the authors describe the delicate negotiations they managed in the face of constant fear and diminishing life-sustaining resources. The book is above all a story of humanity in the midst of an insane genocide. In the end, there are no heroes; there are only people willing to take a risk for the sake of humanity."

—AMY SHUMAN,
PhD, professor at Ohio State University

INSIDE THE
HOTEL
RWANDA

INSIDE THE HOTEL RWANDA

The Surprising True Story...
and Why It Matters Today

Edouard Kayihura
and Kerry Zukus

BENBELLA BOOKS
DALLAS, TX

Map on page xxvi was provided by http://www.d-maps.com/carte.php?num_car=25459&lang=en

BenBella
BenBella Books, Inc.
10300 N. Central Expressway
Suite #530
Dallas, TX 75231
www.benbellabooks.com
Send feedback to feedback@benbellabooks.com

Printed in the United States of America
10 9 8 7 6 5 4 3 2 1

Library of Congress Cataloging-in-Publication Data
Kayihura, Edouard, 1965- author.
 Inside the Hotel Rwanda : what really happened and why it matters today / by Edouard Kayihura and Kerry Zukus.
  pages cm
 Includes bibliographical references and index.
 ISBN 978-1-937856-74-8 (trade cloth : alk. paper)—ISBN 978-1-937856-73-1 (electronic) 1. Rusesabagina, Paul, 1955- 2. Kayihura, Edouard, 1965- 3. Hotel des milles collines (Kigali, Rwanda) 4. Genocide—Rwanda. 5. Rwanda—History—Civil War, 1994—Refugees. 6. Rwanda—History—Civil War, 1994—Civilian relief. 7. Rwanda—History—Civil War, 1994—Personal narratives. I. Zukus, Kerry. II. Title.
 DT450.435 K+
 967.5710431—dc23

                                                                    2013039794

Editing by Brian Nicol
Copyediting by James Fraleigh
Proofreading by Kristin Vorce and Cape Cod
  Compositors, Inc.
Indexing by Debra Bowman
Cover design by Sarah Dombrowsky

Cover photo courtesy of Getty Images, location:
  outside Kigali, Rwanda
Map of Kigali on page xxvii by Ralph Voltz
Text design by John Reinhard Book Design
Composition by Integra Software Services Pvt Ltd
Printed by Bang Printing

Distributed by Perseus Distribution
www.perseusdistribution.com
To place orders through Perseus Distribution:
Tel: (800) 343-4499
Fax: (800) 351-5073
E-mail: orderentry@perseusbooks.com

Significant discounts for bulk sales are available. Please contact Glenn Yeffeth
at glenn@benbellabooks.com or (214) 750-3628.

In Memory of the Victims of the Genocide
Against Tutsi in Rwanda
Requiescant in pace

CONTENTS

FOREWORD

THAT THE 1994 Genocide Against the Tutsi of Rwanda was allowed to proceed unhindered, accompanied by near universal indifference, will remain one of the greatest scandals of the twentieth century. The failure to intervene even amid revelations about the speed, scale, and brutality of the killing and the suppression of information about what was actually happening is a shocking indictment of those governments and individuals who could have made a difference and yet chose not to do so.

In April 1994 as the genocide got under way, I was in New York at the United Nations Secretariat, completing a book on the fifty-year history of the organization. My first interviews to investigate the circumstances of the genocide took place then. It soon became obvious that no tragedy was ever heralded to less effect, and my research showed just how many warnings of the danger to the Tutsi there had been. I would discover how the ideologues of Hutu Power had managed to seize the levers of power in order to put in place their plan to exterminate the Tutsi, mobilizing and manipulating the machinery of state for their campaign—even in the presence of a UN peacekeeping mission.

In the course of my research, I was fortunate to have access to a number of important archives. One set of documents comprised hundreds of UN cables sent from the headquarters of the UN Assistance Mission for Rwanda (UNAMIR). These were given to me by a Polish military intelligence officer, Major Stefan Stec, a UN military observer who had stayed in Rwanda during the genocide from April to July 1994. He had been a member of a tiny garrison of volunteers who, with their force commander Lieutenant-General Roméo Dallaire, had refused to withdraw with the bulk of the peacekeeping mission. The cables revealed how a core group of blue helmets, including Stec, had risked their lives to save as many Rwandans as possible. It was an inspiring story of sacrifice and bravery. Stec told me how UN protection had been provided for sites in the capital city where terrified Rwandan Tutsi had sought sanctuary—including in churches and schools. The site that afforded the most protection was the five-star Hotel des Mille Collines, located in the zone occupied by the deadly Hutu Power forces. It was designated a protected area with military observers providing a permanent UN presence and where the blue UN flag had flown for as long as the genocide lasted.

It was Stec who had stood in the lobby of the Hotel des Mille Collines early on and read the names of those who were to be evacuated to the airport.

"I had a Schindler's list of the people we were allowed to save," he said, "only those with the right visas to enter Belgium." A few blocks away, at the St. Famille Church, 5,000 starving people were trapped. Every night militia came to kill. Stec said, "We did nothing for them because no one there had any visas . . ."

It was with some dismay, therefore, that in 2004 I watched the film *Hotel Rwanda*, released for the tenth commemoration of the Genocide Against the Tutsi. The film was purportedly a true story and yet it did not once recognize the righteous stand and heroism of Stec and his fellow UN officers. It made a hero instead of the hotel's Rwandan manager, Paul Rusesabagina, who claimed that he alone had been responsible for saving the lives of hundreds of people who had sheltered there.

While being presented as unequivocally true and unenhanced, this dramatization did not tally at all with any of my research. Stec told me that he believed sparing the people sheltering in the hotel had been expedient for the *génocidaires*. The hotel had been a favorite with expatriates and had been the focus of Western press attention. There were several high-profile people sheltering in the crowded rooms, including prominent opposition politicians—both Hutu and Tutsi—doctors, lawyers, and a senator. Stec told me that exempting the people in the hotel from slaughter had been part of a strategy by the interim government, a way to obscure the fact that genocide was underway. With these people left alive, it was harder to claim that a targeted and determined genocidal campaign was taking place.

It was clear that there had been three components of the protection afforded the hotel refugees: the presence of the UN military observers, the attention of the Western press, and most of all, the discreet action of a senior French government official and a career diplomat in the Elysée Palace, Bruno Delaye, who headed the Palace's Africa Unit. On April 23, 1994, a military siege on the hotel was suddenly lifted within half an hour of making contact with an official in the French foreign ministry. The timely French intervention was later confirmed by French journalist Alain Frilet, quoting an anonymous, guilt-ridden foreign office personnel who had admitted that the rescue was proof, if any were needed, of the French authorities' influence over events in Rwanda.[1] Frilet later described being in Delaye's office during a grenade attack on the hotel and that he had personally witnessed Delaye make a call to Kigali. After the call, Delaye told Frilet the attack had been halted.[2]

Eventually, the advancing Rwandan Patriotic Front (RPF) forces became the fourth and final component of the safety and eventual freedom of the hotel's refugees.

This, then, is a danger to avoid: the mixing of fact with fiction. The Rusesabagina story has served only to obscure reality. It has usefully diverted attention from what really happened. And that is why

---

[1] Alain Frilet, "La France prit au piege de ses accords," *Libération*, May 18, 1994.
[2] Jacques Morel, "La France au coeur du génocide des Tutsi," *L'Esprit Frappeur*.

this book, *Inside the Hotel Rwanda*, is so important and why I heartily recommend it to all those who seek a better understanding of what happened in Rwanda. Written by someone trapped in the hotel, it is a truthful and heartbreaking memoir. The stories of the targeted refugees' solidarity and courage are awe inspiring. The role of the hotel manager is shockingly exposed.

Yet *Inside the Hotel Rwanda* is much more than a sensitive and poignant memoir, for it also seeks to address an important and pressing issue: the exact nature of the relationship between Rusesabagina and those who had carried out the genocide.

Some years ago Rusesabagina came to London to give evidence in court to try to prevent the extradition to Rwanda of four alleged *génocidaires*. During his testimony, he described the chief of staff of the Rwandan army, General Augustin Bizimungu, as "a good man" and he denied there had ever been "a systematic government-driven genocide."[3] The judge later decided that Rusesabagina's testimony in court had gone against all facts and evidence. He determined that Rusesabagina was "strongly allied to the extremist Hutu faction."[4] The judge's damning opinion of Rusesabagina added to serious questions about his links with Hutu Power—a subject this book powerfully addresses.

The revelations it presents are deeply disturbing, and the book provides enough evidence for those who have bestowed Rusesabagina with honors and awards to seriously question their judgement in this matter.

Fictional accounts dressed as fact do not advance our knowledge and understanding of this awful crime. Indeed, they set it back. The Genocide Against the Tutsi in Rwanda is a terrible story, but it

---

[3] The Government of the Republic of Rwanda v. Bajinya, Munyaneza, Nteziryayo and Ugirashebuja, (2008), http://www.trial-ch.org/fileadmin/user_upload/documents/trialwatch/Rwandan4Decision.pdf, para. 388–429.

[4] Ibid.

is made worse because its true nature continues to be deliberately distorted and confused.

—LINDA MELVERN
London
December 2013

Professor Linda Melvern is a widely published British investigative journalist and author. She is the second Vice President of the International Association of Genocide Scholars. Her book on the Genocide Against the Tutsi, *A People Betrayed: The Role of the West in Rwanda's Genocide* (Zed Books, 2000), is in its sixth printing. In April 2004, Melvern published her second book on the genocide, *Conspiracy to Murder: The Rwandan Genocide* (Verso), a detailed account of genocide planning, those who were responsible, and how the genocide was perpetrated.

GLOSSARY OF ORGANIZATIONS AND TERMS

African Great Lakes Region	Rwanda, Burundi, Democratic Republic of the Congo, Uganda, Kenya, and Tanzania
APC	Armored Personnel Carrier
AVEGA Agahozo	Association of Widows of the Genocide
AVP	*Association des volontaires de la paix,* or Association of Peace Volunteers
BBC	British Broadcasting Corporation
BK	Bank of Kigali
CDR Party	Coalition for the Defense of the Republic
CICR	*Comité international de la Croix-Rouge,* or International Committee of the Red Cross
CJC	Canadian Jewish Conference
CLADHO	Federation of Leagues and Associations for the Defense of Human Rights in Rwanda
CND	*Conseil national de développement*; the House of Parliament
Conseiller	Sector authority

CPPCG	United Nations Convention on the Prevention and Punishment of the Crime of Genocide
DRC	Democratic Republic of the Congo, formerly Zaire, formerly Congo
Entrée	Entrance
FAR	*Forces armées rwandaises*; the regular Rwandan army
FARG	Fund for Support to Genocide Survivors
FDLR	*Forces démocratiques de la libération du Rwanda*, or the Democratic Forces for the Liberation of Rwanda
G2	Rwandan military intelligence
Gacaca	Traditional system of community justice
GAERG	National Survivors Association of Graduate Students
Gendarme	Police officer
Génocidaires	Those committing genocide
GPI	Global Peace Index
HRRF	Hotel Rwanda Rusesabagina Foundation
Humura	Canadian Association of Rwandan Genocide Survivors
IBUKA	Kinyarwanda word for "remember"; umbrella body of genocide survivor associations
Ibyitso	Kinyarwanda for "intelligent people working for the enemy"

Impuzamugambi	Extremist Hutu militia group
Inkotanyi	Kinyarwanda for "invincible warrior"
Interahamwe	Extremist Hutu militia group
Inyenzi	Kinyarwanda for "cockroaches." Derogatory term used by Hutu to describe Tutsi or those who supported them during and prior to the genocide
Kangura	Extremist Hutu Power newspaper
Kinyarwanda	Native language of Rwanda, spoken by all three ethnic groups: Hutu, Tutsi, and Twa
Kubohoza	Kinyarwanda for "the taking over of unknown property"
Kurth Lampe	PR firm for Paul Rusesabagina
LIPRODHOR	League for Promotion and Defense of Human Rights
MDR	Republican and Democratic Movement; the MDR Party
MDR Power	Hard-line Hutu Power branch of MDR Party
Médecins sans Frontières	Doctors Without Borders (NGO)
MILOB	International Military Observer
MRND	National Republican Movement for Democracy and Development
Muhabura Radio	Rwandan Patriotic Front (RPF) Radio
NGO	Nongovernmental organization (generic)
NRC	National Human Rights Commission
ODR	Democratic Opposition Rwandan

PAGE-Rwanda	Association of Parents and Friends of Genocide Victims in Rwanda
PDR-Ihumure	Party for Democracy in Rwanda
Presidential Guard	Elite fighting unit separate from the regular Rwandan (FAR) army
Radio Rwanda	National radio of Rwanda
RFI	Radio France International
RPA	Rwandan Patriotic Army, military arm of the RPF
RPF	Rwandan Patriotic Front
RTLM	*Radio télévision libre des Mille Collines*, or Radio Television of Mille Collines
RUD/RPR	Rally for Unity and Democracy/Rally for the Rwandan People
RUD-Urunana	*Ralliement pour l'unité et la démocratie-Urunana*, splinter group of the FDLR
SURF	The Survivors Fund
Umuganda	A form of nationalistic community service under Rwandan President Habyarimana
UNAMIR	United Nations Assistance Mission for Rwanda
UNDP	United Nations Development Programme
UNICEF	The United Nations Children's Fund
United Nations Foundation	The largest source of private funding to the United Nations

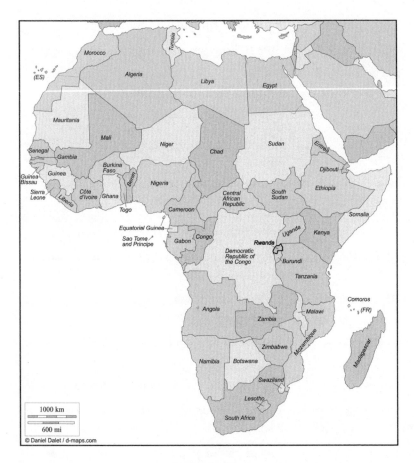

Map of Africa

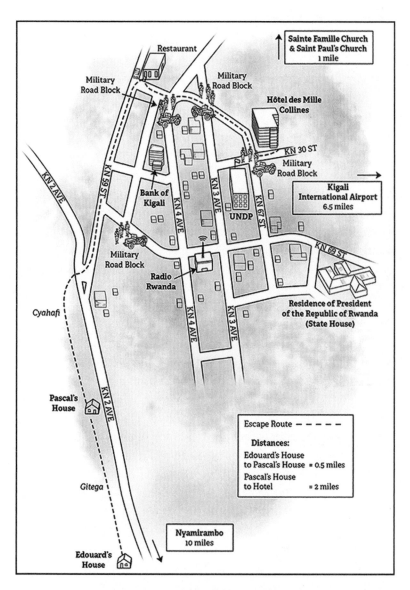

Map of Central Kigali, Rwanda

INTRODUCTION

I N A SPACE of just one hundred days, approximately one million Rwandans—one-seventh of my homeland's total population—were murdered by their fellow countrymen, slaughtered at close range with low-tech weaponry: machetes, spears, clubs, handguns, and rifles. The phrase "blood on their hands" was never more true than during those harrowing hundred days, for human blood splattered all over the killers and their clothing as they hacked at the objects of their hatred.

This genocide in the small east-central African nation of Rwanda, perpetrated from April 6 to July 14, 1994, by certain fanatical leaders and members of the Hutu, the largest ethnic group in Rwanda, against the Tutsi, a much smaller ethnic group, was by far the bloodiest chapter in the conflict between the two. The nearly one million who perished represents only the death toll of unarmed innocents.

The killing of civilians finally ended when the Rwandan Patriotic Front (RPF), an army of Rwandans organized primarily in diaspora in Uganda and led by future Rwandan President Paul Kagame, marched into Rwanda's capital city of Kigali and drove out the *génocidaires*.

With a death sentence staring them in the face if they remained in their homes or in public places, Tutsi desperately attempted to hide or flee. I, along with a scant few other Tutsi, was fortunate enough to survive the brutal genocide. I am among an estimated 1,268 Rwandans who sought refuge at the Hotel des Mille Collines, a luxury hotel in Kigali, one of a handful of places where large numbers of refugees found sanctuary. For years, the name "Hotel des Mille Collines" did not mean anything to anyone other than Rwandans, unless you were a foreigner who had stayed there, a United Nations soldier who had guarded the hotel during the genocide, or an affiliate with the hotel's Belgian parent company at the time, Sabena. But in September 2004, ten years after this holocaust, Hollywood released the movie *Hotel Rwanda*, purportedly based on what transpired at the Hotel des Mille Collines during the genocide. The film, which received much acclaim from film critics and garnered three Academy Award nominations, claimed to show the lives of those who sought refuge in the hotel as a microcosm of the genocide itself.

By the time this film debuted, I had been living in the United States for four years. Though I had stayed abreast of developments in my native country and had kept in touch with many others who had survived the genocide by staying at the hotel, I knew nothing of the making of this movie, so I was surprised when I learned of its existence. My curiosity was unbridled: Would the film be a documentary? A work of fiction? No Rwandan I talked to had the remotest idea. Neither the film's director and co-screenwriter, future Academy Award winner Terry George, nor his screenwriting collaborator, Keir Pearson, contacted any of the survivors I had befriended, with the exception of Odette Nyiramilimo (portrayed in the movie by South African actress Lebo Mashile). Yet before I learned about the movie, months before its release, Odette and I had not spoken for quite some time.

Few people are ever placed in a situation like this. *Hotel Rwanda* was not going to depict the entire genocide but only a small fraction of the story, involving a relatively tiny number of real people. It would be limited to the events that occurred in the hotel that had been my personal refuge during the genocide, much like a World War II film that focuses on the experiences of one army battalion, barricaded within the same foxhole for a hundred days.

It had only been ten years. The wounds, which will never go away, were still raw and fresh. The political analysis that historians normally do was still underway. Many questions had not yet been answered, and some remain unanswered today. I wondered how I would feel seeing this movie in a theater in the United States, sitting among Americans, watching something that, for all but me, would be depicting horrors that happened to others, far away, far removed from their comfortable world. Americans, if they so chose, could erase the horrible images once the closing credits ran. For me, though, it would be like watching a home movie of the worst nightmare of my entire life.

Hotel Rwanda was promoted as a story about "the quiet heroism of one man, Paul Rusesabagina, during the Rwandan Genocide."[5] I knew Paul Rusesabagina. All the people who survived inside the Hotel des Mille Collines during the genocide knew Paul Rusesabagina. No one among us has ever thought of him as altruistic, let alone heroic. On the contrary, of all the people who were within the hotel during the genocide, he would quite possibly be considered the *furthest* from a hero any of us could imagine. Rusesabagina had been a war profiteer, a friend to the architects of the genocide, a man willing to starve those without money while hoarding piles of food, drink, and riches for himself and his friends.

Given this, I couldn't help but wonder: How in the world did someone manage to put this film together and make this man a hero? Truth would not be served. I say this not because I believe myself to be a hero of this episode in time. I am merely a survivor. Perhaps all survivors of horrific circumstances could be considered heroes, but I tend to believe heroism requires much more than that. Heroism is the selfless pursuit of justice and right, the willingness to lay down one's life for the lives of others. Many people consider themselves to have this quality without ever having their resolve tested. Inside the

---

[5] "Center for Diversity," Rose-Hulman Institute of Technology, accessed http://www
.rose-hulman.edu/diversity/events07-08.htm.

real "Hotel Rwanda," some were placed in just that position: to see if we would act heroically when an opportunity was before us. I was not tested in that way, and for that I make no excuse or apology. But it is my honor to describe the actions of those who did find themselves at the crossroads of true heroism.

Shortly after *Hotel Rwanda* opened in theaters, I managed to find someone who sold DVDs of movies and purchased a copy. The film had not yet been released for purchase, and I did not realize at the time he had sold me a bootleg copy. I was a civil servant for the Rwandan government prior to coming to the United States and I would not have purchased something I knew to be illegal. Yet at that moment, excited, tentative, and unaware of the legalities, I took the film home to watch. I was with my wife as well as two young Rwandan friends—students who were only about twelve years old during the genocide. Just as I feared, the drama hit far too close to home for us. It was too much too soon. The students could not finish it because they remembered what had happened during the genocide, how many people close to them they had lost. At the end, I was watching the film alone, the only one able to stay bolted to my chair, refusing to give in to emotion and turn away from the horror.

As the film ended, I was filled with several strong, conflicting emotions. On the one hand, I was glad the movie had been made. It was educational, although inaccurate. So many people, particularly here in America, knew nothing of this genocide. They knew of the slaughter of white people at the hands of the Nazis during the Holocaust. They knew of the slavery of American black people before and during the Civil War. But *Hotel Rwanda* was about black people in Africa. Nothing could be more foreign to most Americans. Thus I was glad the movie introduced Americans to this tragic part of Rwanda's recent history.

On the other hand, the movie presented a story filled with falsehoods. I called many genocide survivors, both in the United States as well as back in Rwanda: Alexandre Nzizera, Isidore Munyakazi,

Jean Marie Vianney Rudasingwa, Egide Karuranga, Augustin Karera, Tatien Ndolimana, and Eugene Kitatire—all of whom had found refuge in the Hotel des Mille Collines. I told them about the movie, and every one of them wanted to watch it. Once they did, their reaction was the same as mine: Although it was good to see the movie raise awareness of the Genocide Against the Tutsi, as we have come to refer to it, the specific story about the hotel and Rusesabagina was wildly inaccurate.

After watching the film, we all felt the need to correct the record, to let the world know where the film had gone wrong. But who would listen?

Besides wanting to clearly present our vision of what really happened, we were, and are, concerned about the effects of the movie in regard to Rusesabagina. The "hero" of the Hollywood story, Paul Rusesabagina, in real life became an international sensation as a result of the film, a living saint on par with Oskar Schindler. Only unlike Schindler, Rusesabagina's cinematic tale was released while he was still alive, so he was able to reap the financial benefits by selling his life rights to the movie's director, Terry George; writing his memoir, *An Ordinary Man;* and public speaking, as the movie launched him as a person important enough for his opinions on politics and world affairs to be considered worth hearing. In fact, Rusesabagina has become a very popular speaker on college campuses and at major houses of worship across America and the world, speaking to audiences who saw his movie and are now anxious to hear his spin on African current events. For these talks he fetches upward of $15,000 per speech, plus first-class airfare and expenses, according to the American Program Bureau, his Massachusetts-based speakers' agency.

He has risen in prominence throughout the United States. The University of Michigan bestowed upon him the Wallenberg Medal, awarded to outstanding humanitarians whose actions on behalf of the defenseless and oppressed reflect the heroic commitment and sacrifice of Raoul Wallenberg, the Swedish diplomat who rescued tens of thousands of Jews in Budapest during the closing months of World War II. President George W. Bush gave him the Presidential Medal of Freedom, America's highest civilian award, presented for meritorious achievement in public service. He was even interviewed and glowingly praised by media icon Oprah Winfrey.

He has also been given a place in world history. Today *Hotel Rwanda* appears on school curriculums alongside such American and Eurocentric educational perennials as *A Raisin in the Sun, A Man for All Seasons, All the President's Men,* and *Of Mice and Men.* In educators' efforts to expand multicultural studies in the United States, *Hotel Rwanda* is now *the* African film to which high school and college students are exposed. It is one of only four films recommended by Amnesty International USA for human rights education, for which the organization has even created a curriculum guide.

In discussions with those who know nothing of the genocide except what they saw in the movie, some survivors are asked, "Are you jealous of his fame?" or "Are you angry the film has made him rich?" In truth, no; however, we wonder how someone could become rich and famous for something he did not do. In that sense, the movie could have been made about any one of us, with the same bounty as the end result. While this leaves a bitter taste in the mouths of many survivors, such feelings can in time be overcome by prayer and meditation. What is less easy to swallow is Rusesabagina's denial of the Genocide Against the Tutsi, which made him famous, as well as his threat to the peace and stability of our mother country, and it is because of this we cannot remain silent.

We should be concerned that, because of this error-filled movie, Rusesabagina has become a wealthy icon and has used that status to become a dangerous, divisive political figure, spewing false truths not only about himself, but about the past, present, and future of Rwanda. In public forums as well as in his memoir, Rusesabagina continually refers to himself as nonpolitical. Rwandans know this assertion is starkly untrue. Rusesabagina has always been political, not just since the events of the genocide, but also before and during it. While the film portrays him as a *bon vivant* hotelier, which gives him access to and relationships with the evil men who planned and executed the genocide, the truth is he was always active in the same political parties and movements as they were, present at meetings and conventions where their hate philosophy was discussed openly.

In speech after speech before audiences around the world, Rusesabagina has used his influence to champion "Hutu Power" politics (an ethnic hate-mongering against the Tutsi), raising money for causes that have less to do with peace than with revenge against current Rwandan President Paul Kagame. Most flagrant of the words Rusesabagina speaks are his attempts to paint the murderous actions of the Hutu Power extremists during what we came to call the Hundred Days as a natural byproduct of civil war and *not* genocide. Rusesabagina even testifies at trials on behalf of those who took up machetes against the unarmed, all the while blaming the victims and claiming they were the true murderers. As one of the most famous men in Rwanda today, Rusesabagina is the smiling public face of the murderous opposition groups who were driven out of Rwanda to end the genocide.

Shortly after the genocide, Rusesabagina left Rwanda and settled in Belgium, a nation that was the final colonialist ruler of Rwanda and that has been accused of exacerbating much of the hatred between the Hutu and Tutsi that led to the extreme violence of the latter half of the twentieth century. After the release of *Hotel Rwanda,* he also established homes in the United States. Rusesabagina has recently been charged by Rwandan authorities with using his nonprofit, American-based Hotel Rwanda Rusesabagina Foundation to raise money for his personal political ambitions, which include assisting in the creation of and having leadership roles in at least two political parties, and arming the terrorist army known as the FDLR—the *Forces démocratiques de la libération du Rwanda* or the "Democratic Forces for the Liberation of Rwanda." The FDLR is the primary anti-Rwanda, anti-Tutsi rebel group, composed almost entirely of ethnic Hutu opposed to Tutsi political representation and influence in the African Great Lakes region (Rwanda, Burundi, Democratic Republic of the Congo [DRC], Uganda, Kenya, and Tanzania). The group counts among its number the original members of the *Interahamwe*, one of the armed civilian militias that carried out the Genocide Against the Tutsi, and is regarded by the United Nations as a terrorist organization. It is composed of child soldiers and uses rape as one its main tools of oppression and terror. In June 2011, Rusesabagina was arrested by Belgian authorities and questioned on these charges as part of the process of repatriating him to Rwanda for trial.

With this book, I want to shine a light on what really happened at Hotel des Mille Collines: who and what got us there, who and what sustained us, and who and what really saved us and how. It is a story with no singular hero, for while there were heroes without whom all of us would certainly be dead, it is really about us as a group sharing horrific days in the same metaphorical foxhole, wondering how and when we would die. As for Paul Rusesabagina, each time we survivors hear him speak today it takes us back to our most primal fears, the recollection of a divided society where murderers faced no consequence and the protection of law excluded many. Everyone is entitled to his or her political opinion and philosophy. But fortune and fame give some people a louder voice. It is one thing when that fortune and fame are honestly earned. But Paul Rusesabagina is a fraud. He did not "single-handedly prevent the slaughter of more than 1,200 refugees at the Mille Collines Hotel for one hundred days during the Tutsi genocide from April to July 1994," as he advertises when he makes personal appearances.

His voice has been heard. Now is the time for the voices of the other survivors.

1

DIVIDE AND RULE

WAS BORN IN 1965 and raised in Gitesi Commune, Kibuye Prefecture, which is today referred to as the district of Karongi in the Western Province of Rwanda. Gitesi is an attractive city on the eastern shore of Lake Kivu, well known because of the beauty of its landscape, the sparkles of its waves, and the lushness of its islands. I grew up in a family of seven children—three sisters, three brothers, and me. I was baby number six. My family lived much the same as the average Rwandan family of the day. We were subsistence farmers. Corn, beans, peas, and potatoes or sweet potatoes were our daily main meal.

There was never a time in my life when ethnicity was not a dominant part of my existence, or the existence of any Rwandan of my generation. All Rwandans were mandated to carry a national ID card with them at all times. The most important piece of data on the card consisted of three words: Hutu, Tutsi, or Twa—the three native ethnic groups of our land. Two of the three words were crossed out. The one word remaining defined your total experience in Rwanda, much like a caste system, though, during my lifetime, far more evil. This, I had no choice but to accept. The sorts of tactics Hitler had used, with his various colored cloth badges sewn onto the clothing of citizens his Third Reich viewed unfavorably, had always been a part of my daily living. I knew no other way.

The Twa were the first indigenous people of Rwanda. Better known to the world as "pygmies," they are the least numerous in terms of population, and politically, they have been dealt with indifferently on the whole.

It has been said that the Hutu and the Tutsi of Rwanda are different ethnic groups, yet even something as simple and basic as this is open to debate. The physical differences between the two are often negligible due to generations of intermarriage. They also share a common language. There are no significant or relevant religious differences. Gerald DeGroot, a professor of history at the University of St. Andrews, wrote in the April 28, 2008, *Christian Science Monitor*, "those labels, 'Tutsi' and 'Hutu,' were meant to define the number of cows a family owned"—nothing more, despite anthropological theories that they were, indeed, different tribes. "During [Rwanda's] colonial period [particularly after World War I], the Belgians turned those otherwise fluid divisions into rigid ethnic identities as part of a strategy of divide and rule."[6] Unfortunately, the "divide and rule" attitude continued even after the Europeans were gone, but DeGroot's basic premise, repeated by many other Western academics, is questioned by us Rwandans. I asked people older than me about it and none confirmed this theory about cows. During much of Rwanda's history, Tutsi lived by their cows, while Hutu tended to farm. But no one ever said those who had cows were Tutsi and those without cows became Hutu. To be Tutsi or Hutu was a designation given at birth based on your father's ethnicity.

According to a 1991 census, Rwanda was 90 percent Hutu, 9 percent Tutsi, and 1 percent Twa.[7] I am Tutsi. Thus, I spent my entire life as a minority; and worse yet, because of when I lived during my formative years in Rwanda, I was part of an oppressed minority.

During my lifetime, a culture of strategic disenfranchisement and dehumanization was entrenched among our nation's leaders, even down to our schoolteachers. As children in school, we Tutsi

---

[6] Gerard DeGroot, "Rwanda's Comeback," *Christian Science Monitor,* April 28, 2008, http://www.csmonitor.com/Commentary/Opinion/2008/0428/p09s01-coop.html.

[7] "World Without Genocide," accessed December 2, 2013, www.worldwithoutgenocide.org/genocides-and-conflicts/rwanda-genocide

were asked to stand up separately, while the Hutu were sitting down. Or Hutu were asked to stand up while the Tutsi were told to stay down. While this did not cause anyone physical harm, it followed the classic pattern of how genocide breeds. Step one is classification: "us" versus "them." In my native Rwanda, I was "them."

In 1962, a few years prior to my birth, Rwanda became an independent nation, no longer a colony of Belgium. Just like in America, the 1960s were a time of social revolution in my country, though I was far too young to comprehend it. Beginning in 1959 and continuing throughout my lifetime, unrest between Hutu and Tutsi was a major part of our rebirth as a nation ruled solely by Rwandans. That year, 1959, marked the real beginning of upheaval, the throwing off of the shackles of Belgian colonialism, which finally culminated in full Rwandan independence in 1962. But a large portion of the rallying cry among the Hutu in our nation was that, in their opinion, the Tutsi were seen as an extension of the Belgians, and in freeing themselves of Belgium, Hutu had to take out their frustrations on all Tutsi. This was the wreckage of the Belgian-sponsored ethnic divisionism and its India-like caste system imposed upon us. Belgians could return to their own nation unscathed, but we Tutsi unfairly bore the full brunt of Hutu fury.

We Tutsi suffered greatly during those days. Some Tutsi were killed, while others were driven out of the land of their birth. Still others left voluntarily, hoping to keep one step ahead of those who would mean them harm. Because I was so young, whatever I came to discover about this time I learned from schools or from what I was told by my parents. Some of my father's family was killed during those days, while others fled to Congo—later known as Zaire, and later still known as the Democratic Republic of the Congo—but I never got to know them.

I witnessed true violence against my family for the first time at the age of eight. It was in 1973 and I was in the third grade. We had early release from school, and our teachers didn't tell us why we had to leave early.

When we arrived home, all the Tutsi men had gathered together to protect their homes. Women and children were asked to go hide in the bushes. Some men gathered on the nearby hill of Gitwa to watch assailants coming from far away toward our neighborhood. That is one of the things that stuck in my childhood memory—that the really bad people who meant us the most harm were strangers to us, rather than the people we saw every day. Our closest neighbors, the Hutu who lived in the same village with us, were less violent toward us. Perhaps that is what happens once people actually get to know one another.

A group of Hutu armed with machetes and spears overran our village. The Tutsi men soon went into the bushes when they saw the attack was so overwhelming and cruel that they could not put up adequate resistance. All night we could only see the smoke and flames of burning houses. It was a time of great harvest, but the assailants focused on burning our homes and spoiling our properties. We spent a week in the forest—frightened and scared. When we came out, we could only see the ashes. Our homes had been burned. Cows, goats, and everything we owned had been taken away. We spent many days in a shelter before a new, modest house was built to replace our old one.

My oldest brother, Alphonse Butera, the second oldest child in our family, was in his third year of high school. The violence of 1973 became intense in high schools and universities, and my brother was lucky to survive the roving bands of young thugs who spent much of their days beating those they labeled as their enemy, sometimes to death. Eventually he was expelled from school and wasn't given a chance to go back again.

It was in this same year that Army Chief of Staff Juvénal Habyarimana, a Hutu from the north, carried out a bloodless coup d'état and declared himself president of Rwanda. People thought he might bring positive change. Although he claimed to be a uniter who would put an end to ethnic discrimination, in the months leading up to his coup thousands of Tutsi were driven into exile, and

Habyarimana's extremist supporters called for our destruction, just as had happened during the Tutsi Massacres of 1959, 1963, and 1967.

In 1975, he created his own political party, MRND (National Republican Movement for Democracy and Development), which every Rwandan was nominally obliged to join, much like the communist parties of China and North Korea. No one was allowed to do politics outside it. The MRND and the Habyarimana government were one. Local administrations simultaneously represented the official party as well as the local authority. Governmental and party policies were communicated and enforced from the head of state down through these local administrative units.

A strict policy of ethnic and regional quotas was enforced in public service and education. Tutsi were restricted to only 9 percent of jobs in the public sector and public education. Hutu leaders pushed Tutsi out of their jobs, as well as out of schools and universities.

Seeing what happened to my older brother, I tried mightily to do whatever was necessary to stay in school and receive an education. It was not easy. An entire generation of Hutu had been programmed by the government to hate the Tutsi, hate them deep within their souls. As I look back, it is a credit to the goodness of humanity and the power of God that many Hutu resisted this genocidal ideology. Poison was being poured into their systems, yet some people remained immune.

> An entire generation of Hutu had been programmed by the government to hate the Tutsi, hate them deep within their souls.

Raised and schooled together, young Hutu and Tutsi occasionally embarked on a romance, but it was done relative to our native culture. A boy might be friends with a girl, but you would not see them together in public unless they became engaged, regardless of their ethnic difference or similarity.

Although the heart wants what the heart wants, other considerations were usually taken into account when a boy and girl from different ethnicities desired each other. Your identity was based on the race of your father. If your father was Tutsi and your mother Hutu, you were Tutsi. If your father was Hutu and your mother Tutsi, you were Hutu. Both my parents were Tutsi.

It was unusual to see a Tutsi boy marry a Hutu girl. Far more common were Hutu boys interested in Tutsi girls, and I would see far more intermarriage of that sort. Still, the families would often become upset; the government, too. If a Hutu who held public office married a Tutsi woman, he would rarely get promoted. In the military, intermarriage was actually prohibited. There were even regional biases. For example, if a Hutu from the north—Habyarimana's region—married a lady from the south, even if she was Hutu, she was labeled as Tutsi, or else somehow less desirable for marriage than a Hutu girl from the north. Some Tutsi women also felt pressured politically or in the workplace to marry any Hutu who wanted them.

As for religion, I was raised as a Christian in the Catholic Church. This gave me a chance to take the national high school state exam as well as the Catholic exam required to enter seminary school. I cannot say it was always my ultimate dream to be a priest, but Catholicism offered me an opportunity for higher education that might otherwise be off limits to me as a Tutsi.

As part of the political indoctrination of President Habyarimana's one-party system, all public institutions were required to participate for half a day each Saturday in community service called Umuganda to learn party ideology, and for another half-day during the week, to engage in nationalistic cultural and athletic enterprises. Government and private institutions competed in different activities like basketball, soccer, or dance to enforce MRND ideology. These competitions opened doors of employment to people who could perform well in certain sports and the arts. The minister of justice was building a basketball team, and I was recruited to play. I was good at the sport and the fact I was Tutsi seemed secondary to creating a winning team. I went there, I played with the employees from the Ministry of Justice, and weeks later I was asked if I was interested in officially joining their team. In order to legally be a team member, I had to be one of their employees. Thus, my first real job was in the prosecutor's office in Parquet Kigali, solely so they could retain my athletic talents. As an ambitious young man living in a society where I was discriminated against, I regarded this as a win-win.

In time, I grew to love the law. It was a strange relationship, though. In loving the law, I learned what it could do in the abstract, but also how it was not being fairly applied in my country. I could never imagine being given the opportunity to exercise my full abilities and knowledge, no matter how hard I worked. As a Tutsi, there was a glass ceiling above me, which I doubted I'd ever break through.

On October 1, 1990, the RPA—the Rwandan Patriotic Army, the military arm of the RPF—an army of mainly Tutsi expatriates who had been living in diaspora, began invading primarily from neighboring Uganda. Hundreds of thousands of Tutsi had been the victims of this expulsion, driven out of their homeland and made to settle as exiles elsewhere. Their exile lasted three decades. All successive Hutu governments barred them from returning, repeatedly stating that Rwanda is a small country that could not accommodate its own native-born refugees if they were to come back. Habyarimana stated that Rwanda was like a full glass of water: If you added any more, it would spill over; there was simply no place for those who had been driven out. The cause of the RPF was the right of return, just like Jews who wish to settle in Israel.

On the night of October 4, 1990, we heard the sounds of heavy artillery all night long. I felt so scared and found it impossible to sleep during the din of the nearby shelling. Despite not being part of the invasion, many Tutsi living in Rwanda were arrested in retaliation. As logical as it might have been for Hutu rulers of our land to feel just as scared of the hostilities as I was, I got the impression some within the government were almost enraptured, seeing this as an opportunity to crack down on all Tutsi. We were no longer a potential threat—now we were a real one. Early the next morning, the military and the government intelligence services went to Tutsi houses throughout the country to arrest intellectuals and businessmen.

One week earlier, I had come back to Rwanda from Burundi, where I had been visiting a family friend. I was accused of going there to plot with Tutsi refugees who were living in Burundi. I denied the allegations.

Ananie Dusabumuremyi and a man named Sibongo from the Rwandan Central Intelligence Service, along with military and the local authorities, came to my house to arrest me. Ananie was an old friend of mine. He was my classmate in high school and, like me, he was from Kibuye Prefecture. Seeing him gave me slight comfort, for I knew he would at least see that I was treated fairly.

I was renting a house with three bedrooms. Two of the bedrooms were open. They entered these rooms and searched everywhere for weapons. They found nothing. Their theory was that a Tutsi like me had been firing weapons the night before, adding to the ruckus caused by the heavy artillery fire. I was accused of having hidden the weapons they heard blasting that night.

The third bedroom was locked. A friend and coworker of mine, Aloys Havugiyaremye, a Hutu, was attending a training session in Murambi. Before he left, he asked me to watch over his belongings. During the weekend he sometimes came to Kigali to pass the night in that room, and he kept the keys to the room; I did not have a second set. Because his room was locked, they had to force it open. They went outside to get tools. Because of all the noise the authorities were making, my neighbors milled around and became convinced there were weapons hidden in that room. After forcing their way in, the authorities searched the room and saw a picture of my friend and roommate. Miraculously, they knew him personally.

Sibongo called one of the local militiamen, Hesron Ndenga, and asked, "Is this really who you call '*Inyenzi*' [meaning "cockroach"]?"

Ananie Dusabumuremyi added, "I know him personally. He is not a troublemaker. Let's go; we are wasting our time." Seeing the pictures and the belongings of a Hutu in my house convinced them I was innocent. They already knew they were arresting innocent people, but this crossed too far over the line for them. They let me go free.

Hesron Ndenga was working with me in the prosecutor's office as a typist. He was also a member of the local authority. He was from the north and had joined the CDR Party—the Coalition for the Defense of the Republic, a hard-line division of President Habyarimana's MRND Party. He had convinced my neighbors I was a bad guy and someone they would be wise to watch all the time. Having to work alongside this man who hated me so made my work environment tenuous and uncomfortable, to say the least.

Even though I had been "acquitted" in the eyes of those who broke into my apartment to investigate me, every evening from then on the local authorities would watch to make sure no strangers came to my house. There were now open threats against Tutsi working in the private sector or in government offices. In my office, we were labeled as "*Ibyitso*," meaning "intelligent people working for the enemy." Each night in Kigali, we heard the blasts of grenades. We lived in perpetual fear.

Earlier in 1990, under pressure from Western aid donors, President Habyarimana had begun to allow multiparty democracy, and other political parties began to crop up in Rwanda, challenging his dominance over the political system. Even though employees of the judicial system were not allowed to join any political party, most of the employees were siding with hard-line anti-Tutsi extremist parties, also known as opposition parties, depending upon how you felt about them. The majority of my coworkers affiliated with the radical hard-line CDR part of MRND, while a few of them from the south identified with the MDR (Republican and Democratic Movement), which was split between Hutu extremists and moderates. Violent crimes were committed everywhere, with no investigations or prosecutions. We saw the assassinations of some politicians. We witnessed the militias getting training and arms. We witnessed the preparation for genocide.

My coworkers included Tutsi as well as Hutu. I knew Hutu, I befriended Hutu; I supped with Hutu throughout my entire life. There were moderate Hutu as well as radical Hutu, just as people today differentiate jihadist Islamists from mainstream, peace-loving Muslims. Yet the general tenor of the country was creating more and more hatred of Tutsi among the Hutu.

When the RPA began making its way back into Rwanda in 1990, it progressed steadily and successfully until Habyarimana's forces held the RPA to a stalemate once assistance from France and Zaire had fortified his army. This deadlock forced a negotiation, one that should have put an end to hostilities. Called the Arusha Accords, the agreement was a set of five accords signed by the RPF and the government of Rwanda in Arusha, Tanzania, on August 4, 1993, ostensibly ending their war. The United States and France orchestrated the talks, under the auspices of the Organization of African Unity. The accords removed much power from the once-dictatorial Juvénal Habyarimana. Most of the power was vested into the Transitional Broad-Based Government, which would include the RPF as well as five other political parties that had formed a coalition government, in place since April 1992, to govern until proper elections could be held.

The Hutu-extremist CDR, controlled by President Habyarimana, was strongly opposed to sharing power with the RPF rebels, however, and refused to sign the Arusha Accords. Nevertheless, a cease-fire was signed while they were still negotiating.

As to the daily life of citizens during this time, I think of how some Westerners view most of Africa. We are not characters in a Tarzan movie, running through the jungle in loincloths. We live in cities with paved roads, we drive cars, we buy DVDs, we have television. Our clothing has designer labels. Our understanding of the rest of the world likely exceeds that of the average American public-school child. Unlike us, most Westerners do not know what it feels to have war standing upon their doorstep—not figuratively, but actually. The 1990s in Rwanda were rife with violence and terror, lawlessness all around, and hatred on so many faces. Tutsi were afraid to mingle, to meet with one another and talk. No more than two people were allowed to stand together in public. Still, we needed that. We needed the camaraderie of those who were in as much danger as we. Sharing those feelings somehow made us feel we were not alone. Death is a lonely experience, as is waiting for death.

After the Arusha Accords were signed, the RPF sent six hundred soldiers to the CND (*Conseil national de développement*—the House of Parliament) in Kigali to protect its officials who would join the transitional government. People who were no longer afraid went to the CND to visit them. I knew a few of them, such as Gaspard Musonera, Théoneste Mutsindashyaka, and Pierre Ndolimana—friends of mine who had joined the RPF. We no longer had to hide that we supported the goals of the RPF as we did before the Accords were signed. During that short period, our support for the RPF was merely looked upon as civic and political, not an activity to be banned or killed for. We all hoped for peace, while others continued to prepare for genocide. We were naïve; we were hopeful. We felt we had been given a respite from the pressures and tensions of living in this divided society, but it was short-lived.

When the Accords were first signed, at the *entrée* of the CND, the government assigned undercover presidential guards to work at the Ministry of Public Works and Energy. These men were to take down the license plate numbers of cars visiting the RPF and then follow them home to see where their drivers lived. From these activities, lists were created. Lists. We were not quite sure what these lists represented and what they would ever be used for. But they existed; they were real. Yet while plans for genocide were being drafted, we spent our evenings in Kigali with nothing riling us more than our debates about football and politics. Little did we know these were, perhaps, our last good times.

2

THE NIGHT THE FUSE WAS LIT

A FTER WORK ON Wednesday, April 6, 1994, I found myself in the Café Rion in Nyamirambo, Rwanda, about ten miles from midtown Kigali, our nation's capital (see map). An African Cup of Nations soccer match played on the television set but, as much as I enjoy the game, I could barely watch it. Instead I found my heart beating rapidly, energized by an ever-growing yet murky fear. Many denizens of the café were feeling good and cheering, clapping their hands when a player did well. With each passing moment I felt sicker and sicker to my stomach, unable to drink soda or even water. Maybe, I thought, all Tutsi were feeling the same dread that was gripping me that night.

I do not claim to be clairvoyant, but I felt that a national anxiety that had been building for days, weeks, and months was coming to a head. At 8:20 P.M., an airplane carrying Rwandan President Juvénal Habyarimana and Cyprien Ntaryamira, the president of Burundi, crashed as it prepared to land in Kigali, killing both men instantly. No nation or group accepted responsibility for the catastrophe. But a very short fuse had been lit, and the bomb that would change a nation forever was about to explode.

I left the café around 9:30 P.M. I was not yet aware of the president's airplane crash, though I couldn't help but notice people listening intently to their radios. I asked a taxi driver for a ride. I was living at the time in Secteur Gitega, a suburban neighborhood of Kigali-Ville.

It normally took me ten minutes to get home from the café. The traffic was light because the military had begun putting up roadblocks everywhere. Other people might have found such a sight unusual, but in Rwanda, I had grown used to it. Tension had been ratcheting up in fits and starts since 1990, and I was also frequently haunted by memories of the more distant past, based on tales from my father. We always seemed to be in a state of heightened military presence, right on our residential streets.

The taxi driver did not take me to my door, but dropped me off several blocks from my house. He claimed it was because of the roadblocks. I continued on by foot.

Unlike other parts of town, Secteur Gitega, the neighborhood I was in, had never been quiet; many militiamen lived there, each evening moving around patrolling the area. It was quieter now, though, because they were all gathered before their houses or in cafés listening to their favorite radio station, *Radio télévision libre des Mille Collines* (RTLM). RTLM was a private station owned by Hutu hardliners that received support from the government-controlled Radio Rwanda, which initially allowed RTLM to transmit using its equipment. Widely listened to by the general population, RTLM broadcasted hate propaganda against Tutsi.

Normally, the Interahamwe and Impuzamugambi—the two major Hutu extremist militia groups—would be marching around, controlling the area. Instead, that night, people were standing around in groups, whispering.

I passed in front of Buregeya's store. People could take a drink in that store, but no one was drinking at that time. The militias were lingering around, visibly enraged. Buregeya came to me and asked, "Do you know what happened?"

"No," I said.

"The president's plane was shot down and he is dead. The militias are in a meeting. We don't know what is going to follow next."

I was so shocked I could not reply. I went directly home. President Habyarimana was Hutu. I was certain his death would be blamed on

Tutsi. I was sure the next thing to happen would be the killing of my people. Genocide.

I cannot minimize the suffering any other person has endured since the beginning of time, for surely there has been far too much. Most humans go through life without ever harboring the acute fear of imminent death at the hands of another. It is the dream of each man and woman to live a long and fruitful life, followed by painless death in one's dreamful sleep. Death from debilitating disease can be a long, painful, undignified struggle, filled with agony and suffering. But few of us, thank God, will ever experience what it is like to realistically take into account one's entirety of being and say, "Soon I shall be viciously and painfully murdered. No one will come to save me, and no one will care." The impending explosion of raw violence that Tutsi were agonizing over was sure to be as vicious and primal as any hatred the world had ever seen. Tutsi, vastly unnumbered, would now be blamed for murdering the president of our nation. We, the unarmed few—not soldiers, but average citizens—would all be marked for death.

There were those who had been preparing for genocide, compiling lists of Tutsi citizens and spewing out hate on RTLM Radio. Now they had the tipping point they had been waiting for—one, perhaps, they may even have created. Now only the shrill voices of death and insanity would be heard over the din.

As I walked to my home, the air was filled with radio broadcasts. The nation had gone collectively insane. I heard voices saying unspeakable things. Savagery was all I could hear: *"Kill the cockroaches! Kill the cockroaches now!"* The words hissed like a slithering snake. I was no longer a human. We—all of us, all Tutsi—were now simply referred to as "the cockroaches."

By the grace of God, I managed to make it to my house and

> **The nation had gone collectively insane. I heard voices saying unspeakable things. Savagery was all I could hear: *"Kill the cockroaches! Kill the cockroaches now!"***

bolt myself inside. I walked around looking for evidence—evidence against me. My very existence as a Tutsi was now a crime. With the president dead, the government's standing army would no longer have control of the land. Militias, well-trained and heavily armed with machetes, grenades, rifles, and handguns, would now rule the streets. Genocidal chatter among the militias had been stirred to a boil for months leading up to this night. Plots had been hatched—we heard of it all the time, for the true believers were not ashamed of their politics of hate. Now the time for mass killing had come.

Newspapers criticizing the president or praising the RPF were illegal—banned upon publication. They were, as you say, "underground" publications. After President Habyarimana's plane crash, when I found any of these anywhere in my house, I destroyed them, tearing them into little pieces and flushing them down the toilet. Then came the music. Citizens were not allowed to listen to certain songs and recording artists who were considered "subversive." Any of those recordings that I possessed, I also destroyed.

Most of the music I listened to was on Muhabura Radio— Rwandan Patriotic Front Radio—a "pirate" radio station that did not censor music and artists. The RPF was a political party that began in exile, made up of mostly Tutsi, but eventually joined by some moderate Hutu who did not agree with the extremism, divisiveness, and genocidal ideology of the Habyarimana dictatorship. Those who had that subversive music or listened to Muhabura Radio were known as "cockroaches" or accused of "sustaining the cockroaches."

Now, I was sure the militias would come to search my house, just as they did in 1990 when the war began. I put everything down the toilet that I believed they could use as their so-called evidence against me. Even though I was spared arrest or murder before, I doubted I would be so lucky twice within such a short period of time.

I lay down on my bed, but I could not sleep a wink. Within hours, the sun would rise on a new world order: the first full, deadly day of genocide in Rwanda.

3

SHELTER INSIDE A WALL

A T DAYBREAK, I stood in my living room looking out of my window and saw my coworker and tormentor, Hesron Ndenga, walking up the street. A radical who hated Tutsi, Ndenga had instigated the search of my house in 1990, and now he strutted with the arrogance of one who reveled in discovering newfound power. Living in a neighborhood such as mine, you came to know very quickly and easily who were your friends and who were your enemies. This man made it no secret that I was his mortal enemy, although I had never meant or caused him any harm.

"Wake up! Wake up!" he shouted in the morning air. "There are cockroaches on this street and we must get our guns to kill them all! Wake up and find the cockroaches hidden in our secteur!"

I did not take his threats lightly. Ndenga was active in extremist groups, most of which were now armed. Even if he was by himself at this particular moment, he could have half a dozen comrades by his side in an instant, for there were far more Hutu in this neighborhood than Tutsi. We were surrounded and unprotected.

The government itself, which was supposed to protect us, was no longer functioning. With the president gone, there was a power vacuum, and constitutional protocols were being ignored as extremists were grabbing power. The police, who were exclusively Hutu, could or would assist Tutsi very little, if at all.

I ducked out of my home and hid. As Ndenga passed by my house without seeing me, I figured the last place he'd look would be right over his shoulder, so I followed directly behind him, hiding behind trees, telephone poles, and houses so he would not notice me.

At an intersection, he turned right toward Buregeya's store, while I kept going straight, constantly watching to see if he would notice me. Outside the store, I noticed militiamen gathering together to begin killing the Tutsi in Gitega. I scampered and ran, doing whatever I could to evade Ndenga's gaze.

I walked into the next secteur, Cyahafi. It was not far, perhaps ten minutes by foot. Slipping between houses and through people's yards, I headed toward the home of Pascal Hitimana—a good friend, a true friend, who also happened to be Hutu. Despite all the hatred and divisiveness within our country, there were always a few good people, people who saw beyond the madness and had a civilized, decent sense of humanity. Pascal Hitimana was such a man.

I knocked on his door. "Please, Pascal, they are looking for me," I said. "Can I stay here?" I did not have to explain the situation to him. By then the entire nation knew what was going on.

"Yes, come in quickly and shut the door behind you," he replied, and he quickly secreted me in his house.

I did not have a plan. I did not know for how long I would need the sanctuary of my friend's home. At this point, everyone was living moment to moment, second by second.

Secteur Gitega, where I lived, was known to be an unsafe area because it had so many Interahamwe, and most of the people living there were members of the CDR and the MRND. Some opponents of the president's government were living in Gitega, too, but they were few. I had chosen to live there because it was close to my job, and I had been living in that area even before the war started in 1990.

Initially, I did not hide, per se, in Pascal's house, but simply enveloped myself in his gracious hospitality. We talked, but neither of us had any grand schemes for my survival. It was like knowing death was omnipresent and unavoidable. The only question was what door or window it would choose to venture through—and when.

At 10 A.M., two people came to Pascal's house. I quickly hid, although I could easily have been found. I listened to their voices.

"Is Edouard here? We went to his house. Someone threw in a hand grenade, but when they inspected the wreckage they found no body."

A hand grenade. Tossed into my house with no more thought than someone flicking a cigarette butt. To the militiamen, it was nothing more. To me, it was my home. I felt violated to my core.

"No, Edouard is not here."

"After the explosion, they broke in and robbed him. The Interahamwe have shared all his belongings. We brought him these clothes we found at his home when we heard he was here."

> A hand grenade. Tossed into my house with no more thought than someone flicking a cigarette butt. To the militiamen, it was nothing more. To me, it was my home.

"That's very kind of you, but as I said, Edouard is not here."

It was a trick to learn whether I was hidden there, but Pascal was no fool. We—Pascal, Pascal's wife, and I—knew this would not be the end of it, though. I had left my house impulsively. Frankly, I was lucky to have even been dressed. I did not pack anything; I was not prepared to never again return home. I was in a white T-shirt and jeans, with a light jacket. It was entirely possible I would spend the rest of my short life in that one set of clothing.

I stayed trapped within Pascal's house throughout the day. Sitting like hens on soft eggshells, we heard shotgun blasts everywhere. For a time, no one else came to search his house. Apparently, they searched my neighbors' houses, but they could not find me.

Pascal's house was small, but he had recently renovated it, and his mother was living in a hut in the backyard. This gave the house some architectural quirks, of which we would soon take advantage.

In his bedroom there was a large dresser with a Sheetrock wall behind it. Inside the wall was a small phone-booth-sized room—not large enough to be a real, regular room, but enough to hide a man. I was able to get in and out of the room through a hole in the wall, which could be covered by moving the large dresser. Whenever someone came to the door, I hid in that wall space like Holocaust victim Anne Frank and her family in their annex.

Another night passed and I went again without sleep, simply staring up at the ceiling—praying, tossing, and turning. I listened for sounds and heard shouting, screaming, and gunfire, always gauging how close or far away it was. At any moment, I had to be ready to run, to hide—to do whatever was necessary to stay alive. I stayed right out in the open, in a room close to the front door, so I would notice any attempt to break in. If I heard something, I was to run quickly to Pascal's room and get back behind the dresser again.

During the night, I asked Pascal to help me leave town. I hoped if I had the chance to reach Butare Prefecture, in what is today the Southern Province, I would be safe, because I thought the killing would not reach that part of the country.

The next morning, he and I went to his car, which was parked by a bar named Imararungu. As we approached, we noticed his car had been vandalized during the night—destroyed, to be exact. It would not start; it would not run. We were trapped.

Even Pascal, despite being Hutu, was extremely scared. The radio hate-mongers were encouraging the "true believers" also to kill their fellow Hutu who gave comfort and solace to "the cockroaches." Pascal was now also marked for death.

Pascal and I tiptoed around his car and slinked around the neighborhood, doing whatever we could not to be seen by the wrong people. By the time we returned to Pascal's house, his wife informed us the militias had returned looking for me, but they had moved on after stealing her money. This is another dirty secret of slaughterers. Unlike real armies, they are far less disciplined and dedicated to their cause. Most are nothing more than common criminals and can oftentimes be bought.

In Secteur Cyahafi, they did not kill during the first day. There were not many militiamen living there, as opposed to my home secteur. It was shortly thereafter, when they tried to kill the secteur authority by throwing a grenade into his office, that the killing in Cyahafi began in earnest.

At 3 P.M. on April 8, a group of people armed with machetes, guns, and spears, and wearing the leaves of the banana tree, came to Pascal's house. They were making so much noise, whistling and yelling, "Search for cockroaches and wipe them out; wipe them out!" and singing, "Everything which is in the world is for Hutu!"

I was behind the dresser. They searched everywhere, but by the grace of God they did not find me. Once again, my fear was so great I could not eat or drink. Pascal told me to pass the night outside in the line of trees that fenced his house. The next morning I went to his mother's hut in the backyard. When they came again to search Pascal's house, they forgot to search the hut. His mother was old and was always sitting in front of her hut. I spent the day in her hut, and at night I went into the bushes and trees surrounding their property again.

Each visit from the militiamen was more frightening, more severe, and carried more blatant threats of violence. Pascal finally confronted me, emotionally racked.

"I am afraid, Edouard. They threatened my wife. I fear I cannot protect her. That is my first and most important job. I'm sorry, but the longer you stay here, the more danger she and I are in. They are going to kill us all."

Anne Frank found shelter from sadistic murderers for two years. In such a heightened state of chaos, I knew there was no way I could possibly evade the Hutu extremists for that long.

4

DODGING MACHETES

THE NEXT NIGHT, Pascal decided to take me to a man called Sibomana, a former *gendarme* (police officer) who had once worked with me. He was living at the bottom of the hill, just a few short strides from Pascal's house. I was reluctant to go because I knew Sibomana was a member of the extremist CDR Party—but I also knew I had no other options. When it became dark we started out toward Sibomana's house. Our movements were slow and stealthy, and we took cover wherever we could so as not to be noticed.

The closer we got to Sibomana's house, the more I shook with terror. "Pascal, Pascal," I whispered, "this is the one who is going to kill me! Please, let's go back!"

Conflicted, Pascal stopped to knock on the door while I hid behind a bush, but no one answered. Sibomana might have been my savior, but my instincts told me he was more likely to be my executioner.

We went back to Pascal's, and I returned to my restless bed among the trees that lined his property. I begged him to let me pass the night there and I would leave tomorrow. I paced and ruminated all night long, wondering where I could go when light reappeared. Fatigue and sleeplessness were beginning to cloud my brain. I was convinced these were my last moments alive. But for the sake of Pascal and his family, I decided to leave anyway.

21

Before I left the relative safety of Pascal's house, I took one final shower—I had no idea when I next might be able to bathe. Even during the short time I was in the outdoor shower, the militiamen showed up once more. Somehow, they had become convinced I was hiding out there, despite however many unsuccessful visits they had made to Pascal's house before. Little did I know how vulnerable I was, naked in that shower, completely and utterly defenseless.

They were menacing and overpoweringly angry, shouting constantly. The radicals had complete control of the suburbs, the small towns, the villages, and the countryside. Time appeared to be on their side. They could be like the lion, dangling a mouse by its tail outside the razor-like teeth of its expansive and voracious mouth.

"We know Edouard is here. Where is he?" they demanded.

Pascal addressed the head of the group. "You know I am Hutu; I cannot hide cockroaches." As they were talking, he discreetly put money into the pocket of their chief. This had become almost like a game, as the local thugs knew all they had to do was come knocking on doors in order to fill their pockets with money, whether they killed you that time or not. It was like American Halloween—trick-or-treat night. They had all the power. Killing Pascal, Pascal's wife, and me would have been so easy; it was merely sport to them now. They could have simply killed Pascal where he stood, taking all of his money, while tearing up the house and property until they found me and killed me as well. Pascal's house was set back rather remotely from the other houses in the neighborhood, up on a small, sloping hill. There was nowhere for us to run except out into the open, where they could shoot us down like rabbits. Why they did not do this, I do not know. Perhaps each man was making sure he got his equal share of Pascal's money, spreading the treasure around among his cohorts before finally executing us. We were that pathetically weak and trapped in contrast to them and their weaponry.

The chief pretended to be gathering whispered aid from Pascal before shouting, "Let's go, let's go; I know where he is!" The assassin grinned, took the money, and turned his back, the way one child gives another a small head start in a chase game. That is what our existence had become, only the stakes were our lives.

Even during the aborted plan to seek benevolence from Sibomana, I never felt betrayed by Pascal, for he had done everything in his power to save me. He had a wife; I was single. For once in my life, that fact made me the luckier of the two. Whatever I did, I only had myself to worry about. Men with wives and children were like cripples, unable to use all of their power to bolt, to run, to fight. They had to try to spread their concern among others, and that loving concern became the downfall of most of them as well as their families.

Leaving Pascal's house, I felt like a man committing suicide or facing the gallows. The moment I exited, the militias could be waiting for me, machetes drawn.

> Machetes had become the weapon of choice among the killers. They were cheap, like our lives had become. Furthermore, they were a painful way to die.

Machetes had become the weapon of choice among the killers. They were cheap, like our lives had become. Furthermore, they were a painful way to die. It is said most modern men prefer the physical and emotional distance of a gun. Today, the world's most powerful militaries use weaponry that can be activated and directed like a video game, lives being designated for termination from thousands of miles away. The Hutu extremists of Rwanda did not wish for such clean and bloodless murder. This was the level of hatred that had developed within our country. They far preferred to hack off the limbs and eventually the heads of their victims, reveling in the screams and awash in the blood. Wealthy men actually *paid* to be shot so their death could be quicker and more painless. Tales were told of wealthy men who paid as much as a million dollars to be killed by gunfire. Once the money passed hands, though, they and their families were often still hacked to death with heavy, dull machete blades, while their young children were struck against a wall until dead.

I began to think of how I could destroy my national ID that identified me as Tutsi, because it would betray me on my trek. I tore it into little bits and put the pieces in the trash.

I asked Pascal to travel with me until I got out of town safely, and he agreed. Perhaps he was worried I might end up on his doorstep again, further imperiling his family. I would not have blamed him for feeling that way at all. We walked cautiously, trying not to draw attention to ourselves. At times we even walked through vacated houses in order to get off the streets. I was without identification, and this in itself was as damning as carrying the ID of a Tutsi, for in this state of designated slaughter, who else but a Tutsi would be without his ID? It seemed like a good plan a few minutes prior, but now it appeared foolish. Militias ruled the streets and IDs were checked at almost every single block. Every one of them wanted to notch a few kills on his belt. Any excuse to do so would suffice.

I had to pass through Secteur Cyahafi. On my way, I decided to go to the sector authority—what other countries might call a county commissioner, someone with governmental authority and certain police oversight. His name was Michel Haragirimana. I knew him and he knew me, but I had no idea if he knew me as Tutsi. He was, of course, Hutu, as was almost everyone in any station of authority. He had moved his office to his home because the militias had thrown a grenade into his office when he balked at their command for him to begin ordering the killing of Tutsi with impunity, regardless of whether they had broken any laws. He had a policeman in front of his house now, acting as a bodyguard.

I asked the policeman if I could see Michel. The bodyguard went to tell him someone wanted to talk to him. Michel came outside and when he saw me, he invited me in, as Pascal waited nervously outside. Again, the word "suicide" ran through my brain. The police were no more to be trusted than a militiaman wielding a machete.

Each second could very well have been my last, and I knew it. But almost any idea that involved something other than slitting my own throat or wrists seemed worth trying. The result of every single thing I did was now in God's hands.

The purpose of my visit was to tell him I had "lost" my ID. He looked bemused. Both he and I knew there was no way he could possibly give me a fake ID that identified me as Hutu. Instead, I asked if he could give me an official-looking paper that simply indicated I had lost my ID. It was an odd compromise. He would not be vouching for my ethnic identity, but he would be affirming that he knew me, nothing more. This he agreed to.

Looking back, I wonder if people like Pascal and Michel saved my life, and I am sure on some level they did. But there was such a cataclysm of murder in the streets that I doubt either of them thought I would live out the day, no matter how much or how little they helped me. It was an overpowering feeling of doom. Thus, they may simply have been providing balm for their own souls, removing themselves from the personal guilt and blame for the death of one more Tutsi. Be that as it may, I bless them for their acts of kind mercy.

My plan was to leave the city by foot and go to the southern prefectures. I had no idea if we could get there or how Pascal and I could pass through the roadblocks. After getting the lost-ID paper, we varied our route, occasionally walking on the sidewalks like regular citizens, other times hopping fences or simply wandering through residents' backyards. Eventually, though, we had to go through the downtown.

We walked among the shops, sometimes even ducking into them if we felt a gang of people nearby was eyeing us suspiciously. No cars were driving through the city. I began to see dead bodies lying out like trash waiting to be picked up. Chilling. Sickening. And most of all, frightening. With each step, we found the dead carcass of what may have once been a friend. I envisioned this was how I soon would be.

This was to be my fate. My brain shot off hysterical sparks of nervous activity—what on earth could I do to alter this inevitability?

I saw a truck parked in front of a restaurant, with people standing around it. Nearby, there was a roadblock manned by children who had become killers as young as age ten or less. They were drunk, having robbed beer from the neighboring stores.

With my pseudo-ID in my pocket in case anyone asked, I saw the owner of the truck, who was also the proprietor of the restaurant. I looked at him and pondered. I knew he was Hutu. I was familiar with his brother, who was abroad at the time. I knew that he knew me. But how *well* did he know me?

Everything I did, I knew, might be my last act on earth. Not everyone I saw out in the streets was actively murdering Tutsi, but there seemed very little distinction between who was killing and who wasn't. Hate radio had stirred up such a furor that all Hutu were being threatened with their own deaths if they did not take up machetes and join in the massacre. Innocent passersby were terrorized and beaten if they did not demonstrate adequate zealotry in the destruction of the Tutsi people. The most vicious and radical ideology was forced upon every citizen. Free will and diverse thought were berated, threatened, or bashed out of every man, woman, and child. Beatings eventually transitioned into killings, voices of murder drowning out voices of moderation. Might had forced itself into becoming right.

I approached the man as he stood near his truck. It was the truck that I needed. The truck meant transportation, an escape from this small, residential area where everyone knew me and where the militias were actively looking for me by name.

"Are you leaving soon? Could you give me a ride to Butare?"

He looked at me, recognizing me but not seeming to have an immediate reaction of excitement at having caught one of the fleeing Tutsi. "Okay, but I cannot carry any cockroaches. They are stopping all vehicles at every intersection."

I said nothing. I looked in the back of his truck and saw ten other people, including members of his family. They all looked nervous. I did not know any of them. Apparently, many cars had been vandalized the night before, as Interahamwe and Impuzamugambi celebrated their "license to kill." People suddenly without their own transportation were looking for rides wherever they could find them.

Once I had settled in, the restaurateur shouted, "No cockroaches in my truck, all right?" Then he paused for a moment and asked for our IDs. The man was a mixture of hate and stupidity. There was no way I could show him my paper. Either he would not understand it or, believe me, he might call to the armed children in the street who had the roadblock there. And if by chance he did believe me, no doubt the rest of the passengers in his truck would have killed me for endangering them once I got inside. Either way, I was a dead man. I had to think fast.

"Do you know what?" I blurted. "I've decided to stay." It was not the brightest thing to say under the circumstances, and if I were dealing with anyone else I would have been dead where I stood. But this man was so absorbed in his own world that he couldn't care less what I did, so long as it had no adverse effect on him.

"Okay," he said. He started up the truck and drove off without me. As frightened as I was, I knew I had made the right decision. I was scared, but not out of my wits. I was not yet ready to die.

5

THANK GOD I WILL DIE WITH OTHER PEOPLE

ASCAL DISAGREED WITH my decision. "Edouard, *please* get on the truck!" he had implored as we stood outside the restaurant. But I was scared. It is hard for a man to admit such things, but the reality was clear: The killings had begun and I was a target. It was about survival, plain and simple.

As Pascal and I argued, I spotted another man I knew, who was employed at the Kigali electrical station two blocks away. He was also my neighbor. He was staring at us. *Now* this *will be the end,* I thought. He approached me and walked right up to my face, whispering in my ear, "They told me you had been killed. What are you doing here, alive and in the street?"

I tried to gauge his tone and intent. It almost sounded like admiration, as if I had bravely and miraculously escaped death. Bravery had nothing to do with it. Still, I was wary of him.

"Where are you going?" he asked.

"I don't know."

He looked past me and pondered the situation. He was not a close friend or much of a friend at all, more like an acquaintance. Perhaps, in only these few short days, the random killing had become fatiguing to some, while others only got more bloodthirsty with each subsequent murder.

Suddenly, an idea popped into my head. "Please, do you have a telephone I may use?"

"Yes, inside," he replied. "Use the office phone."

I had been listening to RTLM radio, which was being blasted everywhere, filling the air with hate speech, egging on the militias and citizens. It had mentioned that "cockroaches" were hiding out at the Hotel des Mille Collines, a luxury hotel in the center of the capital in a sort of "safe zone" that foreigners frequented. I was not sure whether this might be a true refuge now or simply a place where I could die with others like me. The only problem would be getting in. We might not make it that far.

I called the hotel. A man at the front desk answered. "I hear there are people in the hotel," I said. "Can I get a room there? Is it safe?"

"Yes," he replied, "there are people here. Come in if you can. We have room."

Finally, I had a plan of some sort, a destination. I carried with me no belongings except the clothes on my back, but somehow I was going to check into a hotel in the government center near where I worked.

I tried to convince Pascal to accompany me. Understandably, he was reluctant, but eventually agreed, and we took off together on foot. We both knew if we reached another roadblock I would most likely be killed. But the closer we got to the center of the city, the more we saw uniformed militia, not merely the ragtag Hutu extremists carrying machetes. The men in uniform carried handguns and machine guns. If they wanted to kill me, at least I would die quickly. Nothing caused more fear than the thought of slow, agonizingly painful death by machete or other blunt instrument.

A man on death row knows when his execution is scheduled. My execution was a guessing game, but it appeared just as inevitable. There is a strange feeling that comes over one in such a situation. When facing death, the fear is palpable; yet there remains the undeniable urge to live. At any moment I could have simply thrown up my arms and said, "I am Tutsi," and the torturous waiting would end. I could choose the moment of my own demise. Yet I could not do this. I had to play out each and every second. Was there hope? Hope never crossed my mind. Hope was inconceivable. Hoping would take away the sharpness of the mind of a man trying to make sure he stayed alive one more instant.

As Pascal and I got closer to our destination, things became quieter because no one seemed to be working or living downtown except for children abandoned to the streets. All the shops were closed. The few people still living there were hidden. We could hear the firing of guns.

As we expected, no sooner had we gone a short distance than we saw another roadblock. These impediments were less strategic than simply a flexing of manpower and power itself. Rather than drunken children, this one had military men armed to the teeth, along with an armored car and machine guns. We looked this way and that. There were no practical alternate routes. We had to pass through it somehow.

Pascal wanted to go back home. No one was passing through on foot; all we saw were military or government cars.

"Pascal, go in front of me and I will follow you. If you present your ID first, we may be able to slip on by." This is the same silly trick people have used for ages in order to sneak into movie and concert theaters. It usually does not work. Now, in my time of utter life-and-death terror, I was attempting it to save my own life.

Timidly we walked, first Pascal and then me. The closer we got, the easier it was to notice the soldiers were drunk, too, sharing beers with the children running rampant in the streets. As we approached, the armed men shouted, "Hands up! Put your hands on your head where we can see them!" As they got close enough to touch us, they screamed, "Get on your knees!" followed shortly thereafter by "Get down on the ground, face down!"

We both complied. They went through our pockets—first Pascal's and then mine. Pascal had the requisite ID, the one stating he was Hutu. They then found mine, which only stated my name and that

I had lost my official ID, along with an official-looking stamp from Michel, the *conseiller*. Before I could be asked the obvious question, Pascal said nervously, "We are going to the Hotel des Mille Collines. We left our cars there."

This was neither a confession nor an excuse, and it did not placate our interrogator. He raised his gun to shoot me in the back as I lay sprawled out on the road in the hot sun. Pascal yelled, "Please don't kill him! He is ours!"—meaning I was Hutu.

I am sure many others were lying in much the same position as me that day, yelling the same thing, perhaps even presenting ID proving they were Hutu, yet the fanatical killers murdered them anyway. I expected to hear a gunshot and Pascal probably expected to hear it, too, followed by another into his own back. But God shone down upon us. The soldier hesitated, then lowered his weapon.

"Get up! Get out of here!" he yelled at us, and we did as he said and began to walk away, still expecting him to fire upon us, albeit from a short distance. But amazingly he did not.

Once we walked another fifty meters, there was another military roadblock on the northeast corner of the Hotel des Mille Collines at the Rwanda Office of Tourism, on the road coming from the other side of the State House, which encompassed the office of the president, Rwanda National Radio, the Ministry of Finance, and the Ministry of Foreign Affairs. This area was heavily protected with machine guns, mortars, and armored cars. We passed the national radio station, the source of so much of this terror. It was hard for me to imagine that a radio station, something people were supposed to enjoy, could be as sinister and as responsible for death as a huge missile launcher.

The closer we got to the Hotel des Mille Collines, the more uniformed militias were replaced by regular government military, who stopped us just the same. The routine was identical: Hands up, hands on our heads, down on our knees, a search through our pockets for our IDs, looks of confusion and distrust when they found my non-ID, and some bellowing and bravado, but eventually we were again waved on.

Each second of each stop seemed like an eternity. At any moment, one trigger-happy soldier could decide to kill me simply for *suspicion* of being a Tutsi, or even merely a Hutu moderate, and no one would have said a word. Sweat poured from every pore of my body. I wondered if Pascal fully realized how endangered his life would be if I were to be recognized as a Tutsi. The thought made me feel guilty, but only for a moment. The human impulse for survival overrules all other cogent thinking. I was not betraying my heritage to anyone; I was not implicating anyone else. All I could say to anyone who forced me to talk was, "My car is at the Hotel des Mille Collines." Other than that, I spoke not a word. The soldiers seemed to prefer this.

Finally, the hotel was in sight. We had a short distance to go and we were passing along the fence of the Mille Collines. We saw in front of us another military roadblock at the northwest corner of the hotel. The soldiers at this roadblock were the worst. They shouted, "These, we want to kill!" For what seemed like the hundredth time, we were told to raise our hands, place them on our heads, get on our knees, and allow ourselves to be completely searched. For what seemed like the hundredth time, I answered their questions about my ID. They verbally intimidated us far worse than any of the others, screaming in our faces. That we could have both been their Hutu brethren mattered not a bit to them. We were unarmed and thus lacking all power. Things had degraded to schoolyard bullying and primitive incivility. How many nights had these frustrated little men dreamed of having someone to push around without restraint or fear of reprisal?

After making us sit broiling in the sun with our hands above our heads longer than we had ever done before, their leader finally pointed and said, "There is the *entrée* to the hotel. If they let you in, they let you in." The *entrée* was also blocked, but by the capital *gendarmes*. My final task would be to somehow get past them. If I succeeded, I would be where I believed to be safe. But if the *gendarmes* stopped me, that would be it. I would have come all this way for nothing. The inference I gathered from the attitude and tone of the leader was that if I did not pass muster with the *gendarmes*, they would simply turn me back over to them and I would be shot where I stood, for no one, no organized entity, was standing in the way of public killings. Civilized police or military law was no longer in effect. This was now an urban combat zone with a government in total chaos, being led only by an ideology of mass murder.

As I approached the entrance to the hotel, I recognized the *gendarmes*, who normally worked at the Muhima station. I knew them from my job and they knew me. I thought it was likely they also knew I was Tutsi.

"Are you going to take refuge in the hotel?" the supervisor asked.

"No, I left my car there. I am going to retrieve it."

He looked at me and chuckled. It was not a malevolent laugh, but the kind of snicker someone would make if you told them a really bad joke. He then waved me through the entrance, making sure his actions were seen quite clearly by the rest of the *gendarmes* as well as the onlooking soldiers.

Briskly, I walked by him, afraid for my life to look back. The first things I saw were the UN peacekeeping armored cars in front of the main door to the hotel. Above the hotel was the baby-blue flag of the United Nations. Was this indeed a place of safety and refuge? I prayed it would be. The walk from the entrance of the property to the front door felt like it went on for a mile, although it was not a long walk at all. I kept my eyes on that UN flag, half expecting to hear the sound of rifle fire as bullets lanced through my back, a final act of sadism cutting me down as I was mere inches from safety. But no rifles were fired.

Two UN peacekeepers stood at the door, one on each side. I breathed. I stepped across the threshold of the Hotel des Mille Collines—the "Hotel Rwanda." I entered the hotel and nobody asked me anything. As I entered, Pascal turned and went back home.

I could not feel true elation because I knew not what the future, even the very next few minutes of my life, had in store for me. But somehow I convinced myself that something good had just happened to me. A voice from deep inside of me said, *Thank God I will die with other people.*

6

SANCTUARY

A S I ENTERED the Hotel des Mille Collines on April 11, 1994, the first person I saw was a friend of mine, Jean Marie Vianney Rubayiza. He was standing in the lobby looking toward the entrance. He could not believe I was still alive. For that matter, I could not believe *he* was alive.

Rubayiza took me into his room on the third floor, number 306. I had no money except for a blank check I had absentmindedly placed inside of my coat. But Rubayiza assured me we could still go to the hotel restaurant and get food, despite having no money. Running into him and having him offer me space inside his hotel room had already solved my problem of having no cash or credit cards on me to pay for a room of my own. All in all, this was not a typical situation. Genocide was raging outside, the slaughter of innocent, unarmed civilians. The hotel had become a refugee camp of sorts. You do not profiteer in a refugee camp.

When I arrived, five days after the downing of the president's plane that marked the beginning of the genocide, there were already hundreds of refugees at the hotel. There were also whites from Europe and the West who certainly had not planned on being there on business or vacation during a genocide. They were stuck there along with us, unable to leave, with all the fighting and gunfire going on right outside the hotel's gates.

The Mille Collines was, at the time, arguably the premier hotel in the nation's capital, and thus the entire country. I did not know exactly how many rooms it contained, but I had never been in a larger, more luxurious hotel in my life. To go from the bloody carnage in the streets to this palace was like stepping from the front lines of a battle to an exotic vacation spa, complete with uniformed baggage handlers, background Muzak, and, above all else, peace and civility. The contrast was mind-boggling. And yet I was never completely seduced by the ambiance. I was deathly afraid I would still be killed, even in this comparative palace. UN soldiers walked the lobby—whites; Africans from Senegal, Ghana, and Tunisia; South Asians from Bangladesh—all in their trademark apparel. Even odder, the occasional militiaman passed through, wearing the unofficial uniform, a blousy and colorfully flowered tunic. My first impulse was to avert my eyes and hope not to be identified as Tutsi and be dragged out to be slaughtered. Yet I saw no killing within the hotel, nor did the militias brandish their weapons once inside. It was odd, as if there was some unspoken rule calling for a "time out." If only such a sentiment were honestly true, for none of us believed it.

Alexis Vuningoma worked in the hotel and was especially kind to people like Rubayiza and me. "I have been here since the night of April sixth," he confided. "I've not been able to leave. I am on the list of people who are supposed to die."

"What of your family?"

His face visibly saddened. "I pray they are alive. I want to bring them here but I don't know how. I'm trying to borrow money from the other employees so I can pay someone off to bring them here."

Taking us into his confidence, he said, "The first refugees arrived in the hotel on April seventh. They were foreigners who came to the hotel waiting for UNAMIR to evacuate them to their countries. The hotel director, a Belgian named Bik Colonerius, went to Europe yesterday, April tenth. We had no idea he was gone; we just heard about him getting on an airplane in Bangi, Gabon. He left the keys on the front desk but he never really left anyone in charge. As a matter of fact, he never told anyone he was leaving—we just heard the rumors he was gone. We kind of feel betrayed." UNAMIR was the United Nations Assistance Mission for Rwanda—the baby-blue-helmeted multinational soldiers gathered around and inside the hotel.

Many of the Rwandans who sought refuge in the hotel simply occupied empty rooms free of charge, courtesy of the kindly hotel workers there, while the majority who arrived a little later—such as myself—bunked with others. There were often far more people in a room than there were beds, but when one is hiding for one's life, this is but a small inconvenience.

If a refugee had already taken up a room, he or she was always more than happy to share the room with others. But even paying or previously paying guests often admitted some of us who were looking for a safe place to hide. There was a siege mentality going on, and people sensed that if attackers came in and began killing, they would not be stopping to ask questions. We were all in danger. Certainly, out in the streets, this had become the case. Killing was going on now in random fashion. Hutu were slicing up all Tutsi. To be perfectly safe, you either had to be in uniform or you carried a machete. If you were simply walking around, trying to go from one place to another, you were checked for ID. If it said you were Hutu, it would be best if you were directly associated with the militias or a known supporter of their ideology. If a Hutu met another Hutu he knew personally as a moderate, that person was sliced to death as a "sustainer of the cockroaches."

Rubayiza and Alexis told me the Hotel des Mille Collines officially became a UN-protected site for refugees on April 7, the

> There was a siege mentality going on, and people sensed that if attackers came in and began killing, they would not be stopping to ask questions. We were all in danger.

first full day of the genocide. Shortly thereafter, it became a place for the discussion and exercise of international diplomacy in hopes of ending the raging violence in the streets.

The consul of Luxembourg in Rwanda, Charles Shamukiga, was killed on April 6. His son, Christophe Shamukiga, was with us in the hotel and would play a big role in alerting the international community, especially Luxembourg, about our plight. On April 7, Christophe called the State Department of Luxembourg for protection and eventual evacuation. On April 12, he followed up with a letter to them as well, providing them with suggestions as to how they might evacuate more people from the hotel so they would not be killed. On April 13, the grand duchy of Luxembourg wrote a letter to Colonel Fontaine of the Belgium Ministry of Defense to evacuate people who were in the Hotel des Mille Collines, especially his own family. He also attached a letter he had written to the Belgian ambassador in Kigali. On April 15, the chief of staff of Luxembourg's army wrote a letter to Canadian General Roméo Dallaire, the force commander of UNAMIR, to do whatever he could to protect people in the Hotel des Mille Collines. That same day, Leonard Knaff, consul of Rwanda in Luxembourg, wrote a letter to General Dallaire on behalf of the grand duchy of Luxembourg, asking him to protect the refugees in the Hotel des Mille Collines. The letter included a list of people Luxembourg had accepted to host.

Christophe Shamukiga was a dynamic young man from an influential family, yet he immediately gave the impression of one who felt a responsibility to earn such privilege by living a life of service and good works. His efforts were not simply to save himself, but to try to save us all. I found Christophe instantly likable. With no jobs or responsibilities except to stay alive at all costs, all of us at the hotel shared information and stories, mostly about how we had managed to make it to the hotel amidst all the terror consuming the entire nation. We also discussed the situation around us—what was going on out in the streets, what was the long-term prognosis, what was the news of the day, and whether we stood any chance at all of living through this.

Christophe said:

> I was at my home in Remera. I had some guests with me at the time—my niece and my friend. As soon as they heard the news of the plane crash they decided to leave. My wife and I took them home, dropping my friend off first before driving my niece home. By the time we arrived at her place, they were killing people already. So my wife and I spent the night at my niece's.
>
> The next day, someone from Luxembourg called and informed us people were being evacuated from a school not more than one hundred meters away. When I got there, they asked me, "Where did that information come from?" I told them it was from the United Nations in New York. So they said, "Okay, if you have any other people, bring them, too." I went to get my wife and niece.
>
> We were waiting our turn to be evacuated when the soldiers helping us started panicking, saying Interahamwe knew the Belgians were evacuating Tutsi. That became a major problem. Also, we didn't have passports or IDs, so they didn't know what to do with us if we got on a plane with no passports or anything.
>
> My parents were already dead on the first day. My father, Shamukiga Charles, everyone knew him, he was one of the founding members of AVP [*Association des volontaires de la paix*, or Association of Peace Volunteers], so I knew if I would try to go somewhere people would recognize me and kill us all. We were still waiting inside the gate of the school when someone was shot. Interahamwe were on the fences trying to get in and they were already stealing stuff on the streets.

One French journalist was sitting there with us. We were sharing lunch. He kept asking us what we thought about the RPF. We told him it was a good party, everything about it was fair, they didn't discriminate against anyone, and we told him it was about time we had leaders like them in our country. We knew this journalist was waiting for his people to come and get him so we asked him a favor—if he could at least take the women so we knew they would be safe. We didn't want Interahamwe to kill them.

The journalist hesitated and said he couldn't do it. Then we asked if he could at least take the two-year-old baby we had. He said, "Sir, you are annoying me with your plans." He told us, "The RPF will come and rescue you, since you like RPF so much," meaning he knew exactly who we were and we were not on the same side as he.

I told the other people who were with us we needed to go home and I would find another way we could be evacuated. Earlier, a friend of mine, Mugabo, told me people were going to the Hotel des Mille Collines because it was safe. Unfortunately, by the time I got home Mugabo had already been shot. He did not make it—he died. While we were getting ready to head for the hotel, soldiers kicked in our door. Everything we had, the soldiers came and took it all. I had about one million Rwandese francs because I was planning a trip to Burundi. But that's exactly how we got to the hotel. They accepted it as a bribe.

Once we arrived at the hotel, we met two men at the reception desk, Pasa and Zozo. They greeted us beautifully and said, "Hurry up and give these people a room!" I was with my wife, my sister-in-law Eugenie, and her child. When we got to our room, it was nice. There were soaps, toilet paper, and the beds were made properly.

Those men were being so nice to us. They didn't ask for any money; they didn't ask for anything. I was upset because that young man, Mugabo, the one who told us to go to the hotel, I wished he would have made it, for then he would have survived. If it weren't for him, we wouldn't have made it here ourselves.

I reflected upon his words. I knew just how Christophe felt. Mugabo was his Pascal. But Mugabo was dead. Was Pascal alive? I shuddered with guilt and worry.

When we first got to the hotel, everything was good—we were using the phones, we were watching television, and even fax machines were still working. People were using all means of communication to help bring others to the hotel, particularly friends and loved ones. Still, most of us were scared because we didn't know what was going to happen. I knew this was not the safest place to be, even though we were living in the rooms with everyone else. I believed eventually something was going to hit the hotel—a bomb or a missile—or the *génocidaires*, or the murderous militiamen, would come in and begin killing everyone. Some people didn't want to show their faces; they would hide all day in their rooms. Christophe, on the other hand, would go downstairs, trying to make friends with any UNAMIR soldiers he could find, so if anything happened they could get us out of there.

The more Tutsi I found in the hotel, the more their stories linked up. Except for the ones who worked at the hotel, most had leaned upon the assistance of someone else, oftentimes a Hutu, to help get them here. Some had their Pascals—Hutu who were their true friends and had helped them out of the kindness of their hearts. Others were helped by Hutu who operated much like the militiamen Pascal paid off when they came knocking on his door looking for me. In this time of chaos, there was profit to be made. There were political true believers, but far more believed in the one thing that remained constant regardless of regime—money. Even the most political, though, occasionally made purely selfish, monetary exceptions, allowing certain Tutsi to live for a price.

Jean Pierre Nkurunziza, a young student, befriended us. His story:

> A lot of Interahamwe broke into our house trying to kill us. So we all fled to our neighbor Kambanda's house, where there were two other families at the time. My brother had been hit in the head by an ax and was not in good condition. A lot of people were dying. Those who could not escape were killed.
>
> When the Interahamwe found out a lot of us were hiding at Kambanda's house, they tried to come and kill us, but they could not get in easily because Kambanda was a soldier—a major. The genocide occurred when he was in town to visit his wife. When a lot of people were dying everywhere, he agreed to protect us. Kambanda told his escorts to look after us, to make sure we were safe. Because he had a phone in his house, he kept calling everywhere trying to find out how the situation was. Someone told him that he thought the Hotel des Mille Collines was the safest place to be, so he drove my entire family—eight of us—and three of our neighbors to the hotel.
>
> When we arrived at the hotel on April ninth, we couldn't get over how normal everything was inside. We were treated as guests. A lot of embassies were bringing their people over so they could be transported home from here. We couldn't believe they did not ask us for money, even for the food. We are in room thirty. There are eleven of us here—me, my family, and three other men. It's crowded, but we are alive.

Indeed we were. Unlike so many others, we had found sanctuary.

7

WHY??

INSIDE THE HOTEL, I was surrounded by white people who could not understand exactly what was going on around us, even people who came there from the embassies. They saw killings going on in the streets, and they knew a war of liberation had raged not that long ago. Yet many were afraid to utter the word "genocide." Why, they wondered, was this not a conventional war? Why was the Hutu militia, as well as the army of the central government, not utilizing every bit of its available manpower to simply meet the RPF head-on with full force, as armies usually do? Why were Hutu extremists so determined to kill so many unarmed people, diluting their military manpower in doing so?

I had no answer. I could only conjecture based on what I saw, what I heard, and my years of living as a minority in a divided society. Many have attempted to debate me, raising the myriad issues that faced Hutu and Tutsi during the twentieth century, seeking to justify how the *génocidaires* felt. But genocide is a coward's way, the armed slaughtering the unarmed. It has no dignity, nor has it any glory. Anyone who attempts to rationalize and bless it is an animal.

After the signing of the Arusha Accords, the RPF sent soldiers to Kigali to protect its officials who were to participate in the transitional government. They were stationed in the CND, a parliamentary building on what Americans might refer to as our Capitol Hill.

After the crash of President Habyarimana's airplane, the Presidential Guard began shelling that building. RPF soldiers returned fire and held their ground until they got help from other RPF soldiers camped in other areas. The Presidential Guard's camp was very close to the CND and the two factions, impassioned by their beliefs, had been in a permanent state of friction. During an earlier cease-fire, a buffer was created between the two encampments, referred to as *Zone tampon* (the Tampon Zone).

Over the years, Hutu Power extremists demonstrated that they feared even the simple existence of human beings who either disagreed with them or who someday might grow to disagree with or oppose them. Most of all, they feared being outnumbered, although simple mathematics proved this to be ridiculous—Hutu would always far outnumber Tutsi in this part of Africa. To this end, though, they killed the newborn, they cut open pregnant women, and they killed old men, just to eradicate the ethnic Tutsi. Paranoia was allowed to sweep the land via "hate radio" and "hate newspapers" such as *Kangura*. "Hate television" was well into development, yet another form of media soon to be infected.

Mass hysteria and hate are always fertilized through something called "the Big Lie." One uncomplicated, hate-filled lie is far simpler than the truth. Truth has nuance and requires explanation. The Big Lie is black and white with no shades of gray. It is facile and it is powerful. It is short and can be spoken as a chant—what people today refer to as a "sound bite" or a "talking point."

The Big Lie being viciously whispered was that Tutsi living in Rwanda among Hutu were the real enemy, for the invading rebel army would only be successful if their Tutsi brethren working "behind the battle lines" rose up and cut down Hutu defending "their" nation. This was fallacy. I am Tutsi, but I was not a terrorist. No one was communicating with me, stealthily arming me, teaching me how to make bombs, or filling my head with thoughts of suicide attacks. To the best of my knowledge, no Tutsi citizen of Rwanda was. But nearly all Hutu believed the Big Lie. This lie compelled extremists to want to cause the complete extinction of the Tutsi people.

The other way the Big Lie works is that it couches itself in fear and paranoia. If one were in Norway and said over and over on the radio, "Kill the Swedes! Kill the Swedes!" that person would be far less successful than if he or she were to say, "The Swedes are coming to kill us! The Swedes are coming to kill us! Prepare to defend yourself against the killer Swedes!" This was the message that had poured out of Hutu hate radio for months and months. "Your Tutsi neighbors are terrorists! They are coming to kill you! Arm yourself and beware of the killer Tutsi!" Once Habyarimana's plane had been downed, hate radio simply shifted to its own version of "See, I told you so!" Despite no proper investigation, no proof, and no group accepting responsibility, the president's plane crash was blamed on Tutsi. They claimed Tutsi shot it down with missile fire—another Big Lie, a lie that began on RTLM hate radio within moments of the plane crashing into the ground.

The first days of the genocide were especially bloody, wiping out nearly fifty thousand per day, or so we were told by UNAMIR soldiers and others coming in and out of the hotel. The Hutu militia had lists of all Tutsi citizens: their ethnicity and their places of residence, employment, and birth. How did paramilitary groups get this valuable data? The administrative authority assisted them. The government structure coincided with the structures of the president's political party and the militia—from the lowest levels to the highest. All groups worked together; although some would try to claim these groups were autonomous, separate and independent of one another, the opposite was true. None of these groups could operate without the cooperation and agreement of the others. Official authorities within these groups were also campaigning for the destruction of all Tutsi and encouraging the population at large to be involved.

Ours was the first genocide of the Information Age.

Many people debate the definition of the word "genocide." The United Nations Convention on the Prevention and Punishment of the Crime of Genocide (CPPCG) defines genocide as "any of the following acts committed with intent to destroy, in whole or in part, a national, ethnical, racial or religious group, as such:

(a) "Killing members of the group;
(b) "Causing serious bodily or mental harm to members of the group;
(c) "Deliberately inflicting on the group conditions of life calculated to bring about its physical destruction in whole or in part;
(d) "Imposing measures intended to prevent births within the group;
(e) "Forcibly transferring children of the group to another group."[8]

Having lived my entire life in Rwanda and seeing the bloodbath that was going on around me, I had no doubt in my mind what was going on was genocide.

Genocide has many fathers. The dirtiest secret of all is it often occurs because large and powerful nations have financial or military interests within some other country that are best served by one group or leader there having political control. The United States has done this for many years, not necessarily by backing *génocidaires*, but by propping up foreign despots who might be good trade partners or geopolitical allies, such as their support of the former shah of Iran or their many years of supporting Egyptian President Mubarak. A group or a leader is armed and backed financially. One of the most obvious problems is this backing removes autonomy

---

[8] "Convention on the Prevention and Punishment of the Crime of Genocide," December 9, 1948, accessed October 17, 2013, http://www.oas.org/dil/1948_Convention_on_the_Prevention_and_Punishment_of_the_Crime_of_Genocide.pdf.

from the citizens of a nation. The worst problem, though, is when a group supported by foreign intervention uses that backing to gain or maintain control "by any means necessary." The most heinous of those means is genocide.

When the strategy of genocide is used, these larger, richer nations often turn a blind eye and attempt to explain it away to the world at large. Thus, on the world stage, politicians and public figures have the audacity to argue that even the intentional annihilation of hundreds of thousands of civilians, killed simply because they belonged to one group or another, is *not* genocide.

When President Habyarimana's plane crashed on April 6, there should have been a peaceful transfer of power. Like most countries, Rwanda had an official line of succession. Agathe Uwilingiyimana, a politically moderate Hutu woman involved in the multiparty agreement that preceded the negotiations later known as the Arusha Accords, was Rwanda's prime minister. She was in a politically tenuous position from the start, having been placed as more of a figurehead than someone with a significant power base. She was, in fact, what one would call a "lame duck" or caretaker, having been asked to resign her post shortly after receiving it months before Habyarimana's death, in favor of a more hard-line politician. The full transfer of her power, however, had not yet officially occurred, and so upon the death of Habyarimana, she was still technically the constitutional head of government. The MDR Party, which Uwilingiyimana represented, was heavily split between Hutu Power extremists and moderates such as she. The MDR hard-liners convened an extraordinary congress in Kabusunzu on July 23 and 24, 1993, where the Hutu Power hard-liners forced her resignation from the party and, they had hoped, the prime minister position. Among those present at that congress, and who helped drive Uwilingiyimana from the party, was a man I had yet to meet, but who would soon play a major role in my life and the lives of all of us in the hotel—a hotelier by the name of Paul Rusesabagina.

When the death of President Habyarimana was announced, the UN peacekeeping force sent a Belgian escort to the home of Agathe Uwilingiyimana around 3 A.M. on the morning of April 7, 1994, to take her to Radio Rwanda, where she planned a dawn broadcast appealing for national calm. Uwilingiyimana's house was further guarded by five Ghanaian UN troops in addition to ten Belgian troops. Inside the house, her family was protected by the Rwandan Presidential Guard, but the Guard—Hutu hard-liners all—surrounded the UN troops and told them to lay down their arms. In a fatal act of trust and diplomacy, the peacekeepers ultimately complied, handing over their weapons. We would later learn the Belgian UN troops sent to protect Uwilingiyimana were castrated, gagged with their own genitalia, and then executed.[9]

Seeing the standoff outside her home, Uwilingiyimana and her family took refuge in the Kigali UN volunteer compound. Eyewitnesses say Rwandan soldiers entered the compound at 10 A.M. and searched for her. She and her husband were eventually found later that morning by the Presidential Guard and were immediately shot and killed.

A few moderate Hutu and one Tutsi, Landouard Ndasingwa, were in the government that negotiated the Arusha Accords with the RPF. During the first days of the genocide, most of them were murdered. No lines of succession were being followed. Rwanda was in the midst of a coup d'état.

UNAMIR force commander Roméo Dallaire, who spent significant time at the hotel, said Uwilingiyimana and her husband surrendered themselves to the *génocidaires* to save their children, who stayed successfully hidden in the adjoining housing compound for employees of the United Nations Development Programme (UNDP).

---

[9] Scott Peterson, *Me Against My Brother: At War in Somalia, Sudan, and Rwanda* (New York: Routledge, 2000), 292; Daniel Graeber, "Never Forget! The 13th Anniversary of the Rwandan Genocides," *Foreign Policy Blogs*, April 6, 2007, http://foreignpolicyblogs.com/2007/04/06/never-forget-the-13th-anniversary-of-the-rwandan-genocides/.

The UN employees' children survived and were picked up by Captain Mbaye Diagne, a UNAMIR military observer, who smuggled them into the Hotel des Mille Collines, where they stayed as refugees with the rest of us. Later, a dozen Rwandan soldiers came to the hotel looking for the children, threatening to bash in every door to every room until they found them. Brave UN Captain Mbaye convinced them to retreat.

The prime minister's children, meanwhile, were also sought out for death. Captain Mbaye also secreted them into the Hotel des Mille Collines, where they found shelter. The United Nations chose the Hotel des Mille Collines because they were protecting it. In fact, the UN flag flew over that hotel, as I noticed when I first approached it. The United Nations was a major factor in saving the lives of all those children, as well as our own lives.

> Later, a dozen Rwandan soldiers came to the hotel looking for the children, threatening to bash in every door to every room until they found them. Brave UN Captain Mbaye convinced them to retreat.

We were shocked beyond words to hear the Presidential Guard had had the audacity to kill UN soldiers. Surely this would mean the armies of the world would come storming in to bring about peace and stability to our nation and punish the murderers. Yet days went by with no word or even rumor to that effect.

The concept of murdering a handful of UN peacekeepers was, as later analyzed by experts such as General Dallaire, an example of a new military tactic: the "Mogadishu/*Black Hawk Down*" strategy (ironically, a strategy named after a different Hollywood movie of a different terrible African event). Simply put, Western powers, while desiring business and trade relationships with all nations of the world, did not have the stomach for bloodshed, the death of their own people on foreign soil, peacekeeping, policing genocide, or entanglements like civil wars in which they did not have a direct national interest. When eighteen American troops were killed and their dead bodies dragged through the streets of Mogadishu, Somalia, on October 3 and 4, 1993, only six months before the Genocide Against the Tutsi, US President Bill Clinton immediately began pulling the rest of his troops out under political pressure from Congress and the electorate. America had completely withdrawn from Somalia by March 1994, only one month before Habyarimana's death.

Were the Hutu Power extremists to engage and kill *all* of the UNAMIR troops, certainly this would have caused a worldwide reaction via a show of power, in which more and better-equipped troops would be sent in with orders to engage. But killing only a handful of brave Belgian soldiers accomplished exactly what the *génocidaires* wanted—it caused Belgium, sponsor of one of the single largest international contingents in Rwanda, to pull out completely, while scaring off any other nation from increasing its commitment in order to replace them.

The Hotel des Mille Collines was not the only place where Tutsi refugees successfully sought and found safety. In reality there were many such places, including the Hotel Amahoro, the Hotel Méridien, St. Andre's School, St. Paul's Church, St. Famille's Church, and ETO Kicukiro, a technical school. When the genocide began, Tutsi who managed to escape their homes (not to mention the militias) went to whichever location they thought would be safe. The Hotel Amahoro, located behind Amahoro National Stadium in Kigali, was protected not only because the United Nations had its headquarters there, but also because the stadium itself was located in the section of Kigali that had been taken over by the RPF early on during the fight to stop the genocide. The entire area was considered a safe haven for Tutsi refugees, provided they could get there.

General Dallaire has likened Amahoro National Stadium to a concentration camp. In the documentary he would later help create in 2004, *Shake Hands with the Devil,* he said, "When the war started, the place filled up and at one point we were up to twelve thousand in here—twelve thousand people trying to live in here. You get this latent smoke that hangs in here. All you see is people and clothes and so the place looks absolutely, totally out of control. We were out there protecting them, but while we were out there, they were inside dying. And the stench, the stench was so powerful you actually had to force yourself not to puke or anything."

Diplomats and NGOs (nongovernmental organizations) gathered in the Hotel Méridien and the Hotel des Mille Collines to be evacuated to their countries of origin. The UN peacekeepers protected the refugees at the Hotel Méridien, the King Faisal Hospital, ETO Kicukiro, and the Hotel des Mille Collines. Like Amahoro National Stadium, the King Faisal Hospital was situated in territory controlled by the RPF. The Hotel des Mille Collines was a unique case. Despite being under the protection of a UN flag and filled with Westerners, we were in an area unquestionably in the hands of Hutu Power extremists.

As for ETO Kicukiro, several thousand Tutsi refugees were living there under the protection of UN peacekeepers, primarily Belgians—that is, until the April 7 murder of Prime Minister Uwilingiyimana and her Belgian guards at the hands of the Presidential Guard. As a result of this incident, Belgium withdrew its troops from the UN mission in Rwanda. Soon after their retreat, all those refugees at ETO Kicukiro were killed—a massacre of 3,500 to 5,500 unarmed Tutsi, left behind in mass graves. It was not just one of the largest single acts of mass slaughter of the entire genocide; it was also among the largest in all of recorded human history.

8

BROTHER VERSUS BROTHER

OUT IN THE streets, I feared every face I saw as I made my way to the hotel, for there was little to no chance any of those faces were Tutsi. But here, inside the hotel, was a haven not only for Tutsi, but for Hutu and foreign whites as well. Being around white people gave me a sense of relief, particularly being around the UNAMIR soldiers, although the peacekeepers were of various races and from numerous different countries. But hearing of the slaughter of the Belgian soldiers made even this security seem illusionary.

The Hutu, though…I just did not know. I had nothing against Hutu in general, despite all my family and I had been through. Far too many Hutu had been kind to me throughout my life. Yet this was a time far worse than any I had ever experienced. Tension. Fear. Distrust. Insane violence permeated the very air I breathed.

Many of the hotel workers were Hutu. Initially, I distrusted them. But as days went by, not only did they win me over with their personal kindness, but simple logic came into play. If they were truly radical hard-liners, wouldn't they be out in the streets killing and looting? That was where the money was, and that was where one with a heart full of hate could manifest his or her destiny. But these employees were still working. I didn't even know if they were still getting paid. The country had more or less shut down for business. Outside the hotel, I had not seen any businesses still operating normally, taking in money.

Even within the hotel, I feared Hutu would break into the room I shared with Rubayiza, rob us, and kill us—not that we had anything to rob, but still...And yet as day turned into night, this never occurred. Hutu within the hotel thought as we did—that this slaughter of the unarmed was immoral and repugnant on all human levels.

One who should have scared me terribly was Wycliff Kajuga. His brother, Robert, was president of the Interahamwe. What was he doing here? He arrived at the hotel the very same day as me, April 11. Yet he carried no weapon; he wore no uniform, official or otherwise. His manner bore no ill will toward me or any other Tutsi. Many imagined Wycliff had powerful connections with the *génocid-aires*. Would he make us starve or kill us in our sleep, purely for his own enjoyment, and get away with it?

Refugees came to discover that Wycliff had never joined any radical party. He was pro-RPF even though his brother led the Interahamwe. Instead, he became an ally and a friend. What is it the Bible says? "For I was hungry, and you gave me to eat; I was thirsty, and you gave me to drink; I was a stranger, and you took me in." Despite our ethnicities, despite the political philosophies many of us were raised with and had brought with us to the Hotel des Mille Collines, common decency and love filled nearly every hotel refugee I met. No one took power over another, and all shared their meager belongings and acquisitions with one another.

As I got to know him, I learned Wycliff had not even been able to rely upon his own brother for assistance, or at least the level of assistance he had hoped for. Their politics put them at odds with each other, although Robert had not done anything to directly harm his brother. Still, some members of Wycliff's family were killed on the first day of the genocide, and if militias had found Wycliff out in the streets he, too, would have been murdered for his politics.

"When the insanity began, we first ran to the county jail," Wycliff said. "The jail was near the house of an official from the president's party. We heard there was a car going to the Hotel des Diplomates. We followed that car until we arrived there on April tenth."

We had heard the provisional government—those who placed themselves in power following the coup d'état and assassination of Prime Minister Uwilingiyimana—had set up their temporary base of operations within the walls of the Hotel des Diplomates. The Diplomates was operated by Sabena, the same Belgian hotel company that operated the Mille Collines. The leaders of the genocide plotted and managed the killing of innocents from within that hotel. Everyone who was there after April 6 had to have known that—had to have been aware of what was going on and what they were planning.

"We originally sought refuge at the Hotel des Diplomates," said Wycliff. "I came with my family, plus some Arab children who were with us. The Arab children were left with the soldiers for protection, but my family and I were turned down because we were told the hotel was only for governmental ministers. We saw other white folks helped by soldiers but we, the black folks, were unable to get protection. Because the downtown area of the city was calm at the time, my family and I decided to go to the Mille Collines. The hotel was filled when we arrived, but luckily we found one room, number 311, which I share with six other people. The first day I arrived here, I had mixed feelings because of the anxiety. We ate the leftovers from the white man's food."

Robert Kajuga's brother? Eating table scraps while filled with anxiety? I found it hard to believe, and yet it humanized and equalized the struggle we all faced during this time of crisis. When first I took Wycliff into my trust, I thought I might be better protected against whatever might happen next. Now I had my doubts. As in the American Civil War, brother fought against brother as blood spilled throughout the entire country.

Another person I befriended early on was a hotel worker named Pasa Mwenenganucye, a receptionist working the front desk. Pasa gave us the behind-the-scenes story on much of what was going on inside the hotel and behind closed doors:

There were even more white people here before you arrived. I think it was two days after the plane crash, at most three days, when they started sending home foreigners who wished to leave the hotel. Even the general directors of the hotel left. The few white people who are still here are journalists, and they're here just to report on the genocide.

The night the president's plane went down, I was working the night shift. As I arrived, the general director, Bik Colonerius, was leaving and he handed me the keys. He told me he was considering evacuating—he did not know quite when—and asked me not to tell anyone, so that the other hotel employees would not ask about their salaries. He assumed I would leave after my shift, but because of the rioting in the streets, I have been stuck here. He asked when I left to leave the keys with someone I trusted. Even though I stayed, I asked another worker to take the keys—I did not want to take the risk of holding onto them. But he felt as I did and I have been stuck with all these keys, which makes me feel quite vulnerable.

I decided to leave the front desk because I felt it was too risky with the keys. I got a room in one of the hotel suites— a place where people could reach me, but at the same time somewhere I could hide. I never got any further instructions from Bik. As a matter of fact, I asked him if I could continue to stay at the hotel in the suite I procured, room 221 in the newest section of the hotel. He told me, "Go ahead." Some of my family managed to make it to the hotel and they are staying here with me—two of my brothers, my parents, and one of my brother's friends.

None of us here at the hotel have received our salaries since Bik left. The few days when he was still here, Bik never

made anyone pay for anything, so I kind of picked up where
he left off. The stock room is very large and full of food,
drinks, and alcohol. Nobody is being charged. Everybody is
eating, drinking, even living here for free.

It sounded like paradise, and amidst the feeling we could be
raided or bombed at any time, there were indeed momentary feelings of tranquility. Would the food hold out? We did not know.
But no one gorged themselves; no one profiteered. Where anar-
chy could have reigned, a communal feeling swept the premises.
This was comradeship. Hutu, Tutsi, and foreigners all lived in harmony those first few days. All shared, be it food or be it space
and bedding. Pasa, being a hotel employee, could have kept his
suite all for himself, along with all the food and drink he could
consume, yet he overfilled his room with family, as many refugees did, and shared completely, letting all of us know where the
provisions were kept.

> Where anarchy could have reigned, a communal feeling swept the premises. This was comradeship. Hutu, Tutsi, and foreigners all lived in harmony those first few days.

People such as Pasa and Wycliff Kajuga lived among us as *our*
brothers, helping everyone with equal charity.

9

PROTECTORS IN BABY-BLUE HELMETS

THE HOTEL WAS a place of fragile sanctuary, yet it was a rudderless ship. The closest we had to leadership were the UNAMIR soldiers, but their stewardship was limited to their primary mission, which was directed by the United Nations in the United States. It did not involve running a hotel.

Pasa, Alexis, and the other hotel employees simply did their jobs to the best of their abilities, trying to act as if nothing had changed. When people came in, they helped them in any way they could. They cooperated with the UN peacekeepers. All the rooms, it seemed, were spoken for, so as more refugees arrived, they were told they could stay but would have to figure out for themselves where to lay their heads. Rwanda is a small country, a little smaller than the American state of Massachusetts, but densely populated. Most everyone who managed to get to the hotel, though, was from Kigali or its suburban areas, and it was amazing how many people found someone they knew milling about in the lobby. Peaceful alliances of convenience were formed, and most everyone found someone to share space with. Families mostly stayed together, sometimes even extended families; otherwise men shared rooms with other men, women with women. Somehow or other, although we had no formal leadership or social structure, the grave situation at hand brought out the best in people.

No one seemed to be hoarding, behaving badly, or exerting force against or power over anyone else. For a terrible situation, things were about as good as one could envision.

On April 14, Alexis told us some people from the Mille Collines's sister hotel, the Hotel des Diplomates, had stopped by and spent the night—a fellow by the name of Paul Rusesabagina, who was the Diplomates's manager, and a white fellow. They were accompanied by soldiers supporting the old Habyarimana regime. This was less ominous than it might at first appear, as the uniformed soldiers were far more disciplined at this point in time than the crazed militias looting, robbing, and killing everything in sight.

"They say they are just passing through, on their way to Gitarama, which is a safer zone," said Alexis. "They say they need gas."

Alexis knew Rusesabagina, as did most of the Mille Collines employees, it seemed. The two hotels, both managed by Sabena in Belgium, shared employees quite a bit, and it was not unusual for someone to work at one hotel for a while and then get transferred to the other. Rusesabagina was in management, having once been an assistant manager at the Mille Collines, but was now acting as the manager at the Diplomates. He was Hutu, as were most Rwandans who worked in the upper-managerial echelons of the local European-owned hotels. He was a short, round, dark-skinned man of about forty. He was at the hotel one night and gone the next morning.

As I have mentioned, the Diplomates had become the headquarters of the Hutu extremist government, the CDR. According to some in the hotel who knew him, Paul Rusesabagina was a high-ranking member of the hard-line Hutu Power branch of the MDR Party, which came to be known as "MDR Power." Being politically active in one of the genocide-supporting parties also helped one out financially and career-wise. Because Rusesabagina was managing the Diplomates, and because he was a well-known, active member of a political party that advocated genocide ideology, it was logical to conclude he knew much about the genocide being planned and managed at this very moment. He oversaw the servicing of the very organizers of what was going on around us, outside the hotel, the murder in the streets. He stayed with them, he was friends with them from before the killing began, he accompanied them, and he accepted their personal protection. Many held him in deep suspicion.

By now there were more than five hundred refugees in the hotel, though it is likely no one stopped to count exactly how many. More poured in each day, while others, such as the foreign whites, left when opportunity presented itself. Rooms opened up, rooms filled up, overflow crowds asked to join those already occupying rooms and always seemed to be accepted somewhere. While we moved about in the common areas during the day in that first week or so, everyone seemed to find a private place to rest his or her head at night. We were also never asked to pay. The kitchen facilities ran as always. Smiles and nods replaced cash and credit cards. I humbly took only as much as I needed to stay alive. The staff was generous; the refugees were thankful.

No one was killed in the hotel those first nine or ten days of the siege. No violence, either. I suppose the UN peacekeepers were our grand protectors, and if so, they did a perfect job, considering the positive result. They had their own office in the hotel. They were there to protect us and to inform their commander, Roméo Dallaire, if anyone came inside the hotel and threatened us. Short-staffed as they were, General Dallaire's peacekeepers were far from impotent. The Hotel des Mille Collines was like some isolated outpost of peace surrounded by gruesome violence, and Dallaire sought to keep it that way, as if it represented something sane and good to him amidst all the bloody insanity.

Dallaire cut a dashing figure. A squint-eyed, mustachioed, light-haired, muscular man, he was every bit the commanding general. When he walked the lobby of the hotel, the seas parted. He was often in the company of his aide-de-camp, another Canadian, Major Brent Beardsley. We saw Beardsley frequently; he was a bit less formidable to approach, although those who spoke with Dallaire always came away remarking on his very obvious compassion for us Rwandans. He seemed to take this genocide personally, if such a thing could be understood. As time went by, we wondered if the Western world even knew what was going on with us and, if they did, did they even care? But Dallaire cared. The moment you looked him in the eye, you simply knew.

As time went by, we wondered if the Western world even knew what was going on with us and, if they did, did they even care? But Dallaire cared. The moment you looked him in the eye, you simply knew.

According to Beardsley, General Dallaire placed unarmed military observers at the hotel on April 8, when he visited the hotel and discovered many civilians had sought sanctuary there, including the children of Prime Minister Agathe Uwilingiyimana. Dallaire threatened the militias who had set up a roadblock at the gate and told them not to enter the hotel, as it was under UN protection. This was a bit of bluster because the observers had instructions from their headquarters in New York not to use their weapons to actually shoot someone, although they did have communications set up to UNAMIR force headquarters and that was a deterrent.

Regarding the situation as it stood about a week later, Beardsley said:

> We received intelligence the hotel might be attacked by the Interahamwe and this was confirmed by the hotel MILOBs [military observers] that more Interahamwe are at the entrance. The MILOBs's commander is a magnificent and brave Congolese major who I think would rather die than let the militia in. General Dallaire dispatched a Bangladeshi armored personnel carrier [APC] to the hotel, but the Bangladeshis whined and cried that they would be in danger, so he sent a Tunisian section under their fearless commandant.

Luckily, the attack hasn't materialized. It's MILOBs during the day, and MILOBs and the armed section at night. General Dallaire calls the MILOBs every night before he goes to bed to ensure they are safe and to boost their morale and they his.

Even with a section of armed troops with an APC, the small group at the hotel could never stop a determined attack. Their mission is to deter an attack through their presence and warn UNAMIR if the hotel is attacked so more troops can be sent if available. It's largely a bluff, but it seems to be working.

Beardsley was nothing if not honest, direct, and blunt. Having seen what happened to the Belgian peacekeepers, he knew his life was on the line as much as ours were. General Dallaire and his cadre weren't planning to leave. We were all in this together.

Dallaire and Beardsley were but two of a number of "white eyes" who, simply by their skin color, seemed to protect us. The hotel was a meeting place for diplomats and dignitaries; the most plush and civilized place in the midst of the blood in the streets. One of the things the killers feared most was international intervention and the long-term ramifications of international pressure and economic imbroglios, which would place the government they were attempting to put in power in jeopardy, unable to legitimize itself, trade, or rule. They did not want the rest of the world to know their dirty little secrets—and genocide is the dirtiest of dirty secrets. So long as Westerners could not call what was going on "genocide," the killers felt safe. Thus, very little overt killing of the unarmed went on in plain sight of white eyes.

10

AND THEN EVERYTHING CHANGED

A DAY OR TWO after his first visit, Paul Rusesabagina, the manager of the Hotel des Diplomates, returned to the Hotel des Mille Collines. This time he was alone. Pasa, who had the master keys and was the closest the hotel had to a manager at the time, had a look of anger on his face.

"He just showed up and asked me to hand over the keys! I told him I was not supposed to give the keys to anybody. He told me that he was in charge. I let him know I needed proof of that and then he got a fax from our superiors in Belgium, after which I gave him the keys. I kept a master key, though, because I need access to some places, like if I have to get something to eat."

At first blush, none of this mattered much to us refugees. How many people know anything about the individual who is managing the hotel where they are staying? This seemed like nothing more than office politics to us. Pasa clearly did not like this Rusesabagina fellow, though, and the feeling appeared mutual. Pasa felt Rusesabagina was an opportunist who saw no one formally in charge of the hotel and decided to appoint himself. When Pasa challenged him, Rusesabagina apparently called Sabena headquarters in Brussels and got them to send a fax stating he had their official blessing to be manager.

Another possible reason Rusesabagina was suddenly now at our hotel was that the hotel he managed, the Diplomates, had been bombed that very day or the day before, or so we'd been told. It had ceased to operate as a regular hotel shortly after the downing of the president's plane, and it had become the temporary capital of the Hutu Power government-in-transition and its military leaders. Now the military leaders were all scattered, as the hotel became an obvious battle target. We prayed they would not all congregate here at our hotel, making *us* a target, but that seemed unlikely due to the UN presence. Still, with the arrival of Rusesabagina, who stayed with the *génocidaires* during the first week or so of the genocide, many worried. Said Egide Karuranga, a businessman who was also among us: "I do believe this Rusesabagina fellow had trouble in joining his Hutu family and friends in Gitarama, as he is accompanied by his Tutsi woman. Passing the multiple barriers of killers, especially the one in Giticyinyoni, would be almost impossible for him. That must certainly be the main reason why he's decided to come and shelter his family with other Tutsi here at the Hotel des Mille Collines, hoping to make it to Europe eventually, as others, particularly the foreigners, are using it as a departing point."

Soon, not only Pasa was wearing a look of anger, but so was Alexis. "Rusesabagina just held a meeting for all the hotel employees, telling everyone what to do, making himself boss. We know what to do! We've been doing fine without him.

"He told everyone working in the restaurant to start making all the people pay. We told him that we couldn't. That makes no sense, making people pay. They are in the hotel to save their lives. Nobody really thought about bringing any money."

Jean Pierre, our student friend, confirmed what Alexis said. "I just went down to the restaurant. The cooking service has stopped. Someone has shut the kitchen down. How are we to eat?

"I went to see this 'Paul' person who says he is now in charge. He is making people pay for everything."

Later in the day, Pasa was still fuming. "Now he wants to charge the hotel employees! We are stuck here. We cannot go home. If we try to leave here, we will be killed. We must stay here as well as sleep here. He wants to charge us for our rooms! He wants to charge us for food! Not only that, we are no longer getting paid! How can we pay him when he is not paying us?! It is like a form of slavery."

We began to get upset. It all seemed so illogical. The more we thought about it and talked about it, the less sense it made. Pasa and Alexis said Rusesabagina was trying to emphasize to them that the hotel must continue to look as if it was operating normally. But who was this charade for? Anyone with eyes could see we were at war, that the war and a genocide were right at our front gate. The Rwandan military, as well as some militiamen, strolled our halls. They weren't stupid. They could tell what was going on. They couldn't help but know people were seeking refuge here, particularly Tutsi.

Far more upsetting for the hotel employees was the question of where the money was going. According to Pasa and Alexis, employees of the hotel were no longer doing any bookkeeping. We had no idea if banking was even operational in our country. How could anyone make deposits? And even if they could, how would they get money to corporate headquarters in Brussels? How could payroll be made? Payroll *wasn't* being made, so again, where was the money going? Paul Rusesabagina would not say.

Many people do not think much about food until they are in a situation where they may not have any. Never before in my life had I wondered where my next meal would come from. Then I was in a hotel, a beautiful luxury hotel, one that had a restaurant where I had been dining for days despite my pathetic financial situation—brought about by being chased from my home by killers—and suddenly food was an issue of grave crisis to me. For the next few meals over the next few days, those who had money—and there were indeed some who still did—shared graciously with those of us who did not. I got to see the greatest demonstrations of man's humanity toward his fellow man. I thought about Christophe's story of how he had begged a French journalist for assistance to protect a two-year-old child from slaughter and was turned down. Here in the hotel, everyone—Westerners, Hutu, Tutsi, refugees, guests, employees, UN soldiers—faced each new struggle together, living communally, living with love. I will never forget it so long as I live. Our fear, though, was over how long this situation would last. What would happen when *everyone's* money ran out? What would the hotel manager do then? And who could we appeal to positioned above him?

> Our fear, though, was over how long this situation would last. What would happen when *everyone's* money ran out? What would the hotel manager do then?

Refugees continued to swarm in—only now, many found it even harder to take up residence in the hotel. I do not know for sure if anyone was turned away. If they were, I am certain they are now dead; I am certain they were killed within minutes or hours of not getting safe refuge within the hotel walls. I and the others I'd befriended found the most difficult part of our various journeys to the hotel to be the long treks to the main gate. Once we'd gotten inside the gate, we were in the clear; we were safe. Those who managed to join us after the new hotel manager arrived, though, told a far different tale.

Serge Rusagara was nothing more than a high school boy. He got to the hotel with the assistance of the actual head of the dreaded Interahamwe, Robert Kajuga. As he told us:

> Kajuga has been a friend of friends for years now, despite our differences. He asked about me and my family once the killings started, wondering if we were safe. My sister, she took a gunshot wound to the head. She is in bad shape. The wound is deep, but I believe now that we are here and getting attended to, she is getting better.

We waited and waited for Kajuga to come to our rescue and eventually he did, promising to take us somewhere safe. It was me and my four siblings—two brothers and two sisters. The other members of my family have all been killed: my father, my mother, my uncle, and my aunt. I also have with me my three cousins and three other children.

When we got downtown, Kajuga Robert handed us over to other Interahamwe and they accompanied us to the hotel. When we arrived at the gate, the guards and the soldiers wouldn't let us in. Even the Interahamwe that were with us were begging those soldiers to let us in, but they wouldn't—we were still standing on the street. A lot of cars passed by—they were full of soldiers and Interahamwe, pointing their guns at us, and we were certain that if they had the opportunity they would have gotten out of the car and killed us if they could.

When we arrived at the hotel gate around 5:30 P.M., it was getting dark. A car approached us, pointing its headlights in our faces. We were asked to step aside so that it could get through. As the car drove by us, I stepped on the side toward the soldiers and managed to sneak in, along with my little sister. I ran through the parking lot, carrying my sister, a bloody white bandage wrapped around her little head. We saw three UNAMIR soldiers. I started crying and spoke to them in French, begging them to let us in, along with our family. Luckily, they let us all in.

We walked toward the front desk, only to find that the hotel did not want to let us in because we did not have any money. I pleaded with them, "Please, let us in for my sister's sake; she is wounded." They said, "This is not a hospital."

Fortunately, we knew that some other members of our family were staying at the hotel—there were some of my father's friends, such as Mutarikanwa, Rubangura Vedaste, and

Bertin Makuza. We asked if we could go upstairs and get them. Mutarikanwa sent his brother down to check on us. He said that it was okay, that he would pay for us.

Once we were stable at the hotel, we had to be divided into families. My cousin and I went with Bertin Makuza's family, while my other siblings went to Rubangura's family. I am in room 224, on the second floor. There are twenty children in that one room. Sleeping is hard. We have no blankets, no nothing. But I feel safe here—at least compared to what it was like in my neighborhood, where we were scared the whole time. If Interahamwe came to our house to kill us, we just climbed onto the fence and we would go hide on the roof. Some nights we would even spend the night in a tree. But here at the hotel, I am not that worried because I am with others. I am afraid, however, that if the militias come to the hotel, they will throw us out the windows and kill us.

We were shocked. None of us who came to the hotel in the first days of the genocide had any such problems with the hotel staff. Their graciousness was beautiful. Why had the hotel's attitude changed?

Serge, of course, had no idea, for he only had his own experience to rely upon. "For hotel employees to stand at the door and not let anyone in, especially children—and my little sister was hurt pretty badly—I don't think that's a nice thing to do. I would understand if he said, 'Let the kids in, but not the adults.' But they did not want to let us in at all. All they cared about was money."

11

CUT OFF

BY APRIL 20, the Hotel des Mille Collines was no longer a hotel, but a full-blown refugee camp. As such it was no longer capable of offering any hotel-like services. For example, in the room where I stayed, number 306, we had more than eight people crammed in a space created for two. Some refugees were even sleeping as many as ten or twenty to a room, while others were in the corridors where they could find space to rest, just waiting to die, for our outlook on our situation remained grave throughout.

Certain people continued to try to get us help, get us rescued somehow. We were all willing to go anywhere so long as it was safe—passage as well as destination. If you were in the hotel and had friends in other African nations, or in Europe, Canada, or the United States, you could pick up the telephone in your hotel room or in the lobby and make calls. Some refugees were well-connected and managed to make calls directly to consulates and ambassadors in other countries. The rest of us simply hoped some people we knew happened to know other people who could somehow help. We were desperate. Anything was worth a try.

Refugees in the hotel began to organize. Each floor had a representative. The refugee committee was led by Tatien Ndolimana, who had been working with the prime minister's office as an adviser. Our young friend Christophe Shamukiga also served on the committee, as did Wellars Gasamagera, who had worked at the Libyan embassy for fifteen years, and Bernard Makuza, who was also an adviser to Prime Minister Agathe Uwilingiyimana, the brave woman who was murdered at the start of the genocide and whose children were now hiding in the hotel with us. The committee dealt with the United Nations and other humanitarian organizations. No hotel employees were active on the refugee committee.

One of the first visible successes of the committee was to interface with the International Red Cross. The committee got them to come to the hotel and bring us some food, such as corn and beans. Pasa told us hotel employees' access to the stockroom had become limited, and no one other than the manager could be sure how much food was left and how long it would last. Furthermore, he feared some of the hotel food would go bad before being eaten, because less and less was being consumed since the hotel manager had put in the cash register and had forced everyone to pay, despite the ever-dwindling money in people's pockets.

Pasa said, "Even if you are lucky enough to get some food from the outside, he won't let you cook it in the hotel kitchen. He wants everybody to eat the hotel food so they will have to pay for it. We don't know or care about when the hotel food is finished because no one wants to pay—or can pay for it—anyway."

We would have to go outside to cook something if we wanted to eat, because cooking in our rooms was dangerous and could start a fire. Yet going outside was also treacherous. Poolside was especially bad. We were exposing ourselves—the militias walking down the street could easily see us and throw a grenade at us. Life was unpredictable; we never knew what was going to happen next.

The women and girls would wake up and go upstairs to the sixth floor to cook something, and then they would come down at noon so we could all eat together. We started running out of food; sometimes we would only eat once a day. The water pressure and service began to get inconsistent, so to conserve water, the men and boys would get some water from the hotel swimming pool and we would use it to cook and to bathe.

After a while, we made our complaints known to the hotel manager that we did not want to cook outside, and after a long discussion he reconsidered his decision and allowed us to cook in the kitchen, but only the food we bought from him or otherwise acquired on our own. As for the food from the Red Cross, Paul insisted the hotel kitchen staff cook that. And because the hotel staff cooked it, Paul charged the refugees for it. He turned it into a profit center. If you could not afford to pay, you did not get cooked corn and beans that the Red Cross had given to the hotel for free.

Unlike anyone who worked for the hotel, people like Christophe, Wellars, Ndolimana, and Bernard Makuza, as well as Dr. Josue Kayijaho and François Nsanzuwera, my old boss from the Ministry of Justice, were very well connected internationally. They spent much of their days ringing up diplomats and NGOs on our behalf, as well as interfacing with the UN people both at the hotel and abroad. They knew important people personally. We put our faith in them that whatever could best be made of our situation, they would do. The fact that we continued to get responses proved to us these good men were having some effect. Besides, we were all still alive, and each living hour proved greater testament to the efforts of everyone exerting whatever power they could muster to continue that state of being.

And then one day the phones ceased to function. Panic spread as everyone picked up their room phones and found the lines dead. Dear God, how would we be heard now? This would be the beginning of the end. Without phones to contact the world, the evil men with machetes and guns would simply bully their way in and slaughter us all as they had slaughtered so many others already. We wondered if even the United Nations could keep them at bay without phone communication. We assumed the peacekeepers had walkie-talkies and other such communication devices, but still, we saw them using phones, too. And there were so few peacekeepers left to protect us anyway. Being able to call for reinforcements quickly was critical to our safety.

A rumor spread that the hotel manager had cut the lines himself. This made no sense. It was tantamount to damning us all, himself included. This had to have been the work of terrorists from the outside. Still, no one saw anyone do it—not militiamen, not the military, nor anyone affiliated with the hotel.

If the lines had actually been cut, we hoped the UN peacekeepers could help in restoring service. But days went by and we saw no movement toward the solving of this problem. We felt helpless. Just when we had begun to feel some sense of self-sufficiency, it had just as quickly been pulled out from under us.

Then Rusesabagina let it be known there was one working phone, the fax machine in his private office. Joy! We were saved. We could continue to contact the outside world. But happiness was short-lived. He informed the refugee committee that only they could use the phone in his office and no one else. Additionally, they could only do so with his permission and under his watchful eye.

Paranoia arose anew. Happy as we were, how could that one line still be working? How do you cut every line to the hotel but one? The hotel manager claimed it was because that singular line was not routed through the hotel's main switchboard. But hotel employees, who understood the situation the best, remained skeptical. All Kigali telephone communications passed through the center of telecommunication—Rwandatel, a utility whose headquarters was located in the entrance of the Hotel des Mille Collines. There, the Rwandatel operator controlled all communications passing through a central routing station. The only way communication could be cut off from the hotel was if someone physically cut the phone lines. But if someone had, the Rwandatel operator would have known right away. There was no such corroboration.

The rest of us all felt we were in this thing together, a group of equals regardless of ethnicity or station in life, which is how we had acted before Rusesabagina came and changed the tenor of our existence. As angry as we were, we felt there was nothing we could do about it. Though some of us considered banding together and physically overtaking the hotel manager, that would have been imprudent, given his close relationships with some of the most powerful militia and military leaders in the country—many of whom frequently wandered in and out of the hotel while we sought refuge there. We knew if we dared lay a hand on him, it likely could cost us our lives.

Within days of losing telephone service everywhere except in the hotel manager's locked, private office, we proceeded to lose water. Unlike with the phone service, no one seemed to be looking for a conspiracy theory to explain what had happened. Granted, we did not know for sure why the water stopped working, but we could also still look out of our windows and see genocide raging around us. It had been nice and civilized having running water for almost a month, but now we had something new to send us into a panic. Who thinks of these things? Who considers it? We take water for granted. Even in the most rural areas of Rwanda, there are wells. Even if there were water to be found elsewhere, no one was about to walk out from the safety of our enclave in order to quench thirst or bring any back. It would be a one-way trip for certain.

For a day or two, we subsisted on whatever water could still be found in ice buckets or pitchers. Soon that was gone. Humans can only go so long without water. Bathing and cleanliness became secondary to survival.

There was the large swimming pool outside. It was still within the confines of the hotel, but it brought us closer to the violent, marauding crowds. Once we were outside, they could see us and scream epithets at us. "Cockroaches!" was mostly what we heard. "We will come inside and we will kill you all!"

Few had used the pool for its intended purpose, for swimming is done for pleasure and having murderers scream for your head takes away all happiness. But now, as we saw it, the pool had another purpose. It contained water. Yes, it was highly chlorinated, almost toxic water, but still, it was water. It was something. It might stave off death for a short while. When you do not count on anything, you live for the moment and hope for another moment to follow. Still, we did not guzzle it or act like savages by hoarding the pool water. People would delicately tiptoe outside, hoping somehow to not be seen by the outsiders, then quickly and gently fill up a pitcher or bucket and bring it back inside. Then another, then another. This, we did in harmony. No one had to police us. We all knew what we were up against.

> For a day or two, we subsisted on whatever water could still be found in ice buckets or pitchers. Soon that was gone. Humans can only go so long without water. Bathing and cleanliness became secondary to survival.

The water tasted horrible and the heavy chlorination made us sick and even more dehydrated. But our best guess was that it was still better than drinking nothing at all.

Then the electricity went. Again, no fingers were pointed. Water, electricity—these were public utilities and, besides the genocide, we were at war, with bombs and gunfire easily heard just outside our gate. During the day, the lack of electricity was merely an inconvenience, one we hardly noticed. But at night, where before we had lighting in the hallways and in the lobby and other common areas, now there was darkness. Previously, when you heard ominous sounds, you could turn on a lamp in your room. Now you had nothing. The fear level rose precipitously. Nights were far more silent now, with no congenial voices to drown out the bombs, gunfire, and screams. It would take the peacekeepers much longer to realize they were under attack now. Furthermore, we were more vulnerable to stealth attack—a bunch of silent killers quietly slicing up people as they slept, no one able to discern friend from foe in pitch darkness. It was horrible. More and more of us talked of sleeping during the day and staying vigilantly awake at night.

Within days, the United Nations managed to provide us with generators, much to our relief. Still, they were limited; they ran on gasoline, and who knew how long the UN would be able to keep us supplied with that? Thus, the generators ran only at night, to send a signal to the militias that we would see them if they tried to trespass and overtake us in the darkness. We slept slightly more soundly once more. Yet with only swimming pool water to drink, limited electricity, and one telephone we had to beg to use, we felt more and more cut off from the rest of the world. Who knew we were still alive? Who would ever come to our rescue? Did anyone care? When would we all die—from dehydration, from illness, from starvation, or from vicious and brutal murder?

12

BEER AND KILLERS

A S WE RATIONED out swimming pool water, those who still had money had other options. The hotel manager began doing business with an old friend of his, a man named Georges Rutaganda, who was vice president of the Interahamwe and one of the masterminds behind the genocide. Rutaganda was an importer of expensive European beers such as Carlsberg, Heineken, and Tuborg. Before the genocide, Tutsi and moderate Hutu could not buy these items from Rutaganda because he would only sell to those who shared his radical ideology—people such as hotelier and (as we came to discover) MDR Power member Paul Rusesabagina. For Rutaganda, business was good, especially now that the infrastructure of our nation was crumbling.

Because Rusesabagina was still demanding money from refugees for lodging and what remained of our food and bottled beverages, when he went outside the hotel and returned with cases of high-end beers from Rutaganda, we presumed that was where our money was going. How ironic that we were perhaps financially hastening our own demise by enriching one of the chief killers of our people. Yet we were never given a choice. In a situation such as the one we faced in the Hotel des Mille Collines, a luxury beer was the last thing on our minds. What we needed instead were basics like clean water, bread, rice, beans, protein, and fruit—the necessary and healthy foundations of a decent human diet.

Once Rusesabagina used our money to buy Rutaganda's beer, he did not ration it out to us despite our having already paid for it. Instead, he offered to sell it to us at an inflated price few could afford. This left us with only two choices if we wished to avoid dehydration: overpay Rusesabagina for Rutaganda's premium beers, or drink the water from the swimming pool. Once your money ran out, or if you had no money to begin with, your *only* option was pool water.

"Interahamwe leaders are here at the hotel," said Christophe one day. "Karamira, Mutwe, Bagosora, and Karwera. They come in not to harm anyone, just to see what type of people are in the hotel so they can ask them if they want their families brought here, too—but they will have to pay. They are here just for their personal business—to make a profit off us refugees. But other Interahamwe, the ones who are running around on the streets with machetes, they don't seem to dare come into the hotel because of the UNAMIR soldiers and the big tank the UN has facing the gate."

Colonel Bagosora? We had all heard of him. We couldn't believe it!

"Yes, Colonel Bagosora," replied Christophe, "the recognized general organizer of the genocide, was just here in the hotel drinking—probably with our money!"

He was known for establishing the Interahamwe, as well as for his role in distributing arms and machetes throughout Rwanda, so to say that Colonel Théoneste Bagosora hated Tutsi is a bit of an understatement. We heard from the UNAMIR peacekeepers that Bagosora once told one of their commanders the only way to solve Rwanda's problems was to "get rid of the Tutsi." And though he was present at the negotiations of the Arusha Accords in August 1993, it is no secret that Bagosora never supported them—indeed, he is widely cited as saying that once everything was signed, he would return to Rwanda to "prepare for the apocalypse."

Another refugee, Jean Marie Vianney Mutesa, was a journalist from Rwanda National Radio and was staying in room 324 with nine other people. Being a newsperson, he knew all the famous military leaders by sight. "Bagosora is here at the hotel most every evening. When the interim government moved to Gitarama, Bagosora did not. Even though he was part of the government, he was still living in the Hotel des Diplomates, but there was nothing in there such as food or drinks. So he comes here to the des Mille Collines Hotel to get something to eat and maybe to hang out."

Many others inside the hotel, including embassy employee Wellars Gasamagera, young student Jean Pierre Nkurunziza, and our friend Alexis, who worked at the hotel, noted the close relationship between Bagosora and Paul Rusesabagina. They told tales of seeing the two sitting together, laughing and drinking as if nothing was wrong with the world. Afterward, Rusesabagina would strut around, speaking as if he and the colonel were good friends and equals—powerful, important men who liked and respected each other. We shook our heads. Who would take pride in such a thing? And what did this say of his politics? Alexis was even more cynical. He thought it laughable that this pompous little hotelier considered himself on the same level as a military leader who could order the deaths of thousands.

> Rusesabagina would strut around, speaking as if he and the colonel were good friends and equals—powerful, important men who liked and respected each other. We shook our heads. Who would take pride in such a thing?

The leader of the regular military, General Augustin Bizimungu, was also frequently seen inside the hotel—again, laughing and drinking with the hotel manager. Those who got close enough to overhear some of his discussions with UN peacekeepers heard him claim that he, as a leader of the Rwandan Army, did not have control over the militias, nor was he aware of their activities. No one who knew Rwandan politics believed this to be true, but it seemed a good lie to use on foreigners.

Another *génocidaire* friend of the hotel manager who frequented the hotel was Froduald Karamira, president of MDR Kigali City, vice president of the MDR, and the creator of MDR Power. Co-founder, along with Georges Rutaganda, of the extremist hate-radio station RTLM, Karamira was notorious for inciting violence and orchestrating the genocide through repeated daily broadcasts on RTLM. He was also known throughout Rwanda for the speech he gave at Nyamirambo Stadium in Kigali on October 23, 1993, in which he called for total solidarity among all Hutu, transcending divisions among political parties. The infamous speech also popularized the concept of "Hutu Power," which became the slogan of Hutu extremists before and during the genocide.

We first learned of Rusesabagina's relationship with Karamira via another friend of Rusesabagina's, a lovely refugee by the name of Odette Nyiramilimo. Rusesabagina personally arranged for Odette, her husband Jean-Baptiste, and their four children to gain safe passage to the hotel. Nearly everyone in the hotel had someone to thank for getting them into the hotel, and Odette would likely never have gotten there without her friend, the hotel manager. Odette and her family did not join us at the hotel until the April 27 or 28. She said:

> Rusesabagina Paul is a friend of ours. He kept calling our house every day, because we were so scared that if we picked up the phone, the *génocidaires* would know we were still alive. One day, the phone kept ringing. I knew that either way we were going to die. When I picked up the phone, it was Paul. He asked us how we were doing and we told him that people thought we were dead. He told us he was going to send a car to take us to the Mille Collines Hotel. He suggested that Karamira should come to pick us up. We told Paul that if he sent Karamira, we were afraid he would kill us, for we knew him to be a bad man who hated Tutsi. So instead Paul sent a soldier named Nzaramba François.

On our way to the hotel, we came across a roadblock a few miles from our home. The people at the roadblock tried to kill us, but Nzaramba and his escorts jumped out of the car and had them arrested. Nzaramba then took me to the hotel, along with my little sister. The next day, he went back and got my husband and my son so they could join me.

"What is it like out there now?" we asked.

We could see they were killing people everywhere. We passed a lot of roadblocks and there were a lot of Interahamwe with machetes. They asked Nzaramba where he was taking us. He told them I was sick and he was taking me to the hospital. Then, once we got here to the hotel, it was a problem getting in. They asked me why I came here. Nzaramba told them I was a doctor and I was coming to treat Rusesabagina's children. Finally, they let us in.

We didn't have to pay any money to get into the hotel—we didn't have any money left, though I did have ten thousand francs stashed somewhere. When we arrived at the hotel, even though he didn't ask us for any money, I gave Nzaramba ten thousand anyway. We really thanked him. We love him. He saved a lot of people.

When we arrived here, Rusesabagina made me sign recognition of debt for four hundred dollars. Then he took it out of my bank account. Rusesabagina told us there were some other people he brought to the hotel. I tried to talk to them to find out if that was true, but they denied it. One family I was able to speak with was the Remera family from Kabeza. They were the only other ones who said it was Paul who got them here. That I know, because they told me themselves.

Georges Rutaganda, the Interahamwe vice president and beer merchant, began coming to the hotel as well. We surmised it was becoming more and more dangerous for Rusesabagina himself to drive around Kigali. We would see Rutaganda dropping off his beer, but he would also stop and talk with many of the refugees who knew him—people like Wycliff Kajuga.

"If any of you have any money, Rutaganda said he would sell us food and things, but we have to keep it a secret," said Wycliff as he strode away from a whispered conversation with Rutaganda.

This sounded strange. We thought the money paid to Rusesabagina was supposed to bring us food and beverages, which he in turn bought from Rutaganda.

"No, no. Rutaganda said Rusesabagina keeps promising him money but he never pays. Or else he promises to give him a check but then he always makes up some excuse for not having it. Besides, Rutaganda knows that what he gives to Rusesabagina, Rusesabagina sells back to us at a high profit. Rutaganda is offering to cut out the middle man and sell to us directly, but we need to keep it a secret or Rusesabagina will try to close the whole situation down."

Bagosora, Bizimungu, Karamira, Rutaganda—these were all very bad men. Mass murderers, architects of a genocide. All four of them sought out Paul Rusesabagina and spent significant amounts of time lounging away inside the Hotel des Mille Collines with him, sharing laughs and drinking, leaving the rest of us to wonder when one of them might simply pull out a gun and shoot us for the sport of it.

It is said that each of us is judged by the company we keep. Paul Rusesabagina was supposedly active in the MDR Power Party, the radical, violent branch of MDR. As long as Paul was a member of MDR Power, nobody could threaten him or kill him. Judging by his actions, by the way he was exploiting us and mistreating us so mercilessly, we could only speculate that the reason he was sharing beers with those killers was because they shared the same ideology.

13

LIKE NIXON TO CHINA

GENOCIDES, WARS, CIVIL wars, and armed unrest do not happen in a localized vacuum. Nearly every nation in the world plays a part, even if that part is to be a nonparticipating bystander, for as in the biblical tale of the Good Samaritan, to do nothing is to do something. While to most casual observers there were few active participants in these acts of turmoil and death, this, as I learned from being up close, is deceptive. During the Genocide Against the Tutsi many nations had a hidden involvement. One of the foremost actors was France.

France backed the government of Rwandan President Juvénal Habyarimana. The French, under then-president François Mitterrand, continued to back the FAR (*Forces armées rwandaises*—the regular Rwandan army) after Habyarimana's death. The French had even been on the front line of this genocide and war with boots on the ground, and not as peacekeepers. They had participated in training the Hutu Power militias, and they were on the roadblocks asking for national IDs. The French could say, "You, you are Tutsi; you, you are Hutu," and those people met their respective fates.[10]

---

[10] French support of the FAR and provision of military aid are discussed in Stephen Kinzer's *A Thousand Hills: Rwanda's Rebirth and the Man Who Dreamed It* (Hoboken, NJ: Wiley, 2008), and Gérard Prunier's *The Rwanda Crisis: History of a Genocide* (New York: Columbia University Press, 1995). *Rwanda Today* also notes that "The President [Kagame] who was making a presentation under the theme: 'The evolution of conflicts in Africa: Prospect for Peace and Development,' added: 'Genocide was prepared months

We all knew the FAR had a great relationship with the French people. For instance, Mont Kigali is the highest peak in Rwanda. It is a beautiful and picturesque place among our thousands of green hills. And yet that beauty was besmirched in 1994, for it is also where the French provided small-arms and knife-fighting training to the militias shortly before the start of the genocide. The French not only trained the Hutu Power extremists, but they also provided most of their weaponry.[11]

From the moment most of us had settled into the hotel, talk was not of us staying there, trapped like bugs under a glass, but of all of us somehow getting out. We often heard that the RPF was coming to liberate us, but that had yet to happen and many of us doubted it ever would, or if we'd live to see it. We knew we could not simply run out, every man for himself, make a dash for it, and hope to survive. That would be akin to racing across a heavily fortified minefield—instant death at the hands of the crazed men with guns and machetes who never wavered from stalking us from just outside our gates. No, we waited and waited for some plan, some timetable, some real protection that would allow us safe passage out and away from the hotel to someplace safer where there was

---

before the shooting down of the plane; arms were being ferried to Rwanda and French troops were manning roadblocks and screening the Tutsi and putting them aside'";
"Kagame Rubbishes Bruguère's Claims," *Rwanda Today,* accessed October 17, 2013, http://rwandatoday.com/content/headline.php?headlineid=213&PHPSESSID=6f0da11fb dbc58e4817049928604a048.

[11] "French forces superintended the organisation of the militias, known as the Interahamwe. Janvier Africa, son of a Rwandan diplomat, and a former Interahamwe member, described French involvement: 'We had two French military who helped train the Interahamwe. A lot of other Interahamwe were sent for training in Egypt. The French military taught us how to catch people and tie them. It was at the Affichier Central base in the centre of Kigali. It's where people were tortured. That's where the French military office was...The French also went with us Interahamwe to Mount Kigali, where they gave us training with guns. We didn't know how to use the arms which had been brought from France so the French military were obliged to show us.'" (quoted in *The Age,* June 23, 1994, p. 12); Steven, "1990–1994: The Genocide and War in Rwanda," *Libcom,* September 8, 2006, http://libcom.org/history/1990-1994-the-genocide-and-war-in-rwanda.

no genocide and no war. For how long would the undisciplined militias remain at bay? How long before we were the target of some bombing mission?

On May 3, Jean Miseho from the Ministry of Foreign Affairs of Luxembourg wrote a letter saying that Luxembourg's ambassador to the United Nations had announced that refugees in the Hotel des Mille Collines could not be evacuated without a cease-fire between the RPF and the FAR. On May 11, José Ayala Lasso, UN high commissioner for human rights, visited the refugees in the Hotel des Mille Collines. These letters and visits always had the effect of muting whatever nerve the *génocidaires* had regarding coming into the hotel and slaughtering us, or evicting us for the purpose of slaughter. Whoever won the war that accompanied the genocide would need to do business with the rest of the world. Much of the murder of innocents had been unseen and unreported. But those of us in the hotel were becoming more and more known to the outside world. When people came in and out of the hotel—UN people and others—we would learn of other pockets of refugees still surviving the carnage in various places throughout the nation. But we were in the most high-profile location—a luxury hotel where diplomats and peacekeepers could gather. The murderers would forget that from time to time, and then a major diplomatic visit would occur or a telegram would arrive, reminding them of our special place in this macabre ballet.

We also drew attention to our plight because of the valiant efforts of people like Christophe, Wellars, Ndolimana, Kayijaho, Nsanzuwera, and Bernard Makuza—men who personally knew ambassadors and heads of NGOs, who called them incessantly before the telephone lines were cut, and continued to do so to the best of their ability thereafter. If someone like me had tried to call a high-ranking official in some foreign government, how far would I have gotten? I was a nobody who knew no one of importance outside of Rwanda. So, too, most of the others trapped in the hotel or working there. International diplomacy was not our field. But for these other men, this was their trade.

On May 15, Bernard Kouchner, a French statesman who at the time was a member of European Parliament, came into the hotel. Earlier in his career he co-founded the NGO *Médecins sans frontières* (Doctors Without Borders). Because he was from France, he held far more influence in Rwanda than most visitors from other nations. Interestingly enough, Kouchner did not hold a position in the French cabinet at the time of the genocide, but his dossier gave him a high level of gravitas. Everyone assumed he was coming at the behest of Mitterrand, but Paris had not officially sanctioned his trip. It was not until much later that we would discover his mission was a solo flight, the actions of a single man of conscience using his political credentials to bluff his moral will upon an abhorrent humanitarian crisis.

Dr. Kouchner insisted on meeting with Colonel Théoneste Bagosora and General Augustin Bizimungu, the lead *génocidaires*, as well as General Roméo Dallaire, commander of the UN peacekeepers. Refugees were encouraged to attend that meeting, particularly those from our leadership committee. Although I did not officially serve on the committee, I decided to attend because I was very curious to hear what was going on. More than any other visitor, Dr. Kouchner set the place abuzz.

Bernard Kouchner told the refugees to ask any questions they might have. Though we were all afraid of Bagosora and Bizimungu, Dr. Kouchner assured us that we could speak freely—and stared defiantly at the military strongmen for emphasis as he said those words.

The leader of our committee, Tatien Ndolimana, asked about our safety. Dr. Kouchner asked Bagosora and Bizimungu to declare publicly that no one would kill the Mille Collines refugees. To his credit, Bizimungu declared just that—though it should hardly come as a surprise that none of us believed him. After the meeting, Dr. Kouchner went to the RPF zone to speak to leaders there.

Given all the variables, all the different people and agendas, it would be nearly impossible for any one person to singlehandedly change the fortunes of what were now over a thousand lives in the hotel. But there was a feeling that this day, this meeting, would have a grand effect on our existence. No one had spoken so boldly to the Hutu Power military and militia leaders, not even General Dallaire, fearless as he was. These same people had murdered UN personnel before—the Belgian soldiers. The difference was Dr. Kouchner's nationality and perceived position. It was assumed that Kouchner spoke for France, spoke for President Mitterrand himself. If the Hutu Power leaders lost the support of France, they would be almost completely alone in this battle and its aftermath. Dr. Kouchner's assistance and influence could not be minimized. He showed himself to be a real humanitarian who went against the politics of his own nation, and he worked diligently to influence the Rwandan government not to kill us.

It is ironic, but just as American historians have said that only a staunch anticommunist like Richard Nixon ever could have opened China to the United States, during the genocide only a high-profile, politically important Frenchman could have brokered concessions from the *génocidaires*. They needed French support in order to win the war.

Kouchner worked with General Dallaire to find a way that we could be transferred to the RPF zone. If we were able to reach the RPF side, it would be easier for us to be rescued. But because the Hotel des Mille Collines was geographically on the Rwandan government's side during the genocide, someone had to convince the government itself, the high commander of militaries as well as the militias, to let us go.

Another person who played a big role in our protection was Maria, a Tutsi lady who was a guest in the hotel at the time of the start of the genocide and whose fiancé was German. Toward the end of April and into the early part of May, countries who had guests staying at the hotel—mostly white Europeans—arranged for evacuation of their people under the watchful eyes of their diplomatic represen-tatives. For the rest of us, these were bittersweet moments.

From the moment most of us had settled into the hotel, talk was not of us staying there, trapped like bugs under a glass, but of all of us somehow getting out.

Much as we daydreamed that for some crazy reason or another, someone would take us with them, it was never to be. They, too, had their lists—not of people to be murdered, but of people to be saved.

During the evacuation of the whites from Rwanda, the Germans initially refused to evacuate beautiful Maria. Her case would later become an acute headache to the interim Rwandan government. The German government, realizing its mistake in not immediately evacuating her, asked the interim Rwandan government as a matter of diplomacy to protect all the refugees in the hotel, especially Maria. Her protection became our protection.

General Bizimungu personally came to see her. "Are you seeing that we are killing you?" he asked in the most mocking tone one could imagine. "Don't you see that I kill you?!" Then he laughed a hateful laugh. But despite his braggadocio, Maria—as well as the rest of us—was spared for the moment.

Time and again it became clear to us that the international com-munity held the most sway with the génocidaires. After the genocide, after the war that was going on in tandem with it, once one side or the other had won, there would be a whole process of national rebuilding, which always requires trade relations with other nations so the war-ravaged economy can be turned around and the nation sustained. Rwanda, whether it would be led in the future by the RPF or by the Hutu Power extremists, would have to attain and retain a seat at the world's table in order to survive. Thus, the leaders of the génocidaires did whatever was necessary to carry out their avowed mission of killing all Tutsi, while at the same time trying not to incur the wrath of such potential trade partners as France, Germany, Luxembourg, and Italy.

But for all the comfort we imagined because of the efforts of Bernard Kouchner and the Germans, we noticed something else as the European guests left our ranks. The UN peacekeeping forces seemed to diminish in size as well. The embassy guards who gave us such comfort when we saw them marching through our lobby left us as they took their citizens to safety. Once Italy, once Luxembourg no longer had a single citizen or embassy guard or employee in Rwanda, would they look back? Would they monitor what happened to us? Would they care?

14

TO PROFIT FROM THE WALKING DEAD

S TIME WENT by, almost all the cash any of the refugees had brought with them was given over to the hotel's manager. This left him with no other easy options for profiteering, until he came up with the idea of bringing a Bank of Kigali (BK) manager into the hotel in order to run an actual banking operation there. A trustworthy and respected Bank of Kigali (BK) employee, Louis Rugerinyange, had bank receipts for those who had accounts with BK. Those of us inside the Mille Collines signed the receipts, then Rugerinyange went to the bank in Gitarama, forty-five kilometers from Kigali, to withdraw the money and bring it back to the hotel. (All banks and government agencies had followed the interim government to Gitarama.)

I don't blame the bank employee—looking back, it is quite possible that through his actions he may have helped refugees live longer. Frankly, in this time of our circumstance-imposed imprisonment inside the hotel, our only real need for money was to ward off Paul Rusesabagina, who by now was threatening to evict us from the hotel unless we paid for our lodgings.

On May 18, 1994, the refugee committee sneaked into the hotel manager's office while he was unaware and faxed an SOS letter addressed to international organizations as well as Sabena, the corporate manager of the Hotel des Mille Collines, asking for protection and specifically pleading with the hotel management to stop Rusesabagina from harassing us. In short order, a fax came in response from a Michel Houtart at Sabena headquarters in Brussels. Translated from the original French, it made three blunt and salient points:

- *Do not charge money for food received for free*;
- *Do not pressure anyone who cannot defend themselves*; and finally,
- *Make sure everyone is in rooms or dormitories.*

That the hotel's corporate headquarters felt the need to send such a missive to Paul Rusesabagina speaks volumes about what our lives were truly like within the real-life "Hotel Rwanda," and who had made them so. Unfortunately, getting him to heed their warning was another matter altogether.

Those who could not pay for their lodging were forced from their rooms by Rusesabagina himself, literally as well as figuratively. He would send invoices to the rooms. If you did not pay, he called you to his office and asked you to pay or get out of the room. People strongly contested that decision, but some who had money paid, while others signed receipts for the amount owed.

Instead of taking one of the regular Mille Collines employees and making that person second-in-command, Rusesabagina hired himself an assistant, Asuman Ngagi, who had been working at the Hotel Méridien. The Méridien was also under UN protection, in the zone controlled by the RPF, as were the Hotel Amahoro and the King Faisal Hospital. Asuman was even more openly hostile toward us Tutsi than Rusesabagina, threatening us at every opportunity. Visions of him haunted my dreams. Now, armed with a strong and loyal assistant, Rusesabagina became even more aggressive in moving people from their rooms because of nonpayment.

Once displaced, many of us milled around the hotel and slept wherever we could, mostly in the hallways.

I was personally called into Rusesabagina's office with my roommate, Rubayiza. He asked us to pay or to get out of our room. I had no money on me other than the blank check I had found in my coat. I agreed to sign the check over to Rusesabagina, and Rubayiza paid him some cash from approximately 300,000 Rwandan francs he had gotten from Mukaniwa Deo, a businessman from Cyangugu, his home prefecture, who was also seeking refuge within the hotel.

All of us did whatever we could to help one another out, sharing everything we had so that no one would die. Occasionally, after reaching the hotel, someone tried to bring inside a loved one who was still outside, hiding in some other location. We pooled whatever money we had managed to hide away from Rusesabagina to pay off *gendarmes* or militiamen to search for and rescue our family members.

The refugees who managed to bring some money to the hotel could have used that to procure anything from those of us who came in empty-handed—but they didn't. During this time of terrible murders in the streets, we all wanted only one thing: *to live*. Despite vast financial disparity among us, no refugee profited from any other refugee.

On the other hand, there were a few refugees who were not forced to pay because Rusesabagina knew them. I suppose that could be construed as an act of magnanimous charity, but if one were really a humanitarian, why extend such hospitality to only a few personal friends? Most refugees were total strangers to one another when we arrived and yet we shared everything, *every single thing we had*, regardless of our ethnicity. That sort of communal peace and love is what truly sustained our spirits during the dark days.

A typical example was when Major Cyiza, a Hutu military man and the president of the military court, came into the hotel. Sometime in May, he took room 109, which was occupied by Augustin Karera, a businessman, and Wellars Gasamagera, one of our refugee leaders.

They were forced by Rusesabagina to give up their accommodations. The major behaved as if he were a man on holiday, going to work and coming back to the hotel each evening safe and, unlike the rest of us, in no fear of any harm because of his ethnicity and position in the government. Cyiza could have treated us like the "cockroaches" we supposedly were—but he didn't. Instead, and for this I give him credit, the major actually helped some of the refugees by going outside the hotel and buying us provisions with money we gave him.

As for Gasamagera and Karera, they found another room in the hotel, only to be moved again by Rusesabagina. This time they had to resort to sleeping in the corridor until they could find someone willing to share space with them. When they were forced out of their new room, Gasamagera and Karera went out with only a set of sheets and their small cache of personal belongings. When we saw them we were scared, thinking they were leaving the room and taking everything with them because someone inside had died or been killed, or perhaps Gasamagera or Karera themselves were being turned over to the *génocidaires*. That is a sight none of us will ever forget.

I asked Gasamagera a few days later how he was getting on. "A friend of mine named Charles Harelimana took me in. There are about twenty of us in one room and some people sleep in the bathtub. We have a child with us who is mute. We send him around the hotel to beg for food for all of us. That's how we are living." This was rather commonplace. Not everyone had access to food, and if you did not tell someone you were starving and ask if they would share with you, you starved. I asked Karera the same question, how was he getting by. "Victor Munyarugerero came and told us not to worry; that he had found me and my family another room. We are now living with Bernard Makuza."

Rusesabagina continued to harass us despite the fax from Sabena headquarters that clearly ordered him not to. On May 21, 1994, the refugees composed another letter, this time to the CICR, the *Comité international de la Croix-Rouge* (the International Committee of the

Red Cross), asking them to intervene in the matter. Though the Red Cross likewise scolded Rusesabagina for his actions, he did not discontinue them. The conflict escalated to the point where Tatien Ndolimana, acting on behalf of the rest of the refugees, took a letter protesting our treatment to Colonel Moigny, who was in charge of the UN peacekeeping brigade inside the hotel. By their reaction, we could not help but notice in what low esteem the peacekeepers and the Red Cross held Rusesabagina.

Ndolimana, a fine man, was particularly disgusted with the hotel manager. "You understand, not only was he not here in the hotel when the genocide first began, but for almost a month he was going back home every night. Throughout April he worked here from 7 A.M. to 5 P.M. and even then he spent many hours outside the hotel. He only started sleeping here with his family since May second because he thought he and his family could be evacuated to Europe from here."

One day the bloodthirsty militias targeted the hotel despite the UN presence there. An artillery shell was propelled in our direction, but instead it missed its intended target and accidentally hit a nearby bank. Instantly, we all fled to the hotel basement, using it as a sort of bomb shelter. When we got to the basement we saw this little metallic door. It was open. Inside, we found a stock of soft drinks, bottled water, and some cookies. Unbelievable! We had long suspected the hotel manager had been greedily squirreling away provisions in secret. Knowing how hungry and thirsty we were, Christophe Shamukiga began distributing the soft drinks to the rest of us. When the bombing stopped and things began to settle, we made our way out of the basement, only to find Rusesabagina standing in front of the *entrée,* threatening to throw us out into the streets unless we put back the drinks.

A couple minutes later people knocked on Christophe's door. When he answered, they asked if he was Christophe Shamukiga and he said, "Yes." They told him the director, Paul, wanted to see him.

He went up to Paul's room. After what seemed like an interminably long time, Christophe came back out, looking more ragged, scared, and upset than he had ever been seen before.

"I asked why he wanted to see me. He told me it was about the incident in the basement. He said if I didn't pay him five hundred thousand francs he would kick me out of the hotel. I begged him and said we were all hungry and it wasn't our fault. He said he didn't care; either I pay him or he kicks me out. As a matter of fact, he even said, 'I'm going to kick you out anyway. It doesn't matter if you pay me or not.'"

To be kicked out of the hotel at this point in time was akin to being put before a firing squad without trial. It was a death sentence.

"I climbed out the window of his room and stood on the third-floor balcony," said Christophe. "I told him I would rather jump off the balcony than be kicked out of the hotel, especially if I was going to die anyway. He said he didn't care. I told him to at least let me talk to my father's friends, people such as Bertin Makuza, a well-known businessman. They might help me to come up with the money. He said I should sign somewhere that I was going to pay him."

Like those before him who had paid *génocidaires* to shoot them rather than die slowly and painfully by machete, Christophe threatened to commit suicide by jumping from a top-floor balcony to the pavement far below rather than yield to the hotel manager.

We did not know how to properly comfort Christophe, as neither he nor we knew how much longer he would be able to stay in the hotel after having crossed Rusesabagina. Christophe possessed tremendous civility, humanity, and tolerance for people regardless of their ethnicity or politics. With great humility he had used his significant political connections and influence to help save us refugees and keep us alive inside the hotel. In a way, he was our very own Robin Hood, in that he robbed from the rich (distributing freely the biscuits and soft drinks Paul Rusesabagina had stashed away in the basement so he could later sell them for a profit) and gave to the poor (his fellow refugees, many of whom were suffering from dehydration and starvation). It was a daring action that nearly cost Christophe his life.

Later on, fortunately, someone managed to negotiate with Rusesabagina, and Christophe was given a stay of execution and allowed to remain inside. But after the basement incident, Christophe never again felt he had any personal security within the hotel, even more so than the rest of us.

Alexis told me that occasionally he'd hear that some people were trying to escape or run away from the hotel. As soon as they'd leave, before they'd get very far away, they would all be killed. "Why would someone want to get himself killed?" He asked. We knew the hotel was the safest place anyone could be, especially because we were already there. We were supposed to stick together, no matter what. That had been our credo, the thing that helped us combat the insanity of the genocide.

Throughout these tumultuous days, our lives were in the hands of God. Bishop Nicodème, another refugee at the hotel, gathered us daily in the conference room, where we would pray. Victor Munyarugerero, a very religious man, would knock on our door to let us to know it was time for our daily vespers. After we had evening prayers, those who had no food could get some from a shared stockpile to which everyone who had food would willingly contribute.

Victor was a Hutu in his forties. During our time together, cloistered inside the hotel, he showed us how people are different; how all Hutu were not killers or exploiters. Some people collected money and gave it to Victor in order to smuggle their families and friends into the hotel. When Bernard Makuza, one of the refugee committee members, first arrived at the hotel, he had been beaten up by the thugs in the street and was in pretty bad shape. It was Victor Munyarugerero who took him in, along with Bishop Nicodème. We had a doctor inside the hotel, Josue Kayijaho, who was also a refugee, and they would ask Dr. Kayijaho to check on him.

It was people like Victor who risked their lives by leaving the relative safety of the hotel to find militia or *gendarmes* who would accept bribes to let people inside the hotel, or to buy food for the rest of us. Victor did this many times without any complaint, and certainly without any thought of retaining a profit for himself. Many refugees sang his praises. He was so nice, but he didn't want to take any credit for his generous and noble deeds. Bernard Makuza, in particular, felt Victor was owed a special debt of gratitude. "He cares about what people are eating, how they were living, if they have any problems. There is also this man named Cassien Nzaryana; he works in the kitchen. When I was hurt and couldn't move, sometimes he would bring me a drink, but he would have to do it without being seen by anyone. He never brought me any food, though. I guess it was too risky for him, with the hotel manager watching over everything."

I would run into Alexis from time to time and ask him how the hotel employees were doing in light of no longer getting paid. "I don't think the employees really care about their salaries anymore," he said. "All we care about is staying alive and making sure our families are safe. At this point, we are all refugees."

Life in the hotel during the days of May 1994 was strange indeed. We were under siege, and yet those whom we feared most strolled in and out of the hotel as if nothing was the matter. The hotel was an odd and tenuous sort of neutral zone, yet we had no reason to trust that this would last. Every day and every moment, we feared the next time a Hutu Power soldier or militiaman entered, he would be leading a pack of armed jackals, ready to slaughter us. The screams, explosions, and gunshots we continually heard outside on the streets made us tense and wary. Many had trouble sleeping, wondering if they would be roused by a machete held to their neck.

There were basically four groups of people who were in the hotel: Tutsi who sought refuge in order to avoid death, Hutu who did not share the same ideology as the killers and were also threatened with death, Hutu who came into the hotel simply to avoid the war zone for a little stay while they made plans to leave town, and UN peacekeepers and other visiting internationals. All in all, it resembled the classic American World War II–era film, *Casablanca*, in which Nazis, Vichy French, French freedom fighters, locals, and various expats all shared space—a place where cautious civility and a respite from actual armed conflict existed, although its component parts made for a potential powder keg of blood and death if political and military situations suddenly changed.

Managing the peace, of course, was the fourth group: the ever-present UN soldiers and other internationals. While they had nothing to do with the daily running of the hotel, which was a private business, it was they who provided the on-premises security in this highly unique situation. The peacekeepers had their own office in one of the hotel rooms and someone was there at all times, 24/7. One of the rules they enforced for visitors to the hotel was to leave their weapons at the reception desk. The hotel was a kind of de facto protected site for all kinds of international visitors, for nowhere else in the nation seemed as perfectly located and secured.

Kalisa was an example of a Hutu who did not support the *géno-cidaires*. While at the hotel, he risked his life by helping us. Kalisa had kept his friend Emmanuel Musonera, a Tutsi, safe in his house in Secteur Gikondo by hiding him inside his roof, much as Pascal had hidden me. After managing to sneak Emmanuel into the hotel, Kalisa took the money we raised communally and purchased things we needed. Food and water, of course, were our largest concerns, but basic sanitation, cleanliness, clothing, and medical supplies were also difficult to come by. We may have been refugees, but we sought to retain our human dignity and pride. We did whatever was required of us to stay alive, but we would also not allow our spirits to be broken.

Despite the kindness he showed us, Kalisa was a man who scared many refugees, especially his Tutsi roommate, Alexandre, because of his familial connections. One of Kalisa's sisters was married to

Anatole Nsengiyumva, a lieutenant colonel who was known to be one of the planners of the genocide, while another was married to Colonel Karangwa, who was in charge of G2, the Rwandan military intelligence. In fact, Karangwa came to the hotel many times to see Kalisa, as well as to see his friend Paul Rusesabagina. Whenever he arrived, there was likewise a distinct scent of fear in the air.

Kalisa and Alexandre lived in room 305, just across the hall from my room. Alexandre had just barely managed to get into the hotel and he had foreign money in his pocket. Because he was scared of Kalisa (or perhaps more accurately, Kalisa's in-laws), he slept very little at night, succumbing only after exhaustion had overtaken him. Though he would catch some rest during the day, he also prayed that the daylight, not to mention the stirring of those of us who were awake, would alert him if we were being invaded or if he alone were in personal danger.

Alexandre and I used to go into the basement at night to find places to hide in the event of another bombing—though in truth we were certain it was a matter of "when," not "if." On the day when Christophe Shamukiga distributed the drinks and cookies to us he had found stashed away in the basement, Alexandre and I took a package of cookies and hid it in another part of the basement so we would have something to eat during a future attack—or at least that was our thinking at first. As time went on, though, we made a pact: no matter how hungry we were, no matter how desperate things came to be, we would never open that package of cookies. It was sacrosanct, a visual reminder of hope that we would somehow get through this alive—and though we never said it in so many words, to tear open that package and eat those cookies would have been as if we had given up that hope. Even if the hotel were stormed and taken, we would have left that package intact. Hope was all we had, and hope was what had gotten us to the hotel in the first place.

Meanwhile, throughout my days at the hotel, my stomach continued to hurt from drinking pool water. I had by chance met up with a woman I knew named Jeannette, whose husband happened to work at the hotel. Though Jeannette was Tutsi, her husband was a zealous member of President Habyarimana's MRND Party. He supplied her and her children with everything they needed, such as juice and food. On April 6, when the president's plane had crashed, Jeannette had been blocked at Gitega, my town, and could not go back home that evening. She stayed hidden in Gitega with a family friend, close to where I had lived, secreted away until she was finally able to get to the Hotel des Mille Collines. She knew how hard the militias had searched for me and had heard that they had killed me when I was trying to leave town. You can imagine her surprise when she stumbled onto me one day and saw I was still alive.

"Edouard," she said with tears in her eyes. "I cannot believe it is you! Are you all right? Do you need anything?" She could tell I had been wearing the same clothes since I fled Gitega on the morning of April 7, over a month before. "Do you need money for underwear?"

Instead of feverishly guzzling it, we just smelled the aroma of the juice because we had drank so much of the heavily chlorinated water from the swimming pool. It smelled so good. It smelled like civilization.

"I don't worry about underwear, Jeannette," I said. "But I do have a stomachache."

She went and brought me a cup of juice and 20,000 Rwandan francs. To say "thank you" is easy. I think God himself knows what she did for me. And yet I could not drink this cup of juice without sharing it with my friends Jean Marie Vianney Rudasingwa, Rubayiza, and Emmanuel Musonera. Instead of feverishly guzzling it, we just smelled the aroma of the juice because we had drank so much of the heavily chlorinated water from the swimming pool. It smelled so good. It smelled like civilization. And then, as we looked at each other as if for permission to finally quench our thirst, we slowly and equally shared it.

The water in the swimming pool would frequently run out and we would have to wait until the UN peacekeepers could bring back more with their tank truck to refill the pool. When the pool had water in it, we would go outside each morning with a large trash basket, fill it with water, and then bring it inside the hotel. At night we would go back again and do the same. One good thing was that as time went on and the UN refilled the pool, it was no longer treated with the harsh chemicals that made it safer for swimming but made us sick.

Rubayiza, my roommate, had no idea about his wife and children—whether they were dead or alive, or where they or their bodies were. Emmanuel had no idea about his wife, either, while Jean Marie Vianney Rudasingwa had come to the hotel after they had killed his wife and children.

When Rusesabagina forced people out of their rooms, some people paid for other people or signed checks for them so they could stay and not have to sleep in the hall. I split the 20,000 francs I'd received from Jeannette with Emmanuel Musonera. Even though Emmanuel was a businessman, he had no money in his pockets. When you are running for your life, you are living moment to moment. It does not occur to you to bring all the cash you can lay your hands on, and at a time when mayhem ruled the streets, it was not as if you could easily go to a bank, make a withdrawal, and assume you'd come back alive.

Emmanuel's father-in-law, Vedaste Rubangura, was also among us. Vedaste was one of the wealthiest men in the country and the first Tutsi to get into the Hotel des Mille Collines. He had a large family and helped buy food for everyone. Many refugees ate because of this man.

Then there were the families of Mister, Damascene, and Assiel, whom I will never forget. Somehow they were able to bring a grill inside the hotel, which they used to cook food they had managed to buy early on during our time together. Once we were allowed to use the hotel kitchen, they cooked beans and corn given to us by the Red Cross and shared them with many people. Meanwhile, the UN peacekeepers who were in the hotel also helped some refugees, particularly those who had children, by giving them food and potable water.

I remember sometimes we would gather together, apportioning our suffering with others: Jean Marie Vianney Rudasingwa, Emmanuel Musonera, Eugene Kitatire, André Musoni, Jean Pierre, Alexandre, Rubayiza, and me. There were so many people who took care of other refugees—businessmen like Bertin Makuza, Egide Karuranga, Vedaste Rubangura, Augustin Karera, Victor Munyarugerero, and Mutalikanwa. Some kindly Hutu who were not staying in the hotel brought in food from the outside to family and friends who were refugees. Among these were Sadala Abdalahaman, Libanje, Maniraguha, and a priest named Kaberamanzi, who made his way through the roadblocks every morning and every evening to bring food to his colleague, Bishop Nicodème.

The chapter markers that normally highlight our lives continued inside the hotel, much as they do anywhere during any circumstance, but hastened, as we feared if we did not partake in important sacraments, we would die before we got the chance. Bishop Nicodème baptized one child of Tatien Ndolimana. The daughter of Victor Munyarugerero married her boyfriend, and the bishop celebrated the mass and gave the marriage sacrament.

These names mean nothing to anyone outside of our band of survivors. But to us, these were real heroes. These noble men and women sacrificed everything they had so that each of us could live. None of us will ever forget the love we all demonstrated for our fellow man.

We shared everything we could, and though we did our best to keep our spirits up, deep down we all feared we would never leave the hotel alive. It was as close to purgatory as one can imagine. All we were doing was buying time, each of us making his or her own negotiation with God for one more hour, one more day. The magnanimity within our ranks was our way of making our peace with God, our hope of settling our karmic accounts before death.

Each one of us inside the hotel had our own personal, special story. We talked; we listened; we allowed one another to cry when the time came to cry. But more than anything else, we waited... waited for death to take us.

15

NAMES, NUMBERS, COLLABORATORS, AND BETRAYERS

A S THE SECOND month of our voluntary incarceration inside the Hotel des Mille Collines stretched on, the genocide continued, while the war appeared to be getting closer and closer to our door. Yet the thousand or so refugees in the hotel were not always intimately aware of exactly what was going on with either, or how in danger they truly were. UNAMIR General Roméo Dallaire finally gave the dreaded overview:

> There have been several artillery and mortar rounds and some rocket-propelled grenades and sniper fire aimed at the hotel. Also, there were two incursions inside the hotel that were stopped by UN Military Observers, which is why I make so many night and morning radio checks with the observers who put themselves in front of you civilians. I have deployed UN Military Observers with radios at the entrance to the hotel to report immediately any attempt by the Interahamwe or the FAR to enter the hotel. Indications are that the hotel manager has done everything in his power to have these UN soldiers removed from the hotel. I also received unconfirmed

> reports that the manager has given FAR General Bizimungu a
> list of hotel guests and their room numbers. UN soldiers are
> changing around the room numbers of the most threatened.

One might wonder how we were all not aware of guns and weaponry being fired at the hotel, or militiamen attempting to storm the place. The fact is, the hotel is rather large and there were so very many of us all over the place. People slept where they could and when they could. The sound of gunfire and bombs was constant. Sometimes it was louder than at other times. It was difficult to know from sound alone whether an attack was close or whether the firepower was simply exceptional in strength. But we were ever aware that we were sitting in the middle of a combat zone—a terrible feeling that never left us.

While we quivered inside the Mille Collines, we would hear our names announced on RTLM hate radio, one of our only regular portholes to the world outside our walls. Some had difficulty understanding why RTLM would have our names, and furthermore, why they would use them. Who cared? But others knew the dreaded answer to that. It is what made this a genocide and not simply a war. Specific people were hunted down for death. Those who came to murder me on April 7 did not bomb my entire neighborhood or randomly shoot up house after house. My name was on a list and I was targeted for extermination. RTLM hate radio was sending out messages to murderers that certain specific people could be found inside the Hotel des Mille Collines and if they wished to do something "heroic" in support of the Hutu Power political agenda, they could make their way into the hotel and hunt certain people for death. That is the reason why the UN soldiers changed around or completely removed the room numbers: to confuse intruders. Of course, much of this rejiggering proved unnecessary: Because there were not enough rooms to begin with, most of us were jammed into them beyond capacity or were sleeping in hallways or common areas. Our own family and friends would have had trouble locating us quickly if they had to.

But how did RTLM obtain our personal information in the first place? No can could say for sure. Just as the United Nations suspected Paul Rusesabagina of endangering us by revealing our personal information to FAR General Bizimungu, we also knew Rusesabagina counted among his best friends Froduald Karamira, the owner of RTLM radio. Karamira, like Bagosora, Bizimungu, and Rutaganda, was a frequent fixture at the hotel, drinking and laughing with his friend and, as we would come to learn, political brother-in-arms, Rusesabagina. Perhaps this was just a coincidence and perhaps it was not. I have only circumstantial evidence. Perhaps the UN had more; I do not know. If Rusesabagina did provide the killers with our names, though, his motivation might have had less to do with wanting us all murdered than in maintaining his power and control over us. In this respect, he was very much like the lazy and corrupt militiamen who showed up looking for us at our homes and the homes of our friends. Because of their menace, they were able to keep going back again and again, shaking people down and taking what they could from us. Even in those early days of the genocide, before we all reached the hotel, Tutsi borrowed money from wherever they could in order to pay off the thugs at their doors. The militias were mere citizens who had lived among us and us among them, all of their lives and ours. It was only because of these extraordinary circumstances of genocide that they could possibly act in this manner.

The same could be said of Paul Rusesabagina. If the phone lines were all working, if there were someone or some way to keep the militias and Hutu Power military leaders out of the building permanently, then perhaps Rusesabagina would have been "overthrown" by either the refugee committee, the other hotel employees, or both. But hearing our names on hate radio made us cower in fear and gave Rusesabagina license to bully us.

What Dallaire said about Rusesabagina trying desperately to have the peacekeepers removed from the hotel, though, was another matter entirely. If UN intelligence was correct on that issue, it was an accusation that the hotel manager was purposely putting the refugees in peril for no good or logical reason.

Alexis told us of something he saw one day. "Karamira came to the hotel one certain time to see Paul Rusesabagina. They went into his office. They were there for a while. That was not the first time Karamira came to the hotel; he has probably been here at least three times that I witnessed. I overheard them talking about how they started something but they failed to finish it. He said they were supposed to kill all the intellectuals but they could not seem to keep the Interahamwe under control. I know that was none of my business, but I heard them."

There was actually a split opinion among us over the effect of having radio stations such as RTLM announcing our names to the nation. Most of us felt violated, that it was an invitation to attack us and kill certain people among us. A small minority, though, thought the Interahamwe and the soldiers wanted to show people from other countries that the genocide was not planned, because obviously there were many Tutsi in the hotel whom they didn't kill. Some argued that an "unplanned" genocide might not even be genocide at all, although many would disagree. As to being on the radio, I sided with the majority. I did not want to be singled out on any radio broadcasts. I did not even want it widely known that Tutsi by any name had sought refuge in the hotel. The streets were filled with armed, crazy people, and even with the UN soldiers among us, we were horribly outgunned.

RTLM was not the only entity that had our names. UNAMIR Major Brent Beardsley said, "We have the names of all of the people in the hotel. General Dallaire told General Bizimungu we have everyone's names; that he is being held personally responsible for your safety, and if the hotel is attacked, we will know if anyone is killed from our list and he will be held accountable. Bizimungu immediately placed an armed FAR detachment at the hotel and has been chasing away the Interahamwe."

How odd that part of our overall protection was now the very army that wanted us annihilated. But this is how it is with the intercession of the international community. It created the need for strategic thinking on all sides, which made wholesale slaughter of the unarmed less practical in the long run.

Bernard Makuza spoke often to the UNAMIR soldiers at the hotel. One he befriended was an African named Ores Song. "Song told me the RPF knows we are in the hotel and nothing is going to happen to us," said Bernard. "Because of where the FAR army is and how the situation is, there is no way they are going to destroy our hotel. He said the only side that can destroy the hotel is the RPF, and they would never do that because they know exactly who is in the hotel. The RPF knows about us. They want to save us."

Meanwhile, one who grew more and more anxious than most of the rest of us was Christophe. As the days passed after his confrontation with Rusesabagina, he continued to look over his shoulder, always wondering when he might be singled out and thrown to the wolves. He felt liked a marked man.

One day, a militiaman came into the hotel looking for Christophe. Dear lord, this was it, the day of Christophe's execution. Christophe knew the man—he was the son of Dr. Akingeneye, a medical doctor of the deceased president Habyarimana. They spoke for a while and then Christophe, looking far more hopeful than in recent days, told us, "He brings word from Nyamirambo. My brother, Jacques, he is alive! He has been in hiding there. All my other family members are gone, but Jacques lives."

The words were happy and optimistic given the context of time and place. We all either knew or assumed that most of our family members, loved ones, and friends, were now dead. Confirmation that any single one of them was alive was some sort of miracle.

"That man, he has agreed to bring Jacques here to the hotel—for a price."

Of course for a price. No one, particularly no one affiliated with the militias, was going to risk his life bringing a Tutsi to safekeeping out of the goodness of his heart, particularly not at this stage in the killings.

"But will the hotel manager allow him in?" someone asked.

Christophe was already thinking far ahead of us. "I cannot risk it. I cannot bring Jacques here only so we can die together. I asked the doctor's son to take Jacques and me to Burundi, where it is safe. I have access to money there; enough money to pay him the large ransom he requires."

The plan seemed perilous and fraught with danger, but what other options did Christophe have?

A few days later as he greeted his brother, waved good-bye to us, and turned his back on the hotel for what we assumed was the last time, we wondered if we would ever see him again. Was this a trap, a cruel way in which to murder both him and his brother? Would we ever even know? What little optimism resided within us hoped for the best, as the first among us appeared to have found a way to true freedom and safety. With the cynicism, the realism, dominating our thinking, we feared the worst.

Jean Marie Vianney Mutesa from Rwanda National Radio was one of a handful of journalists who remained with us at the hotel. So, too, Louise Kayibanda and Peacemaker Mbungiramihigo, the brother of Pasa, the hotel employee. By now the foreign journalists were all gone, having been moved safely out by representatives from their respective nations. Another journalist among us, more famous than Mutesa, Kayibanda, and Mbungiramihigo, was a man by the name of Thomas Kamilindi from Radio Rwanda, who also was a correspondent for Radio France International (RFI).

One day, as many of us were listening to RFI on small transistor radios, we heard Kamilindi's voice broadcasting from inside the hotel. How could this be? Kamilindi went on to say there were many

Tutsi in the hotel, confirming on legitimate radio what had only been spit out before on hate radio. He gave a full rundown on what was going on in the hotel: who was there, what we were doing, how life was for us there.

Refugees had no real qualms about the accuracy of what Kamilindi was saying, at least to the best of my recollection. What many were more concerned about was, "Why is he doing this?!" They felt he was drawing attention to us, and not in a constructive way. Yes, we wanted the UN to know about us, the NGOs to know about us, people of conscience around the world to know about us. But we were already reaching those people through official channels. This was mass media. This was a popular radio station broadcasting in Rwanda. Refugees milled around and argued, some saying he was rubbing the génocidaires' noses in the fact we were still alive, right there in the middle of their capital city.

> He was rubbing the *génocidaires'* noses in the fact we were still alive, right there in the middle of their capital city.

Some went down to the hotel manager's office, the location of the only operational telephone. Kamilindi wasn't there. And yet they still heard his voice on the radio. How could this be?

After the broadcast ended, Kamilindi exited his hotel room. Bernard Makuza confronted him and let him know in no uncertain terms he did not appreciate the broadcast. He felt that in Kamilindi's desire for a scoop, he was imperiling us all.

It was only afterward that someone brought up the obvious: The only way Kamilindi could have broadcast from inside the hotel was by calling into the radio station or the station calling the hotel. And if Thomas Kamilindi wasn't in Rusesabagina's office...then the telephone in his room must have been working!

This refocused all our fears and anger, and it wasn't at Kamilindi, who was simply doing what he thought was best, even if all of us did not agree. We had suspected ever since the phones went dead shortly after Rusesabagina came to the hotel that this was not a coincidence, because one phone line continued to work. The water and the electricity going out, this we understood. The infrastructure of the nation was being destroyed. But if one phone line worked, they all should be working, *unless*…the lines weren't dead or physically cut at all. We were utterly convinced now that Rusesabagina had simply turned off our telephones, all except for his own. Once he had befriended Thomas Kamilindi, a journalist who could possibly benefit him in certain ways, just as Bizimungu, Bagosora, Karamira, and Rutaganda had, he must have felt it proper to turn the phone on in his room so he could do a live report from the hotel. Now, in addition to patronizing the leaders of the Rwandan army and the dreaded militias, he had his own private herald.

16

HOSTAGES

ALL WE COULD dream about was somehow receiving safe passage out of the Hotel des Mille Collines, to be safely evacuated. Despite the heroic actions of many people and entities, we still felt it was only a matter of time before the militias would come in and kill us. Though some were under the impression the militias answered to the Rwandan military, be it General Bizimungu or others, this was, to a certain degree, an illusion. In truth, they were bloodthirsty killers who not only murdered innocent people, but maimed and raped many of them, causing as much human suffering as could ever be imagined in one's worst nightmare, before blessedly extinguishing their lives.

The United Nations had been trying for weeks and weeks to evacuate us. It was not practical for us to stay at the hotel until the war ended, for no one had any idea how long that would be or, for that matter, which side would win. In addition to the horrible genocide against the unarmed, battles were moving closer and closer to the hotel itself, making it an increasingly dangerous place to be. Even if we were not intentionally being targeted by either warring side, we stood an ever-greater chance of becoming accidental collateral damage. There were other places where fighting had either never started, or where stability had been achieved and genocide and war were no longer an immediate threat. Those were the safest places to be.

General Dallaire did whatever he could, above and beyond our wildest imagination, to help get us out of the hotel. Dallaire would risk his life traveling between the two combatant camps after the number of peacekeeping forces had been reduced. He would go directly into the war zone, hoping to find a solution between the Rwandan Patriotic Front and the Hutu Power interim Rwandan government. The peacekeepers may have been understaffed, but General Dallaire still made sure they were far from impotent. The Hotel des Mille Collines was like some isolated outpost of peace in the gruesome violence, and Dallaire sought to keep it that way, as if it represented something sane and good to him amidst all the bloody insanity.

The first major attempt to evacuate refugees—real Rwandan refugees as opposed to foreign guests of the hotel—was put into motion around May 3. The idea was to actually leave Rwanda for some other country, if one would have you. To be on the list of evacuees, you were supposed to have a passport, a host country, and someone who would take you in and accept personal responsibility for you once you received safe passage. Unfortunately, many of us had no passport, while others lacked either a host country or someone to take them in. I was among that majority, and for that reason, most of us resigned ourselves to staying in the hotel.

A list was written up and given to the UN. Someone I had come to know and respect, Odette Nyiramilimo, whose passage to the hotel had been arranged by her neighbor, Paul Rusesabagina, was on that first list. So, too, was Rusesabagina's wife. The peacekeepers tried to transport those on the list from the Mille Collines to the airport. Not only did RTLM hate radio know which refugees were staying at the hotel, but also when UNAMIR began planning that first evacuation, and when and exactly who would be traveling aboard which convoys. Based on everything else we had experienced in the hotel up to this point, we had grown to suspect exactly how they got this information and disseminated it so quickly.

Interahamwe attackers were waiting at Sopecya Station, about four miles from the hotel. By the time the trucks from the hotel arrived, escorted by UN peacekeepers, the Interahamwe had already set up roadblocks. The extremists began to beat the refugees, and the UN peacekeepers called for help. The militias were enraged. The prefect of Kigali, Tharcisse Renzaho, tried to stop the violence, to no avail.

The only man who managed to keep the extremists from killing the evacuees was, amazingly enough, Interahamwe VP and beer distributor Georges Rutaganda—who, for once, showed his power in a far more cerebral way. UNAMIR Commander Amadou Deme, a Senegalese Army officer, recognizing Rutaganda's power within the Interahamwe, went to get Rutaganda and brought him to the roadblock. "Don't kill them," Rutaganda told the militia. "We are going to exchange them for our people who are in the RPF zone."

Rutaganda, so vilified and so feared, actually saved the lives of the hotel refugees who were in those trucks on their way to the airport. Why? Little did we know, an entirely new scenario was underway.

At the very same time as that evacuation attempt, the RPF and FAR were in negotiations, with General Dallaire as a mediator. RPF soldiers threatened to take the FAR negotiators hostage if the extremist militias killed the refugees from the hotel. Dallaire kept negotiating until the refugees got back to the hotel and the FAR negotiators were allowed to safely leave the bargaining table. If the intent was just to save the hotel refugees, all the parties involved would have simply let them go to the airport. However, Commander Deme and the UN peacekeepers escorted the refugees back to the hotel because it was now believed by General Dallaire that they, and we as well, might be better used in hostage exchanges.

In the hotel, we thought of ourselves as many things: refugees, hotel employees, victims. At times we considered ourselves prisoners— glad to be alive, but at the same time stuck inside this building with nowhere else to go. And as captives in this luxurious dungeon, we had one very bad prison guard, who, like many classically corrupt sentries, exploited us and treated us poorly. But one thing we never considered ourselves to be was hostages.

A hostage is a person in some form of captivity who has a perceived value in barter. In most criminal situations, that value can be measured in dollars. In a wartime situation, it is as a trading chip for other hostages. As time went on, the RPF side began collecting prisoners of war. Meanwhile, we at the hotel, deep within Hutu Power/FAR territory and many of us simpatico to the RPF cause, provided a bargaining chip for the FAR to use in getting some of their people back from the RPF.

Actually, certain people within the militias and the interim government had earlier on considered taking us hostage, as a pawn in future negotiations. The UN peacekeepers felt if this was allowed before any formal agreement for peace or a cease-fire had already been reached, the prisoner exchange would be imbalanced. Whoever had hostages—especially higher-profile ones—would already have the upper hand in any negotiation. This went into the peacekeepers' thinking when they decided their best move would be to get the refugees back to the hotel, where they could protect us until the negotiations were further along. This is something we all wish we had been more aware of when we spent the latter days of the genocide within the hotel compound. We may have been incrementally safer, but we were not, in fact, safe. Yet at the time it was all happening, we were mostly kept in the dark regarding the political intrigue going on around us and involving us.

Some of us wondered why Paul Rusesabagina, suspected of giving our names to RTLM hate radio, had put his own wife on one of the transports. Did he feel that because he considered himself an important man, friend to the *génocidaires*, she would be left unharmed while others were murdered or beaten? Did he think putting her on the truck after providing the passenger manifest would protect all the refugees on board? No one could say for sure, but

Wellars Gasamagera, a mature and wise man, might have said it best and most succinctly: "It shows that he is nothing."

A major turning point in the war occurred on May 22 when the RPF took control of the Kanombe Military Camp, and eight hundred Rwandan soldiers and their families surrendered to General Dallaire. He handed them over to the Red Cross, which handed them over to the RPF and oversaw their captivity. The detention of those surrendered soldiers and their families, along with some of the Hutu refugees who were in the Hotel Méridien and the King Faisal Hospital, put pressure on the interim-government militia to protect the refugees at the Hotel des Mille Collines. The RPF controlled the Amahoro National Stadium in Kigali and used it as an internment camp. Many of the killers who marched under the Hutu Power banner were now corralled there or else had friends who were there. Those of us in the hotel were an asset for the *génocidaires*, who were in need of a truce when they realized they were losing the war. The interim government cajoled the Interahamwe, telling them they could not kill the people in the hotel because those people would be exchanged for their members and families in the RPF zone.

> Those of us in the hotel were an asset for the *génocidaires*, who were in need of a truce when they realized they were losing the war.

On May 22, Ghanaian Major General Yaache, a sector commander and military observer of UNAMIR, and his humanitarian team, which included French statesman Bernard Kouchner, held an important meeting at the Hotel des Diplomates with Colonel Bagosora and the Interahamwe to officially discuss hostage transfers. Rumors spread throughout the hotel community, positive rumors of impending freedom and a road to safety. Yet there were those among us still nursing their wounds from the beatings they took at Sopecya Station. Would the Interahamwe, who appeared completely out of control and only interested in bloodlust, actually go along with a wholesale plan to allow us to leave the hotel? RTLM radio still pumped them full of roaring hatred and murderous thoughts on a daily basis. The tenor had not changed since April 6. These people were easily led, with minds full of irrational fears and paranoia, and deep-seated personal insecurities that made them suspicious and jealous of anyone of reason or intellect. They were the hate-filled bigots of our nation, now fully immersed in government-sanctioned violence. Once they had legally tasted blood, committed vicious murder and rape, could they ever turn back?

Hope was all that got us through each day and each night. But was hope just a mirage?

17

THE BARTER OF BODIES

A T THE VERY end of May 1994, it appeared we were finally going to be evacuated—not just those with passports and foreign connections, but all of us, in a hostage/POW-type exchange. When zero hour finally came, they asked us to write our names on a piece of paper indicating which zone we wanted to go to—RPF or FAR. We were skeptical. We could not risk anyone finding out which side we wanted to go to. Our names had been our most protected asset. It seemed almost every time our names were released to anyone for any reason, somehow they ended up on RTLM hate radio, a tip-off to the militias letting them know who was where and when. But the choice was clear. To stay in the hotel meant we could be killed. Life inside the hotel had always seemed like life on borrowed time. In going to the FAR/Hutu Power government zone, we Tutsi would be killed; we knew this. Our only rational choice was to go to the RPF zone, but we were not sure if we could get there.

Everyone secretly wrote down their information on a piece of paper and passed it under the door of the living room of the UN peacekeepers, which also doubled as their office inside the hotel. Those who felt their lives were in danger, every Tutsi and quite a few Hutu, requested to go to the RPF zone. Others requested the Rwandan government zone, while an even smaller number, for various reasons, chose to remain in the hotel. This began a new round of fears for us. If one chose to go to the government zone, it was like a declaration that you were a Hutu Power extremist, a friend of the killers. If you went to the RPF side, even if you were Hutu, you were declaring allegiance with the "rebels." You were admitting that either you were a "cockroach" or that you shielded them.

Jeannette, who had helped take care of me during my time at the hotel, was in a stressful situation. As a Tutsi, she felt compelled to go where she most logically would be safest, which was the RPF side. But her husband supported the government, whose supporters were going elsewhere. Obviously, she wanted her husband to go with her, but certainly not at the cost of her life. Most of the people in the hotel chose to go to the RPF side, regardless of their politics. But Jeannette's husband refused to join with us there.

On May 28, the FAR and RPF militaries sent their delegations, and UN peacekeepers arrived with three trucks. The FAR was represented by the chief of headquarters for General Bizimungu and the chief of police, Major General Ndindiliyimana. Names were called out. As the names were called, RTLM Radio called out those very same names almost simultaneously. Paranoia and anxiety grew anew. Who was setting us up, and were we all going to face the very same treatment that led the first group of refugees to be beaten and returned to the hotel? And despite the beatings, those people actually felt lucky, the beneficiaries of a miracle, that they were not slaughtered and returned in pieces. Would even that level of luck hold out again?

Meanwhile, Paul Rusesabagina swung into action. He set up his people at the front door of the hotel to check whether any refugee took with them anything belonging to the hotel. Diplomats, military leaders, negotiators, and peacekeepers were struggling to arrange a delicate prisoner exchange, while Rusesabagina did nothing more than check to make sure none of us stole any towels. Before they could leave the hotel, Paul made those who did not pay him in

Diplomats, military leaders, negotiators, and peacekeepers were struggling to arrange a delicate prisoner exchange, while Rusesabagina did nothing more than check to make sure none of us stole any towels.

cash sign somewhere saying they would pay later for their accommodations.

When you heard your name, you went to a truck. Some of the Hutu who were with us in the hotel were now enraged at those of us who decided to go to the RPF zone. Others were more circumspect. Kalisa, who did not support the genocide and showed great mercy on us while we lived together, likely felt it would be far too controversial and dangerous to his friends and relatives were he to join us with the RPF in Kabuga, so he instead went to the government zone in Gitarama. While we lived side by side during the genocide, we rarely discussed politics or ethnic divisions. We all lived in peace with one another, each relating to the other as an individual and a survivor of a desperate situation. But now old divisions began to reveal themselves once more. Would this be our permanent situation in Rwanda, our unchangeable legacy? Would we always have these murderous ethnic divisions? It was so sad to think our time spent relying on one another, human to human in frightened refuge, might only be an anomaly for some rather than a permanent state of being and enlightenment.

The operation was to go like this: Whatever number of people went into a truck at the Hotel des Mille Collines, that same number entered a similar truck in the RPF zone. This was a prisoner exchange, pure and simple. The trucks left at the same time and were to meet at an agreed-upon point at Kimihurura, another neighborhood of the capital city. Those from the Hotel des Mille Collines were escorted by the UN peacekeepers and the FAR governmental military forces. Those from the RPF zone were escorted by RPF soldiers and other UN peacekeepers. Once the trucks from both sides met up at Kimihurura, at a big public traffic circle well-known to all, the prisoner exchange was formally made, names were checked and rechecked, heads were counted, and the trucks containing those of us who asked to join the RPF side were then waved through and were to continue on to our final destination in the city of Kabuga, about twenty-three kilometers from the hotel. At no time during the journey was anyone allowed to get out of the trucks.

There were a lot of us, probably a thousand people, and there were only a few trucks, so we could not all be evacuated at the same time. Some did not even leave on May 28 but were instead evacuated on May 29 and 31. The first group of people who left was brought right back—unharmed, thank God—because of some misunder-standing. It seemed things at Amahoro National Stadium, where those desiring to leave the RPF zone were being kept, were far more chaotic compared to how well-organized the evacuation from the hotel was being handled, and this caused enough tension and con-cern that both sides took a step back, regrouped, and began again. Our nervousness ratcheted up precipitously. Despite our travails, we had been lucky for far too long. Many of us thought this might be the moment our good fortune would finally run out.

Another fracas occurred when some people found out at the last minute their names were not on *any* list. Luckily, I was not one of them, though I worried for those people. I worried for everyone. I also worried for myself.

Jeannette sought me out, sharing the tale of her conflict with her husband. Without telling him, she filled out her paperwork to go to the RPF side, doing the same for their children. Her husband was doing everything he could to prevent her from getting in a truck bound for RPF-controlled lands. As much as the escorts attempted to maintain order, much chaos ensued due to the stress of our situation. Amidst this tumult, Rubayiza and I helped to smuggle her children into our truck without her husband noticing. Jeannette got into an RPF-bound truck as well, much to her husband's chagrin, leaving him screaming in anger and rage.

I was supposed to be evacuated on the second turn. As much as my heart was with those I was leaving behind, who were engaged in heated discussions with the military personnel coordinating the evacuation, I still took my place inside the truck. The last thing I saw as we pulled away from the hotel was people I recognized and knew, arguing, crying, and (once we were too far away to hear their debating) gesticulating. *It will all work out,* I prayed. *It will all work out somehow.*

As we were in the trucks and riding down the street, we saw many militiamen. They were waving their machetes at us, saying, "We will kill you anyway." Were they right? Even if we made it safely out of the hotel, what was the state of the war? Was the RPF winning, as we had been led to believe? Or would the genocide continue?

As we got to the point of exchange, the RPF soldiers dropped back a little bit and the FAR military escorts did likewise. Only UN peacekeeper escorts representing each side could cross the exchange point at Kimihurura Circle, near a beautiful place where many young couples go to have their wedding photographs taken. As the peacekeepers shared data and inspected us in the trucks, I felt the same dread I'd felt when I'd been stopped so many times as I traveled on foot with Pascal on my way to the hotel right after the genocide began. This was but another roadblock, another test of whether I would live or die. I had little to no control over my own survival. It is the most sickening feeling of powerlessness in the world. All of us were frightened, our hearts pounding very fast.

Slowly, the truck lurched into gear once more and we were moving, moving farther away from the hotel that had been our home for nearly two months. We remained tentative, hoping we would make it to Kabuga. Yet as we passed by the traffic circle at Kimihurura, I was relieved like a woman who had just given birth after a really hard, long labor. The peacekeepers in the truck kept in radio contact with their compatriots at the hotel, at Amahoro, and at Kabuga. Only when we heard that the people who left the hotel before us had made it safely to Kabuga were we no longer as tentative. Even though we were still in transit, people began smiling and smelling the life around them. Hearts took wing. Some even began to whisper, "We are saved!"

As we were driving, we saw another UNAMIR truck coming down the street toward us. Right there we met *Inkotanyi*. Many books will tell you that the word *Inkotanyi* was widely used during my lifetime by Hutu propagandists to link the RPF in the minds of Hutu with memories of long-ago Tutsi oppression of their people. It is a measure of the potency of Hutu propaganda that even Tutsi children adopted such terms into their own vocabulary, having been led to envision horrible, terrible images of their own people. *Inkotanyi*, literally translated, means "warrior," and as respectable as that may sound, Hutu initially used it as a derogatory term. The word *Inkotanyi* also means "invincible." After a time, the RPF took to using the term proudly to refer to their entire movement.

This was the first time many of us had ever seen *Inkotanyi*—proud rebel soldiers who believed in the right of return to the land of their birth. They looked totally opposite from the way schoolchildren were taught they looked—not horrible, ugly, disfigured, murderous barbarians. Everyone was so happy to see them; I will never forget that. Alexis said, "I don't care if I die right now; I am so excited to see *Inkotanyi*. I don't care that I am being saved. All I care about is that I just saw *Inkotanyi*, the RPF soldiers who stopped the genocide!"

18

KABUGA

KABUGA, TWENTY KILOMETERS from Kigali, was our destination. Our rescuers were as excited as we were. "Are you the
only survivors? Now you are saved. Nobody is going to kill
you." The chief commander of the Rwandan Patriotic Army,
Paul Kagame, came from his headquarters in Mulindi to welcome us.
The soldiers told us to sit down as an act of respect, but Kagame said,
"You have been sitting long enough. Now you can stand up."

Commander Kagame greeted each of us, one by one. Those who
were familiar with him approached him and began chatting. You
could see how happy he was to see us, but at the same time sad
because of what we had gone through. He comforted us, telling us
we were safe now. We were also welcomed by another high-ranking
officer, General Charles Kayonga. I believe I also saw Kabuye Rose—I
think she was what one would call the mayor of the city. We all sat
down and started talking with these kind people. They told us they
had enough food, that we wouldn't starve, and that's how we knew
we were truly safe. We believed we had finally been saved and that
Commander Kagame would now be our personal protector. It was
one of the happiest days of our lives.

Kagame continued to receive us at this big house; I think it once
belonged to a Hutu businessman by the name of Michel Bagaragaza.
Bagaragaza ran the tea industry in Rwanda; politically he was suspected of supporting the Interahamwe. When the RPF advanced

into his area, he supposedly fled the country. Kagame himself was not staying at that house; it was simply the largest single building in the area, making it a good choice for a gathering. Many of us were invited to stay at that house. It was big; a lot of people stayed in the living room, while others were in the smaller rooms. Still others stayed in different abandoned homes. I continued to live with Rubayiza. We found a small home and we shared one small bedroom, while others shared the rest of the house with us. The families of Mister, Assiel, and Damascene occupied other rooms next to us.

Kabuga is a small commercial center with productive land. We arrived there during the harvest period and were told to help ourselves to whatever nourishment we could find. The local population had abandoned the area because of the war, and so while we were happy to satiate our hunger with the local crops, we were also providing a service by helping with the harvest. We went out each and every day to bring back food and provisions—green beans, bananas, sweet potatoes, water, and wood for cooking fires. Besides the food we fetched, the RPF supplied us with cornmeal. It felt so good to be able to go out and about without fear of torture, rape, and murder. Even when we had eaten inside the hotel, our portions were meager and we had to find someone to go out and get it for us. Now we felt like real citizens again, self-sufficient and free. Our money was no good there; everything was free for the taking. No one was profiteering off our misery and hunger. We felt embraced by love, freedom, and equality for the first time in months—for some of us Tutsi, for the first time in our entire lives. Even though no international humanitarian organizations were intervening there for us, we had no problems getting ourselves food. We were living

> No one was profiteering off our misery and hunger. We felt embraced by love, freedom, and equality for the first time in months—for some of us Tutsi, for the first time in our entire lives.

peacefully with the Hutu from the hotel who joined us there, without any suspicions or anxiety. We didn't have anything to worry about because RPF soldiers were there to protect us.

We remained there almost a month, though some came and went at will for various reasons. For example, Jean Marie Vianney Mutesa, the journalist, was only there a short time; all journalists had been asked to go to training because the RPF wanted them to work for Muhabura Radio. Muhabura Radio was the first alternative to government-controlled Radio Rwanda; it had reached all but the south of Rwanda by mid-1992, and had been picked up by the BBC starting that same year. Odette Nyiramilimo, Paul Rusesabagina's friend, also did not stay long, but soon departed for Nairobi.

One who was not at Kabuga was Christophe Shamukiga. Had he made it to Burundi? Was he still alive? Many, many days passed and then, like a miracle, we saw his exuberant face. As he explained:

> The son of Dr. Akigeneye did as he promised and took Jacques and me to the Burundi border. But he wanted assurance I would not take advantage of him and fail to pay him what he asked. Many refugees escaped by crossing the border into Burundi. The killers are afraid to cross the border and continue their slaughtering there. Akigeneye told me I had to cross the border on my own and get the money. Meanwhile, he held onto Jacques for ransom. This too, it seems, has become very common.
>
> When I returned with the money and paid them, I waited at the border for my brother for almost three hours. It was getting dark. All of a sudden, my brother showed up. We stayed in Burundi for about three days, and then we came here to Kabuga because we wanted to be with everybody else—all of you, my good and true friends who stood with me through the darkest days.

We were so glad to see Christophe, and so heartened he felt so close to us that he left the safety of Burundi to be with us. But many were traveling between Kabuga and Burundi by now—refugees who had survived the genocide by escaping to Burundi, slipping back into Rwanda, going to camps such as ours in Kabuga, looking for their families and friends. Also, people from our encampment in Kabuga would sometimes travel to Burundi to buy supplies and bring them back. It was a safe area for us now, not just in Kabuga, but in that entire area.

There were some people who stayed in the hotel and didn't go to the government side or to the RPF side. One of them was Paul Rusesabagina. He and the others were hoping to go to Europe. However, by the end of June, Kigali was almost completely surrounded by RPF soldiers. There was no longer a safe way to go to the FAR side because all roads were blocked by the RPF. At the end, everyone left was forced to come to Kabuga if for no other reason than their own safety.

About two weeks later, after I and most of the others were evacuated from the hotel at the end of May, the RPF made a daring raid on the Sainte Famille Church as well as Saint Paul's Church in Kigali and rescued many refugees there. Sainte Famille is a Catholic church about one mile from the Hotel des Mille Collines, down the hill from it, and Saint Paul's Church is nearby. Many Tutsi and moderate Hutu refugees sought sanctuary in both these churches during the genocide, just as we did at the hotel. The difference was that in St. Famille and St. Paul, not everyone who stayed inside the walls of the buildings survived. People were being raped and killed. The RPF raid was a big victory because of the dangerous location of those churches, deep within FAR territory, but the RPF soldiers used excellent military tactics, getting there incognito in the early morning like a well-trained SEAL team.

Unfortunately, not every refugee from the churches was extracted safely. When the militia found out about the extraction, they became enraged and attacked the churches, killing all who were left behind in a hideous slaughter. With that, they turned and headed for the Hotel des Mille Collines. The date was June 17, but most of us had already left the hotel and were in Kabuga.

According to soldiers we spoke with, nobody really expected St. Famille to be attacked in such a manner. It was also important to note that the attackers were the Interahamwe and not the regular Rwandan army. FAR forces, knowing the war was winding down and that they appeared to be on the losing end, wanted to mitigate their losses by more strongly policing genocidal attacks. A FAR unit was called in to attempt a rescue at St. Famille. They soon called for reinforcements and brought in a lot of tanks so they could defeat the Interahamwe.

The Interahamwe's decision to regroup and attack the hotel that had been our home for so long gave us pause. We tried to remember who had stayed behind and who was not accounted for in Kabuga, and we prayed for their safety as we listened for news from Kigali.

When the RPF heard the hotel was being attacked, they threatened the FAR—some of whose leaders were still in extended negotiations with them—with being taken hostage if they killed any refugees at the hotel. General Dallaire personally threatened General Bizimungu, apparently successfully, motivating him to go and stop the militia. Major Beardsley confirmed that this had been effective, that owing to Dallaire's threat Bizimungu thwarted the attack on the hotel.

Nonetheless, we heard some Interahamwe had managed to gain entrance to the hotel that day. No one was killed, but a few people we knew, like François Habiyakare and Ambroise Mulindangabo, were beaten up. A few other people were robbed. But because of the brave UN general, no one was killed at the Hotel des Mille Collines that day or any other day.

There were conflicting stories as to whether the hotel manager was even at the hotel at the time it was breached. I was in Kabuga at the time and could not say with any certainty what the truth was, nor at the time did I care. In some versions, he hid for his own protection, for which I do not blame him, while in others he claimed to have been drinking with his friend, General Bizimungu. This version does not jibe with what the UNAMIR officers reported, and I always found the peacekeepers to be impeccably selfless, humble, and honest. I did hear the episode shook him up enough that he begged for another evacuation for himself and the few others who remained, no longer holding out hope for timely transport to Europe. He joined us in Kabuga later on; I think it was around June 19. By then those in the hotel had no other choice—the RPF had closed all other exits from Kigali.

Alexis told us that when the hotel ran out of food, there were still some wines Paul Rusesabagina had stashed in the stockroom. Later, certain people who stayed in the hotel, after they decided to go to Gitarama in the Hutu Power zone instead of joining us in Kabuga with the RPF, sold those wines. It was a man named Jean Baptiste; we called him "Rutubuka." He was a big man. His wife was named Teresa Nyirabikiga—she was a hotel governess. They were both employees of the hotel. "They sold a lot of wine bottles," said Alexis.

"Rusesabagina was also involved with those bottles of wine big time," he explained. "He sold one part to Rutubuka and his wife, and he brought the other part here with him to Kabuga. I mean, he smuggled out a lot of bottles of wine he had hidden inside the hotel while we were stuck there. A lot of his friends go to where he is staying and share that wine with him, and he also brought with him a lot of food from the hotel. There is this guy; he is Rusesabagina's nephew. We asked him if he could go get us some wine since it has been a long time and we haven't had any. Paul's family is living very well since the evacuation. All his friends go to his place at night and drink with him."

19

RETURN TO THE MOONSCAPE

O N JULY 4, the RPF took the capital of Kigali, and on July 6 we were invited to go back into the city. The war there was over and the soldiers gathered us together and told us we needed to go back home. Most of us were hesitant to go back because of what we knew had been going on not too long ago. When people began going to Kigali and coming back safe and sound, we finally knew it was all right.

We had to figure out our own transportation in order to get there. Rubayiza and I were inseparable. Deus Kagiraneza, an RPF officer, gave us a ride into town. He had a big truck. What a change this was from when I made my way from my home to the Hotel des Mille Collines just three months before, and yet it seemed like a lifetime. No running through yards, hopping fences, and ducking into stores to avoid being seen by drunken murderers. Now I rode in a truck with a friendly and helpful military man, watching the sights as we drove, gradually allowing myself to feel relaxed, dreaming of what it might be like to be freer and more at ease than I had ever been as a Tutsi in Rwanda. For not a single day in my life had I been treated like anything but a second-class citizen in my home country— discriminated against, made to leap higher hurdles in order to be treated with proper dignity. But now, who knew? Who truly knew what the future might bring? From the vantage point of the inside of that truck, however, the prospects seemed limitless.

Back in the capital city, all we could see each mile were military men with camouflage uniforms and boots—RPF soldiers. All of them were friendly and willing to help. None of them asked us for ID; none of them asked if we were Tutsi or Hutu. None of them cared. They seemed weary of the fight and, seeing that we were unarmed and at peace, they treated us like fellow world citizens and nothing less.

For years, we had carried those cursed cards because the physical differences between Tutsi and Hutu are not so obvious. It would be similar to trying to tell Irish Americans from Italian Americans. Some people may fit into a physical stereotype, but just as many might not. Also, there were no immovable rules concerning intermarriage. Mix it up time and time again over many generations, and again—what were you? Hutu and Tutsi, during various times in our national history, even became more like social classes than ethnicities. Society could regard a person as one or the other, or that person could wake up one day and *claim* to be one or the other. It happened rarely and it was very risky, but it did happen. Some tried to hide their ethnicity when applying for employment and job opportunities, but they would be investigated. In your own neighborhood, everyone knew you and it was very hard to change, because as soon as you were born you had to be registered and given an ethnic ID, usually bearing the same ethnicity as your father, even if he married outside his ethnicity. But as we wandered around Kigali now, post-genocide, post-war, we wondered if any of that would ever matter again.

The town was deserted and all we could smell was the stench of dead bodies. The optimism of the previous days slowly began to fade. The ferocity and grotesqueness of it was beyond our comprehension. We had struggled through a genocide, through violence in the streets, bloodshed accompanied by the sounds of gunshots and

screams. But now all was silent, yet left in its wake was the aftermath: the bodies and body parts lying about the city as if it all had
been done by some brute, natu-
ral force and not by man himself.
It was all totally unreal to us.
Life had become so very hard;
we didn't know where to go or
where to live. What was now safe
here in Kigali? Was *anything* safe?
Were *we* truly safe?

> But now all was silent, yet left in its wake was the aftermath: the bodies and body parts lying about the city as if it all had been done by some brute, natural force and not by man himself.

The soldiers told us to take care of ourselves, but our homes
had been robbed and destroyed. We had to find our own places
to live because all the houses were shattered. We had nothing to
eat. No cars. No water. No stores were open. Not that it mattered
much anyway, because we had no money, nothing at all. When Jean
Marie Vianney Mutesa went back to Radio Rwanda, he found it had
been robbed and all the equipment was stolen. They were told to
somehow rebuild and make it all work again. It was misery for the
survivors. We began to ask God and ourselves why we had been
chosen to survive, left to walk aimlessly around this bleak scene
that looked like nuclear moonscape.

I went to see if I could find the body of my brother, Alphonse
Butera, and those of my friends, Donat Mutesa, Raymond Rwagasana,
Innocent, John, Eric, Nshogoza, André Kambogo, Eugene, and
Alphonse Gatema. I could not find any of their bodies because the
génocidaire government had used its trucks to take them to the cem-
etery. Some of the assailants had begun to agonize over the coming
end of their occupation of this city, and they worried about how
their actions might be judged, so they threw some of the bodies into
common ditches or toilet trenches so that their dirty deeds could not
be easily seen.

I found the body of my friend Alphonse Gatema laid in a toilet
with those of his wife and two children. That image has stayed

in my memory. These were my best friends; we used to hang out together. When I remembered them, I asked myself why God had let me stay alive alone. Yes, it was not only survivor's guilt I felt, but also abject loneliness, the feeling one has when he pines for the loss of a loved one. But those few of us who had been targeted yet still survived the genocide, we wept for the loneliness that came from losing dozens upon dozens of people who had each played a role in our lives. We lost parents, siblings, teachers, ministers, doctors, neighbors, friends, lovers, and acquaintances we had grown used to seeing every day of our lives—all gone now, all gone all at once. There weren't enough tears. The few of us who remained, many of us strangers when the killing began, had only one another now. All the rest of the people in our lives were gone forever. It is a strange feeling; the feeling of being in a familiar place, yet everything that had once been familiar had vanished, never to return again. What was our reason for living? we asked out loud. For surely there was a reason. To tell the tale, perhaps?

It has been very hard to forget our first evening back in the capital city. I looked around at the skeletons of buildings where I had once gathered with friends and wondered who was still alive, and if they were, how we would we find one another. Before the atrocities, my comrades and I spent much time together in the Kambogo clothing store or in John's Bistro, just analyzing politics, exchanging stories and experiences, full of good cheer. As those happy memories flooded back, I begged to see a familiar face of one of my brethren reemerging in peace. It was like gathering in an airport waiting area, except I had no idea who would enter next through the door; even if I found someone I loved and cared about, instead of rushing off home with them, we would embrace and tearfully share our personal stories of survival. Looking at each building now, even the pleasant, happy memories drew tears.

I could not go directly to the village where I was born. On July 9, the French military intervened with about 2,500 troops and created the Triangle Zone (Gikongoro, Kibuye, and Cyangugu) under UN authorization, to conduct humanitarian operations in what was called the Zone Turquoise. Despite stated best intentions, what occurred on the ground was renewed vigor among the *génocidaires*, causing more civilian killings. The westward FAR exodus under the protection of Turquoise was also marred by more *génociadaire* roadblocks where unarmed Tutsi and undocumented Hutu were murdered. RTLM transmitters also continued to broadcast Hutu Power calls to arms, which the French-led troops did not attempt to stop, adding to the carnage.

It was not safe. None could venture into that area. My hometown, Kibuye, Gitesi Commune, Gitarama Prefecture, was in that zone. The entire prefecture was one of the few parts of the country that had primarily Tutsi inhabitants. Since 1960, the Tutsi citizens of Kibuye had always defended themselves by fighting until the military got involved. I came to learn that in the spring of 1994 they fought against the militias until the army intervened with guns. They had regrouped on the hill of Gitwa, and they staged major resistance on the hills of Bisesero. Most of them died there, while others died on their way to Bisesero. My entire family—my uncles, nieces, and cousins, all of our extended families, close family friends, and the entire village—was eliminated. The ethnic Tutsi were eradicated there, but they died bravely. They are our heroes.

Around the middle of July, the RPF began to contact some political figures among the Hutu to ask them to join their government. Before this time, as the FAR began losing the war, the French decided to withdraw and crossed international borders, mostly into Zaire, with the militias, FAR, administrative officials, and the rest of the population who supported the Hutu Power government. The country was gradually being emptied in a strategic military retreat.

As the Zone Turquoise collapsed and was pushed ever deeper into Zaire, only then, at the end of September, did I decide to go to my village to examine what was left of it. My friend Emmanuel

Musonera and two soldiers accompanied me there. After four hours of driving, we finally arrived. I was suddenly a stranger to where I was born. Paths had become almost impassable, covered with bushes. Along my way I could see one human bone here, another there. I could hear only dogs barking unsociably because they had lost their masters, or because they had eaten their masters' rotting carcasses. But no one was left to tell me their tale.

Three harmless-looking ladies, all Hutu for sure, were cultivating the yard where once had stood my home. I knew none of them. Only two questions came into my mind: "Where are those who lived here?" I asked.

No one answered, and so I asked, "Did anyone survive?"

One of them said, "Maybe their son who lived in Kigali survived. Aren't you him?"

I did not answer. One of my colleagues asked them, "Who told you to cultivate here?"

Prior to the triumphant return of the RPF rebels, one way in which the Hutu Power government sought to eradicate all ethnic Tutsi was to tell the Hutu to take over Tutsi land and property and expel the Tutsi who had previously lived there. In this way, even Hutu who had no desire for killing were made to be accessories to murder by sending Tutsi out into the streets where they could easily be slaughtered. Yes, there were Hutu who courageously hid Tutsi, but they were few.

Conflicted, I wiped the tears from my face and said, "Good luck with the harvest and God bless you," and we drove back to Kigali.

I searched for Pascal, Pascal my hero, the man who risked his own life and that of his family in order to save me. For all those months in the hotel, I had no way of knowing where he was, whether he made it back to his home safely, and whether he had lived or died.

Eventually I did find him, and we reunited happily, sharing our stories as Rwandans love to do. He had managed to remain safe within his house throughout the Hundred Days, as we came to call the genocide, which in fact lasted exactly that long. As the country began to rebuild, he opened an office supply store and made much money after the genocide. Tragically, in 1998, after the genocide and the war had ended, he was killed on his way to his house coming from a bar late one evening. Unknown people threw a grenade at him. He was taken to the hospital and died there.

Why? Why? I cried. We never knew who did this to him. Pascal had helped me. After having survived the genocide and having saved my life, he was now dead, the victim of even more violence.

20

JUSTICE AND REBUILDING

AFTER THE SWEARING in of the RPF government, I decided to return to work with the Ministry of Justice in Parquet Kigali. People like me were given the task of interrogating suspects, but in truth we did not have any legal authority to prosecute their cases. Like much of the rest of Rwanda, our entire justice system had been decimated by the war, and it would be a year before it was finally rebuilt and fully functioning again in late 1995.

Once the new government took office, it was the task of the appointed minister of justice, Jean Marie Vianney Nkubito, to set up a justice system. There were already nearly ten thousand jailed prisoners suspected of genocide. It was not until after the promulgation of the Organic Law of August 30, 1996, on the Organization of Prosecution for Offences Constituting the Crime of Genocide or Crimes Against Humanity that judges and officers of public prosecution were formally appointed. This organic law organized jurisdictions charged with the task of trying those suspected of the crime of genocide or crimes against humanity by creating specialized courts, which we called chambers.

I was among the officers appointed to the Public Prosecution Department for the Specialized Chambers of the Tribunals of First Instance of Kigali. Later, I was named first deputy prosecutor in charge of this department. I reconciled myself not to use my power to arrest anyone simply because they were Hutu, but instead to be fair and guided by the rule of law. I had the opportunity to survive in the Hotel des Mille Collines with my old boss, François Nsanzuwera, the prosecutor of Kigali. It is very hard to describe this man. He is a typical upright man of laws who never showed any ethnic bias during his career. He was a man who respected the rule of law, and he tried to be fair when the country was divided by ethnicity. Even though I was working under his authority, we had mutual respect and we would eventually build a friendly relationship. Today he is still my friend. He worked vigorously to arrest those who were involved in the killing of innocent people before the genocide, but the judges appointed for political reasons diluted his power by releasing them. Once, a public officer had refused to go to pretrial before a particular judge by saying that the judge was a cockroach—and got away with it.

We went back to our jobs in order to help the government rebuild itself. The country was completely destroyed as a state, with no functioning institutions. We lived in a traumatized society. The new RPF government set up ruling guidelines from the 1991 Constitution, the 1993 Arusha Accords, and the power-sharing agreement between political parties. A Hutu from the RPF, Pasteur Bizimungu, became president, and Faustin Twagiramungu, a Hutu from the MDR, became prime minister. A new post of vice president was created and held by former RPF commander Paul Kagame, a Tutsi who now had the rank of major general.

This government faced many challenges: no functioning offices, no paper, no pens or pencils, no typewriters, no computers, no Internet, no cars, no fuel, no telephones, and no cell phones. Civil services were nonexistent. Reconciling the torn society would be jeopardized by insecurity, large portions of the population living in refugee camps, and the sociopsychological need to bring the perpetrators of genocide to justice.

A large portion of the Hutu population was taken hostage by Hutu Power militias and ex-FAR army personnel and placed in refugee camps across the border at Goma in Zaire, soon to be renamed the Democratic Republic of the Congo. These refugees caused many problems for the new government and the international community. The camp housed almost the entire administrative and political structure of the old regime, the FAR, and the Hutu Power militias. It was impossible to manage them or to control the distribution of humanitarian assistance.

The international community had failed to disarm the FAR, and the refugee camps became an opportunity for the FAR to reorganize and make incursions into Rwanda to kill innocent survivors of the genocide. The international community, which had failed to stop the original genocide, also failed to close the camps in order to allow the nonviolent population that had been kept hostage there to return home. This refugee crisis existed for almost two years and only a small number of voluntary repatriations occurred. As the Hutu Power die-hards came to kill inside Rwanda, they also went on to kill Tutsi in Zaire.

Inside the camps, people were dying from disease. The stateless army, along with the militias, continued to launch attacks into Rwanda and killed more and more of the unarmed portion of our population. The level of fear and instability remained high throughout the country. RTLM hate radio also continued to broadcast out of Zaire. Zaire's President Mobutu attempted to manipulate the refugees' situation to his advantage. He turned a blind eye to the organization and rearming of the FAR controlling the refugee camps by providing sanctuary and allowing the FAR to make raids into Rwanda. This posed a serious threat to Rwanda until the RPF crossed the border, destroyed the camps, and liberated the Rwandans encamped there against their will at the end of 1996.

Closely related to the refugee crisis was the crisis of justice. The new government was trying to achieve some justice for those who suffered and survived the genocide. The perpetrators had to be held accountable. Our infrastructure had been destroyed; virtually no trained judges and lawyers remained in the country. With few resources to establish a new system, the rule of law became a priority, but development was slow and painful, as the international community was reluctant to help Rwanda.

Rwanda had ratified and integrated into its national legal system the Geneva Convention of Genocide and Crimes Against Humanity, but had failed to insert in its law the actual penalties for that heinous crime. We were working under less than auspicious conditions: The Hutu were not happy when they or someone they knew was arrested, and the victims were not happy if someone they felt had participated in genocidal activities was released.

> The Hutu were not happy when they or someone they knew was arrested, and the victims were not happy if someone they felt had participated in genocidal activities was released.

We had nothing with which to conduct the investigations—no police or legal infrastructure. We had no technology. We kept records on paper files in manila folders. Most of the records from before the war had been destroyed. All we seemed left with was the simple and often flawed human ability to record accusations and interrogate those who were arrested. Even once this information was logged manually on slips of paper, there was no computerized system with which to compile it, cross-reference it, and permanently store it. Sometimes, after all this painstaking effort, a "mole" or spy would find where the papers were kept and destroy or alter them in order to save a friend.

People were occasionally imprisoned unfairly, lost in a system that was struggling to merely *become* a system, while some of the worst offenders roamed free. Even those who had indeed committed crimes would languish for extraordinarily long times in jails as the government struggled to compile enough evidence with which to go to trial. It was a disastrous mess, yet few could figure out a better way to do things on the budget and the resources available to us.

Everyone's frustration was palpable, yet those of us who believed in justice and reconciliation knew we had to wake up every morning and do our part in order to bring our nation back together again. The problems before us were disheartening, yet the overall picture was that we had been given the opportunity to start anew, to help create an African nation based on the rule of law where we could all try to bring about lasting peace unencumbered by ethnic hatred and ignorance.

Even though we had the best of intentions, I could not say we always perfectly served the cause of justice. But I also believe we were in a situation created by genocide, and we had to find truthful answers to that episode of our collective national history in order to handle that situation. With a traditional court system, we realized it would take two hundred years to clear all the cases clogging our prison system. Thousands of people would die of natural causes before they could have their day in court. The government proposed the idea of using a traditional village way of solving conflict, named "Gacaca court." Gacaca is actually a species of grass that forms lush lawns. Traditionally, wise elders would sit on the lawn under a tree to settle community disputes. The mission of this system is to achieve truth, justice, and above all else—reconciliation. In fact, a summit on reconciliation is held annually to evaluate the reconciliation process. The summit brings together various stakeholders, including Rwandans living in diaspora. Gacaca aims to promote community healing by making the punishment of perpetrators faster and less expensive to the state. It has profoundly impacted reconciliation in Rwanda, and has succeeded in increasing community solidarity in conflict resolution.

In 2000, a law legalizing Gacaca was passed. Under Gacaca, people confess and then apologize for the crimes they committed. A communal punishment for these people was introduced. According to the National Service of Gacaca Jurisdictions, the Gacaca court system has the following objectives:

- The reconstruction of what happened during the genocide
- The speeding up of the legal proceedings by using as many courts as possible
- The reconciliation of all Rwandans and building their unity

In November 1994, the UN Security Council created the UN Tribunal for Rwanda to try those accused of genocide and crimes against humanity. This international tribunal is, ironically, located in Arusha, Tanzania, where the Accords were originally signed that became such a flash point for the hate-filled Hutu Power extremists. The international courts in Arusha are where the leaders and architects of the genocide have been brought to trial, as opposed to the Gacaca courts, which have primarily handled the cases of the lesser offenders—the foot soldiers of the murderous plotters.

After intensive training on the new organic law, organizing the prosecution of Offenses Constituting the Crime of Genocide or Crimes Against Humanity, I was given more and more responsibilities. Soon I started prosecuting genocide cases. I took my job seriously and never allowed my emotions to overrule what was fair and right. This was most tested in early 1997 when I was chosen by the government to open the first trial of the crime of genocide and crimes against humanity in Kigali by prosecuting none other than Froduald Karamira, the dreaded creator of the term "Hutu Power." Karamira had been a frequent visitor to the Hotel des Mille Collines when I was a refugee there, sharing laughs amidst the rape and genocide with his good friend Paul Rusesabagina. Karamira freely ate the best food and drank the finest liquor in all of Rwanda, while those of us seeking shelter inside the very same building secretly pooled our resources together to purchase crumbs, or went outside to gather water from a swimming pool to drink in garbage pails. It was Karamira's voice we heard daily on RTLM Radio, which he co-owned, personally encouraging the crazy people in the streets to kill all Tutsi.

This was God's test for me, to see if I could control my emotions and merely do my civic duty without prejudice. It took all the character I could muster to look into his eyes each day, knowing who he was and what he had done, knowing that he knew me, that he saw me nearly every time he came into the hotel during the genocide, knowing were it not for the UN peacekeepers on site and the threats of the international community who visited us, he would have joyously sliced me to pieces himself, just as he encouraged his followers to do.

It would be cliché to say that now the tables had turned. His fate was now in my hands, as mine was once in his. A lesser person might look at this as a wonderful opportunity for revenge, but I refused to think in those terms. This was my job and my duty, and I had to do it properly and right, without undue passion.

Winning this case was far too easy. There was never any doubt to the verdict; there was never any doubt to his guilt.

I should have felt happy; I should have felt vindicated. I felt none of these things. Karamira was one of the very last people in Rwanda to suffer the death penalty. If ever there was a person who deserved such a fate, it was him, but still, I do not believe in an eye for an eye. I cannot abide the death penalty. It crushed me to have played a part in that sort of justice, but the penalty was not passed down by me, nor did I write the law that provided the sentencing guidance. Immediately after Karamira was killed by firing squad, the death penalty was held in abeyance, and in 2007 it was abolished. Rwanda now joins the two-thirds majority of the world that no longer has a death penalty. Would that that had been the case in 1997; I would not have to go the rest of my life with such a pall on my conscience.

I was also given the responsibility in 1999 of prosecuting one of the most high-profile genocide cases to ever reach a Rwandan court: Augustin Misago, a Roman Catholic bishop. Even the pope weighed in on this case, pleading for Misago's freedom and amnesty regardless of his guilt or innocence.

Those who experience war, genocide, or violent death all around them frequently develop posttraumatic stress disorder (PTSD). They cannot escape the horrifying images engrained in their mind and thus cannot find peace or happiness in the here and now. I was never diagnosed with PTSD, but nonetheless I, too, was having severe difficulty living in the here and now, finding peace and happiness. My job, the prosecution of *génocidaires*, forced me to personally relive the genocide every hour of every day. I could never escape it. Every day of my life I was back in April of 1994, running from crazy men with machetes, tripping over dead bodies in the streets, listening to gunfire, grenade explosions, and screams.

Having been selected to prosecute Karamira and Misago indicated I was reaching the top of my field. I should have been proud and happy. But I had never chosen this particular field. It had chosen me by happenstance. I'd come to love the law. But was this the only form of law that I could practice—the prosecution of genocide crimes? In Rwanda in the late 1990s, the answer was yes. I could have done something else, but I was more committed to playing my part in rebuilding the country, especially in the justice sector where I was working before the genocide, where human capital had been completely destroyed. After the genocide, we were working with no pay. We were dedicated to helping the government raise the country from the ashes. Many NGOs were paying good money, but I chose to be one of the people who were rehabilitating the justice system. Others in my country gradually opened or reopened shops and cafés. Some found work in factories and offices. Still more went back to tilling the fields. The genocide would always be with them, a part of their lives, but they could also escape it for hours each day, fixing computers or selling coffee. I could not; not due to any mental affliction, but by occupation.

Somehow, amid all this, I met a girl and fell in love. She, too, had a career. One day she received an opportunity to move to America. She wanted to go more than anything she had ever wanted. I encouraged her. When the time came for her to leave, I accompanied her to the airport. Tearfully, we said good-bye to each other and agreed to keep in touch.

Alone again for the first time since the daily reliving of the genocide had begun to wear on me, in my mind I saw the flicker of a way out. To follow her to America would take an enormous leap of faith, a jump into the unknown. But what would I do in America? In Rwanda, I was a respected prosecutor. In America, I would have to explore other options.

When I finished the Misago trial and its worldwide publicity, I had finally had enough. I had given all I could for the time being. My life needed a new chapter, a change, a respite. I closed my eyes and leapt. I said good-bye to the green hills of my homeland. Without any idea what I would do to sustain myself, I joined my love in America.

21

HOLLYWOOD

ON SEPTEMBER 11, 2004, the movie *Hotel Rwanda* was released. It eventually received three Academy Award nominations and worldwide acclaim. For survivors like me, though, it had a completely different effect. As I explained in the Introduction, this was a foxhole movie, and I was one of the very few who had been in that real-life foxhole. Ten years had gone by and my fellow survivors from the hotel had all gone their separate ways. Many were still in Rwanda, scattered throughout the country. Bernard Makuza eventually became the nation's prime minster. Wellars Gasamagera became a senator. Jean Pierre Nkurunziza, who was just a young student during the genocide, was now working in Kigali in an ombudsman's office. Pasa Mwenenganucye was now head of financial administration in the Rwandan Network Computer Company in Kicukiro. Serge Rusagara, who was only in high school during the slaughter, got a job with a telecommunications company. Alexis Vuningoma owned an eatery in Kigali named the Karisimbi Restaurant.

Others, like me, came to the Americas. Dr. Egide Karuranga is now a professor at the Laval University School of Business in Quebec, Canada. Some joined me in the United States. Many Rwandans emigrated to Belgium, France, and the French-speaking areas of Canada, as most of them spoke French more fluently than English. But wherever we were and whatever we were doing, this movie brought us back together like some long-buried magnet. Those of us who had not spoken to one another in years were reconnecting again, and we had only one thing on our minds: that movie.

As I spoke with other genocide survivors, particularly those who sought refuge in the Hotel des Mille Collines, I heard nothing but disappointment and anger. In some cases, the criticism was rather petty—people who were enraged because many of the scenes were filmed in South Africa and not Rwanda and it was obvious to them, as native Rwandans, that the landscape was not that of our country. Others almost universally derided the depiction of Paul Rusesabagina as a hero.

I can only imagine that a retelling of a narrow and specific historical event, boiled down to a two-hour Hollywood movie, would leave most anyone who was there in person disappointed in the result. I am a reasonable man and I know that were a filmmaker to interview two hundred witnesses to an event, they would get two hundred slightly different stories and make two hundred slightly different movies. That much I can accept. I also understand, as do my fellow survivors, that in order to make a Hollywood movie entertaining, one must sometimes elongate the truth for dramatic purposes. This is the trouble with historical nonfiction, particularly that based on events so very recent in vintage.

Once we had vented our emotions about the film, we all asked the same rhetorical question: How did this all come to pass? How was Paul Rusesabagina selected from among all who were in the hotel, and all who helped protect those of us in the hotel, for deification in a Hollywood film?

It seems to have started innocently with one fine book released in 1998, *We Wish to Inform You That Tomorrow We Will Be Killed with Our Families*, by *New Yorker* staff writer Philip Gourevitch, who dropped Rusesabagina's name a few times throughout. He had even interviewed Rusesabagina, but Gourevitch spent more time focusing on another hotel survivor, Odette Nyiramilimo, dedicating page after page to her personal story.

My American co-author, Kerry Zukus, had the opportunity to interview Mr. Gourevitch long after the release of the movie.

"The first person who told me about all the people surviving within the Hotel des Mille Collines was François Nsanzuwera," Gourevitch told Zukus.

Ironically, François—the prosecutor of Kigali—was my boss before and shortly after the genocide. I knew him very, very well.

Zukus asked if François had mentioned or praised the hotel manager, crediting him with saving our lives. "No," said Gourevitch.

> In fact, nobody described the hotel to me as a story unto itself, but rather as one of the stations in their own personal stories of survival. It was only as I started to notice how the hotel figured for a number of different people I'd met in different contexts through unrelated introductions— Nsanzuwera, then later Thomas Kamilindi, and later still Odette Nyiramilimo—that I became interested in the hotel story as a whole. The only person who had mentioned Paul Rusesabagina to me was Odette, when she spoke of how he arranged for her family to get from their home to the hotel. She clearly felt that he had helped them crucially. But she didn't represent Rusesabagina as the savior of everyone in the hotel. Nobody said that, and it was a point I made clearly when I wrote the story.
>
> Still, after interviewing those people, I wanted to know more, because the hotel seemed to be one of the largest single gatherings of targeted people who survived the genocide. I think I asked Odette what became of that hotel manager. This was in the summer of 1996, in Kigali, and she said, "He's working back at the Hotel des Diplomates."
>
> You have to understand, no one in Rwanda knew me and when I introduced myself as someone writing for the *New Yorker*, no one knew what I was talking about. Everyone had

heard of New York City, many had heard of the *New York Times*, but when I said, "the *New Yorker*," they just smiled politely or looked confused. We obviously did not have a large circulation in Rwanda. And most people who had experience with the press thought of it in terms of daily journalism. They'd say, "When is this going to be published?" thinking I'd say tomorrow, or this weekend. When I said, "Maybe in five or six months," they just laughed. At that point in Rwandan history that seemed like a very distant future. So no one seemed in a big hurry to try to impress me by bragging about the things they did or did not do during the genocide. They could see little benefit in doing so.

Still, people told their stories with different degrees of self-regard and self-importance. Paul Rusesabagina clearly felt proud of what he did. Not more than many others, and he had done nothing to draw attention to himself. I'm pretty sure I was the first reporter to ask him for his story—and I felt that he was glad to be asked.

Zukus asked Gourevitch if he bothered to fact-check every claim Rusesabagina made about himself.

Every claim—no. But I corroborated every claim he made about the hotel story with the accounts of others, and nothing he said to me was contradicted by anyone I spoke to. What he's said to others since then is another matter—I haven't kept track and can't comment on it. But I've never seen any reason to regard what he told me shortly after the genocide, while he was still in Rwanda, as false or outrageously self-serving. He wasn't a figure of controversy at the time, so I didn't interrogate every detail of his statements like a prosecutor might, the way I did, say, when I interviewed *génocidaires*. I didn't meet survivors of the hotel who say that he took credit he didn't deserve, and much worse than that, because he hadn't yet taken, much less been given any by Hollywood. In fact, I never heard any such complaints in response to my writings about him—only later after the movie.

Zukus brought up comments Gourevitch attributed to Rusesabagina about calling and faxing world leaders for assistance:

> If you look closely at my book, the things Rusesabagina said to me were a lot of "we, we, we," with the occasional "I" thrown in for good measure. It stands in stark contrast to how most of what he says today is all, "I, I, I." Even when he said "we," such as his account of the faxes and phone calls, it did not seem to me that he was taking personal credit. The same goes for when he talked about calling General Dallaire, asking for assistance. It was more like when a football team gets a goal and a supporter says, "We scored!" No, *he* did not score, nor was he even on the team, but the team he supported scored and he identifies with the team.
>
> Rusesabagina seemed to identify with all the good things that brought about survival within the hotel, and also with the fear and angst of being besieged there—he definitely felt that he was on the team, and essential to it—but when I spoke to him back then, he never gave me the impression he was claiming to be some singular hero. That is reflected in my book and I stand behind it.

Indeed, in Gourevitch's book, no one else praises Rusesabagina about the miracle of the hotel except Rusesabagina himself, and even then, he does so in rather small amounts. It is nothing at all like the movie or the book Rusesabagina wrote after the movie, for which Gourevitch said he declined to be interviewed. Gourevitch's book never states Rusesabagina "single-handedly saved us all." Regarding

Paul and the hotel refugees, Gourevitch, in his own voice, wrote, "He hadn't saved them, and he couldn't have saved them—not ultimately."

There is another possible place where someone looking very hard may have heard the name "Paul Rusesabagina," but it is far more obscure. The privately published academic press of Human Rights Watch, an NGO, printed the words of the late Alison Des Forges in a tome entitled *Leave None to Tell the Story: Genocide in Rwanda*. Published in March of 1999, it is 789 pages long. Rusesabagina appears on one single page.

And yet, in the promotion of the movie, Rusesabagina claimed to have been "besieged" by book writers, journalists, and filmmakers because "the Hotel Mille Collines story was *my* story." He says this in the commentary section of the *Hotel Rwanda* DVD. If none of the rest of us who had been at the hotel, who had survived the genocide there and had kept up with all the news about the hotel's survivors, never said or read anything claiming Rusesabagina was a hero, what exactly was he talking about? How did he manage to get himself attached to this Hollywood movie that would soon make him a worldwide celebrity? None of us knew.

Based on what we have pieced together, we can only speculate, and I say SPECULATE with capital letters, that when Keir Pearson, the screenwriter who originally conceived of the film, thought the Hotel des Mille Collines story was script-worthy, he tried to track down witnesses in the most logical fashion. How did he hear about the hotel? In an interview in the May/June 2005 edition of *Harvard Magazine* (he is an alum), he is quoted as saying that in 1999 his friend John Robinson, also from Harvard, who had spent the previous seven years in Tanzania, told him about Paul Rusesabagina. Not about the hotel, but about Paul. Suspiciously enough, 1999 is also the year Philip Gourevitch's *We Wish to Inform You That Tomorrow We Will Be Killed with Our Families* hit the bestseller lists. Gourevitch, who continues to have interest in Rwanda today, said he'd been told of Pearson's remarks: "What can I say? I never looked into it."

At the time Pearson found Rusesabagina, it was years after Philip Gourevitch had, and Paul was working in Brussels as a taxi driver. It is alleged (and I am choosing my words carefully because I am not 100 percent certain of these details) that Sabena, who had managed the hotel during the genocide, had contact information on Rusesabagina, being that they were located in Brussels as well. For that matter, Philip Gourevitch still had his contact information, too, but Gourevitch told us neither Pearson nor director/co-screenwriter Terry George ever contacted him.

It is likely Sabena would only have had information on hotel employees rather than refugees, and even then probably only those at a managerial level (e.g., Rusesabagina). If I were Pearson and I were looking for an eyewitness account, this is how I would begin. But it is not how I would end. It seems, however, that Rusesabagina—presented with a rapt audience and no one to contradict him—felt his meeting with Keir Pearson, a *screenwriter*, rather than a journalist for a magazine Rusesabagina had never heard of, was a wonderful opportunity to spin far more fanciful tales than those he told Philip Gourevitch. Perhaps other survivors would have been tempted to do the same. For this, I focus my blame less on the bragging Rusesabagina than on Pearson. A screenwriter is not a journalist. But this was a true story, not a made-up one. Journalists get confirmation. Then more confirmation. And then more. Philip Gourevitch interviewed countless people in the writing of his book, which looked at the full expanse of the entire genocide. Pearson was only writing about the hotel. He should have tried to find as many survivors as possible simply to ask them about what happened there. This alone would have provided Pearson with completely different stories that had *nothing* to do with Paul Rusesabagina, or that would have contradicted his tales of heroism. But building simply off of Rusesabagina, with his self-aggrandizing tales, was just too juicy, too cinematic, too…Hollywood. One brave and selfless savior, saving 1,200 people all by himself. Unarmed. The whole world against him.

What Hollywood studio would not have said "Wow!"? This wasn't some typical African movie. This was *Die Hard* in the sub-Sahara. A more complex and truthful story might not be as tantalizing.

In an op-ed he wrote for the May 10, 2006, *Washington Post*, director and co-screenwriter Terry George stated, "Before making the film, I grilled Rusesabagina and read all I could about his experience. I traveled to Brussels and Rwanda, and I met survivors from his hotel, some of whom still worked there. No one contradicted his story."[12]

When pressed by survivors like me (and they *were* pressed, although it received little media attention), Pearson and George released a few actual names of people they went to for corroboration of Rusesabagina's version of events: Thomas Kamilindi, the journalist friend of Rusesabagina, who inadvertently almost got us all killed; and Zozo, the jovial hotel worker who still works at the hotel to this day. Zozo is quite a character and we all like him very much. But part of Zozo's appeal is that he will tell you whatever you want to hear. If you go to the hotel today and ask about "the hero, Paul Rusesabagina," Zozo will regale you with grand tales of the wonderful Mr. Paul. If you ask instead about "that lying scoundrel, Paul Rusesabagina," he will commiserate with you completely. In short, Zozo is a wonderful host who loves to please. And if Pearson and George wanted Paul Rusesabagina praised, Zozo would have been more than happy to do so. I have spoken to him recently and he regrets it. And no, in this case, knowing him as I do, I sincerely do not believe he was only saying that to make me happy.

But then there was one other person Terry George mentioned by name: Odette Nyiramilimo. Most everyone in and around the hotel saved *someone's* life. Pascal saved mine—and in Odette's case, it actually was Paul.

Throughout *Hotel Rwanda*, there is a minor character named Odette, who is married to a man named Jean-Baptiste. The characters

---

[12] Terry George, "Smearing a Hero," *Washington Post,* May 10, 2006, http://www.washingtonpost.com/wp-dyn/content/article/2006/05/09/AR2006050901242.html.

are based on two real people: Odette Nyiramilimo, a Rwandan physician who later became a senator and also served as minister of state for social affairs, and her husband, Jean-Baptiste Gasasira, who is a medical doctor. The film treats Odette kindly—as it should, for she is a wonderful lady.

Today Odette serves as president of People's Well Being, a human rights organization in Rwanda, and she is also a member of the East African Community parliament. I interviewed her after the release of *Hotel Rwanda*.

> Regarding the movie *Hotel Rwanda*, I actually knew about it before it even came out. The director, Terry George, was in Rwanda for a couple weeks before they started making the film. I read the script and I told him that this is not what happened. He told me, "It's a film; it's not a documentary. It is supposed to be fiction." But what I liked about it is that he tried to show the rest of the world that they didn't even bother to save us. He also told me that what motivated him to make the film is that no one was killed in the hotel.
>
> What I didn't like about the film was that they tried to give Rusesabagina too much credit. I know he didn't go out to get us food, because he was scared as well. But at the end they show what really happened. They show all of us going to the RPF side. They really showed that RPF was involved in us being saved. They also show that not all Hutu had the intention to kill Tutsi. That's what I liked about the film.

"It's a film; it's not a documentary. It is supposed to be fiction." This is Terry George's smoking gun, even if one were to disregard every single thing every other hotel survivor says today. "It is supposed to be fiction." If only the movie had included a disclaimer to that effect either at the beginning or at the end, such as "Based on a true story," or "Inspired by a true story." Qualifying phrases such as those rarely if ever have a negative impact on an audience's enjoyment of a film. Not a day goes by that I and my fellow refugees do not shake our heads and ask, "Why couldn't they have added such a simple disclaimer in the spirit of truthfulness?" It would have changed so much.

Apologists for the film and for Paul Rusesabagina have stated publicly that far more refugees from the hotel were interviewed by Pearson and George than even they have mentioned. Rusesabagina, under oath in a UK courtroom in 2008, stated he and the filmmakers (he did not specify exactly who) went to Rwanda in 2003 and interviewed fifty to one hundred people and compiled fifteen hours of interviews with those who survived at the hotel from April through June of 1994. But he provided no names, and thus no way of proving or disproving the claim. Furthermore, in other interviews, Rusesabagina claims he made only two visits to Rwanda since he left in 1996, and this 2003 visit was neither of them.

The *Maravi Post* out of Malawi reported on November 19, 2011, that "During the preparations for filming the Academy Award nominated *Hotel Rwanda* the director of the film interviewed over 1,000 people who resided at the hotel at the time of the genocide with Mr. Rusesabagina in order to verify his accounts of what happened there. All 1,000 people confirmed that Mr. Rusesabagina was a hero and saved their lives. They corroborated his accounting of events without hesitation."[13]

One thousand of us. That would be practically all of us. That would likely include me as well as everyone I know who was in the hotel in April and May of 1994. I was not contacted, nor were they, save for the few I mentioned. Finding a thousand of us would also be completely and utterly impossible. But this is the propaganda we face.

---

[13] Jennifer Fierberg, "The Ordinary Man That Rwanda Would Like to Silence," *The Maravi Post*, November 19, 2011, via Zimbio.com, http://www.zimbio.com/Paul+Rusesabagina/articles/jySWGyLk3B-/Ordinary+Man+Rwanda+like+silence.

In one of the movie's first scenes, Rusesabagina goes to buy provisions from his best friend, Georges Rutaganda, a shareholder in RTLM hate radio and vice president of the Interahamwe. That scene is followed by another showing Rusesabagina being friendly with General Augustin Bizimungu, one of the chief planners of the genocide. These relationships were all true. What the film attempts to do is show the "fictional" character, Rusesabagina, as having very bad friends whom he comes to see as being evil, all the while using them in order to "save" Tutsi such as myself and others. The character arc of the ambivalent man who finally sees the error of his ways and takes a brave stand is commonplace in many forms of art and literature—think of Rick, Humphrey Bogart's character in *Casablanca*.

Since the end of the genocide, I have come to learn that the relationship between Paul Rusesabagina and Georges Rutaganda was a complex one, particularly from Rutaganda's point of view. In his statements to the international criminal court in Arusha in December 2004 as he filed appeals against his convictions for genocide, crimes against humanity (extermination), and crimes against humanity (murder), Rutaganda made the following declaration: "Paul Rusesabagina…was an important activist member of the MDR political party in Gitarama and [nationwide]."[14]

Even in Philip Gourevitch's book, Rusesabagina was careful to hide his Hutu Power politics, but they define him and he cannot escape them when they are exposed by the light of full disclosure. Also, at the time of Rutaganda's deposition, the movie *Hotel Rwanda* had already been released, and Rutaganda was obviously attempting to somehow utilize it in order to save himself.

Rutaganda further testified:

---

[14] Georges Nderubumwe Rutaganda, "La vérité sacrifiée à l'autel de la manipulation politico-judiciaire," October 2005, http://repositories.lib.utexas.edu/bitstream/handle/2152/4719/3805.pdf?sequence=1, 52.

Paul Rusesabagina [was] struggling for a solution to feed thousands of refugees who were in his hotel. When he reached me, he used our good relationship to ask me for a loan of quantities of beers and other foodstuffs to help him take care of those refugees. To tell the truth, although willing to help him, it was not easy for a businessman to grant such a loan while people were anxiously waiting to pay cash and above all, during a war for which no one knew its endings.

Not having any other way out, Rusesabagina went up to beg for my good hand and promised me that he was going to leave behind a cheque as surety. During normal situations, it was common practice to leave a cheque as security for a loan, without making payment. He said, "Most of my people don't easily swallow water and if even they wanted to, we don't have proper drinking water." I felt deeply moved and conceded that credit to Rusesabagina and gave him the first delivery, which he hurriedly took in his hotel's minibus, despite that he hadn't brought said cheque with him. He was not only provided with beers but also with bags of rice and cartons of toilet paper. According to him, sanitary conditions had become bad because of the lack of pipe water.

The following day, I went to the Hotel Mille Collines to collect the promised cheque and got the opportunity to visit its compound whereby I met and talked at length with many of my acquaintances among the refugees. I noticed that they were from both Tutsi and Hutu ethnic groups.

The day after, Rusesabagina came again to me requesting another credit. Asked if he had brought me the amount for the first cheque, he said that the collected money was serving in purchasing other items they needed such as potatoes, vegetables, beans, etc., at the local market. This was really unbelievable for me because I was expecting the payment as soon as Rusesabagina got paid by his customers! But after a long

> discussion as at the previous occasion, I again accepted to help
> him as long as he left a new cheque as guarantee.
>
> The same transaction was repeated many times and went
> up to the equivalent of about 15,000 US dollars.

When he spoke these words, Rutaganda was a man fighting for
his life, having already been sentenced to life imprisonment. But
ironically, in his appeal (which came shortly after the movie *Hotel
Rwanda* was released), upon seeing how his friend Paul Rusesabagina
had "reinvented" himself as a hero, Rutaganda attempted to do the
same for himself. As he goes on and on in sections of his testimony
I won't fully list here, he lays claim to the theory that *he*, and not
Rusesabagina, was the true hero of the Hotel des Mille Collines—
Georges Rutaganda, the vice president of the Interahamwe! Yet when
reading his statement, one imagines what Rutaganda thought as he
watched that movie—that if Paul Rusesabagina "saved thousands of
people during the Rwandan Genocide," then, frankly, who hadn't?
Rutaganda even presented as evidence a signed declaration from one
of the UNAMIR soldiers, Commander Amadou Deme, a Senegalese
army officer, who praised him for helping save lives when there was
a standoff at a roadblock during the first attempt at evacuating the
hotel. Deme witnessed the entire drama and testified to the facts of
the case during Rutaganda's court appeal. In his signed testimony,
Deme rails against Terry George's movie, claiming it was not simply
wrong, but a premeditated attempt to confuse many important facts
concerning Rusesabagina's political ties.[15]

But let us for the moment simply consider what Rutaganda
says here about his dealings with Rusesabagina. Contrary to what
he claims in both the movie as well as his book, *An Ordinary Man*,
Paul Rusesabagina did not bring back food to us that he bought

---

[15] Amadou Deme, "Hotel Rwanda: Setting the Record Straight," *Counterpunch*, April 24,
2006, http://www.counterpunch.org/2006/04/24/hotel-rwanda/.

from Georges Rutaganda. Maybe he brought food for himself or for his friends, but he brought back none for refugees. Even his friend Odette testifies he brought us no food.

And then there is the beer. As Rutaganda quoted Rusesabagina in his testimony, "Most of my people don't easily swallow water and if even they wanted to, we don't have proper drinking water." What person can only drink beer but not clean water? But unlike water, beer can be sold. In 1994 Rwanda, the concept of charging people for water was rather foreign.

Rusesabagina was indeed collecting money from us. Yet Rutaganda states Rusesabagina offered him only excuses, not money. Is this true? Rutaganda could be making this all up; yet again, this part of his story is consistent with the Paul Rusesabagina we refugees came to know. It would not surprise us that he might take our money, go to Rutaganda, ask for credit, get beer, sell us the beer, and then walk away with money he received from us and never pay Rutaganda, but who knows for sure?

Later on in his appeal, Rutaganda stated that he asked Rusesabagina to testify on his behalf and that Rusesabagina agreed, but then went back on his word. In a written statement to the court, Rusesabagina says that he bought only beer from Rutaganda, not food, contradicting his own book and movie.

There is also the confusion caused by the film regarding exactly *how* Rusesabagina was heroic. It is inferred that people like Rutaganda did not know Tutsi were in the hotel; that Rusesabagina lied in order to hide us. Yet Rutaganda told the truth when he stated he was inside the hotel, speaking with people he knew, Hutu and Tutsi alike. He knew the hotel harbored Tutsi refugees. This also pokes holes in the movie's only reference to Rusesabagina handing out bills to the refugees for payment. In the film, Rusesabagina claims he must do this as a ruse so people like Bizimungu and Rutaganda would think everyone in the hotel was a regular, paying guest. But it was not a ruse; the bills were *demands* to be paid, and the billing was unknown to *génocidaires* like Bizimungu and Rutaganda. They couldn't care less whether we were being billed or not. They knew Tutsi were in the hotel, and all Tutsi were enemies of the state regardless of whether they paid for a room. Rusesabagina and the film's explanation hold no water. But it was almost as if Rusesabagina was already anticipating some blowback from refugees once the film came out. The bills, the money—he had to get out in front of it somehow.

It irks me that today, refugees' criticism has been minimized to, "They're unhappy they had to pay to stay in a hotel." This misses the mark completely. The money did not keep the hotel open. The money did not go to the hotel's foreign management. The money did not go to employees' salaries. The money did not even go to purchase food or water for us to stay alive. Rutaganda supports this in one of his final statements: "When the banks re-opened at Gitarama, I paid in all Rusesabagina's cheques at the Banque de Kigali. They were on the name of CRHT—Compagnie Rwandaise d'Hôtellerie et de Tourisme, Rwanda's biggest organization, which was in charge of hotel management. At the present moment, I don't know if these cheques have been cashed [cleared]."

We were forced to give cash to Rusesabagina, ostensibly to give to Rutaganda for beer (though we didn't want beer), but Rutaganda claims he never actually saw cash from Paul Rusesabagina. The trail of the money Rusesabagina took from us remains a mystery. Rutaganda claims to be unsure the checks he received ever cleared. In a November 17, 2011, article she wrote for the *Guardian,* British journalist Linda Melvern claims, "The cheques he [Rusesabagina] accepted for rent were cashed in Gitarama, where the [Hutu Power] interim government had established its premises."[16]

As the film progresses, the Rusesabagina character is at the Hotel des Diplomates and has turned the keys over to the Rwandan army.

---

[16] Linda Melvern, "Hotel Rwanda—Without the Hollywood Ending," *Guardian,* November 17, 2011, http://www.theguardian.com/commentisfree/2011/nov/17/hotel-rwanda-hollywood-ending.

He has also given them guests' money that was in the office safe in order to buy his and his family's freedom.

There is a fine point worth mentioning that demonstrates the frustration the refugees feel not only at the movie, but worse yet, at the statements Paul Rusesabagina has made since the release of the film, "rewriting" the film itself as it suits him. In his 2006 book, and in an interview with Oprah Winfrey published in the March 2006 issue of her magazine that references this point in the movie, he claims that when he entered the Hotel des Mille Collines he was confronted by a Tutsi army captain who had been sent by the "new government." He says the captain put a gun to his head, tried to take over the hotel, and gave Rusesabagina his gun and ordered him to shoot his own family.[17] Would someone please explain how a Tutsi was a captain in the army of the Hutu Power government that took over on April 9, 1994? This is like claiming a black slave was a captain in the Confederate Army during the US Civil War. And how did Rusesabagina know the captain was Tutsi? Because he claims it happened at the hotel, there must be other witnesses to this dramatic tale. Who are they?

They do not exist. The story is a vicious lie to smear all Tutsi. He did this to intentionally delude the reader that the Tutsi were also killing, as he developed his theory of "double genocide." Someone who doesn't know Rwandan history might believe that Paul was almost killed by a Tutsi soldier when the genocide started. What was a Tutsi army doing in the middle of the FAR zone?

When the Rwandan army leader in the film wants more money in order to spare the lives of others who had sought refuge at the Diplomates, Rusesabagina asks that he be allowed to go to the Mille Collines, where he knew he could gather more money. The army leader says, "You'll go into the hotel and hide behind the UN." In his

---

[17] Oprah Winfrey, "Oprah Talks to Paul Rusesabagina," *O, The Oprah Magazine*, March 2006, http://www.oprah.com/omagazine/Oprah-Talks-To-Paul-Rusesabagina/1.

commentary, the real Rusesabagina chuckles as he says, "The UN was not there, so there was nowhere to hide."

The reason the army character in the film raises this concern about allowing Rusesabagina into the Mille Collines was because the UN was *indeed* there. In fact, in the very next scene, Rusesabagina, escorted by the Rwandan military, pulls up right in front of the Hotel des Mille Collines, which is surrounded by baby-blue-helmeted UN peacekeepers as well as jeeps conspicuously bearing the large and impossible-to-miss letters "UN." Terry George somehow allowed his own "consultant" to the film to contradict his own screenplay—right on the DVD version of the movie itself.

A movie is a movie. In this case, a hundred days were being boiled down to about two hours. Things get condensed; shortcuts are taken so major points can be made. This any rational person can understand. On the other hand, if one looks at the film as a plan by an individual to aggrandize himself for power and profit, certain details *are* relevant. Downplaying the role UNAMIR played is a perfect example. If UNAMIR was in places Rusesabagina says they were not, doing good things he claims they did not do, he must also share credit with them, if not completely abdicate personal credit in some instances. This is the part that offends so many of us who were really there.

Among the many people to whom I happily give credit for our salvation is UNAMIR Gen. Roméo Dallaire, portrayed in the movie as the fictional "Colonel Oliver" (the character played by actor Nick Nolte). The UN peacekeepers had an office in the hotel (one of many facts omitted from the film). They were there to protect us and to inform Dallaire if anyone came inside the hotel and threatened the refugees. The UN flag flew above our grounds. The implication to all who would cause us harm was obvious.

After the genocide, I had the opportunity to discuss those horrible days with General Dallaire himself, as well as his aide-de-camp, Major Brent Beardsley. Dallaire claims never to have been approached by either Keir Pearson or Terry George prior to the making of the film, despite the fact his "role" in the movie was the second largest. This is something no real journalist would ever do, which further rams home the fact that movies are not journalism, and Hollywood is not where one should go in order to learn historical facts. It also raises a major question: *Why wasn't Dallaire approached?* Did Pearson and George know they were dealing in fiction and did not want someone as credible as Dallaire to tell the world he tried to warn them that they were dealing in falsehoods? Or did Rusesabagina warn them not to approach the general for some reason or another? Only George and Pearson know, and they're not talking.

To say that General Dallaire is not a fan of the film would be putting it mildly. He never makes public statements about it, claiming he has no desire to add further to Paul Rusesabagina's fraudulent celebrity. Privately, though, he states, "No general or force commander would ever sit in bars chatting with barkeeps, and I certainly do not refer to Africans as 'niggers'—ever! The force commander never personally led any convoys as depicted in the movie, either, and so on and so on," referring to scenes from the movie. Each of us, it seems, has a different scene or scenes from the film that particularly stick in our craw.

As difficult as it may be to believe, in my humble opinion, Dallaire suffered as much as any of us who survived the genocide. I saw a news program a few years ago where he and Paul Rusesabagina appeared in split screen. As they were both asked to describe what they saw during the Genocide Against the Tutsi, Dallaire, the white Canadian career military man, broke down in tears and had trouble getting his words out, so distraught from the painful memories of those days. Paul Rusesabagina smiled throughout, looking like a man happy just to be on television.

> Dallaire, the white Canadian career military man, broke down in tears and had trouble getting his words out, so distraught from the painful memories of those days. Paul Rusesabagina smiled throughout, looking like a man happy just to be on television.

General Dallaire's book, *Shake Hands with the Devil*, is a heart-wrenching account of his experiences in Rwanda. Not once does he mention the name Paul Rusesabagina. I highly doubt this was an issue of jealousy. Dallaire's book was published in September 2003; the movie *Hotel Rwanda* was released in September 2004. Given that movies and books are frequently released about twelve to eighteen months after completion, this still means the general was one full year ahead of the movie—a movie he knew nothing about. Paul Rusesabagina's book was released in 2006, *after* the movie. In his book, Dallaire speaks quite a bit about the Hotel des Mille Collines and how its inhabitants were spared. Throughout the book, many names are mentioned and much credit given. The absence of Rusesabagina's name speaks volumes. Twice, Dallaire mentions "the hotel manager"—the same number of times he mentions managers of other hotels. Once was when Dallaire received a letter from "the hotel manager" on April 16, asking the general to remove the more than four hundred Tutsi refugees inside the hotel. It is unclear whether the letter was dated April 16 or received April 16. April 16 would likely have been the very first day Rusesabagina was even in the hotel and in charge. Either way, according to Dallaire, the letter did not ask that we be *saved*, but that we be *removed* so the hotel itself would not be attacked. The second reference was a doff of the cap to "the hotel manager" for helping the more traditional military efforts of Tunisian UNAMIR soldiers who were guarding us by "buying off" some Interahamwe with bottles of wine from the hotel's cellar the one single time they entered the hotel to cause trouble.

But Dallaire made it very clear in interviews and discussions that he and Rusesabagina are completely unlike the movie characters played by actors Nick Nolte and Don Cheadle. They were not friends, ever. Dallaire has always believed that Paul Rusesabagina was the mole, the collaborator in our midst, who tipped off the militias to our every move and the general's every strategy concerning our safety within the hotel. He lays blame on Rusesabagina for trying to remove UNAMIR from the hotel completely, which would have meant certain death for all us Tutsi. When RTLM recited our names, Dallaire believed they, too, came from Rusesabagina.

In a *Huffington Post Politics Canada* story from December 29, 2011, Dallaire says of the film, "I think the only value of 'Hotel Rwanda' is the fact that it keeps the Rwandan genocide alive, but as far as content, it's Hollywood...When people use the term Hollywood in a pejorative way, [it's because] they produce junk like that...The story is skewed and we didn't need that. Philip Gourevitch wrote an excellent book [*We Wish to Inform You That Tomorrow We Will Be Killed with Our Families*] from which they extracted him [Rusesabagina], but I think that the facts were not necessarily well-researched."[18]

Dallaire was appearing at a November 2011 "We Day" youth rally in Waterloo, Canada. Paul Rusesabagina had also been scheduled to appear at a similar Canadian event, but cancelled in light of protests from refugees such as myself, due to comments on the Genocide Against the Tutsi he has made since *Hotel Rwanda* made him famous. To this, Dallaire simply stated that it was very good he cancelled, or else "I wouldn't be here."

The documentary based on Dallaire's book and its interviews with the general are an incredible character study of a man torn and anguished by things he saw and things he wished he could have done to make more of a difference. Whenever someone regards him as a hero, Dallaire is quick to counter that he views himself as a *failure*, never once allowing his ego to receive any adulation.

There's an incredible moment in the documentary when Dr. James Orbinski, representing Kigali's Doctors Without Borders at the

---

[18] Joshua Ostroff, "Romeo Dallaire: Senator Slams 'Hotel Rwanda' Film as Revisionist 'Junk,'" *Huffington Post Politics Canada,* December 29, 2011, http://www.huffingtonpost .ca/2011/12/29/romeo-dallaire-hotel-rwanda_n_1174607.html?icid=hp_canada-politics_ gallery&just_reloaded=1.

time of the massacres, insists that Dallaire's actions saved countless lives. The camera then cuts to Dallaire, who quietly disagrees: "What about the thousands who died?"

The camera captures the look on Dallaire's face and the slight catch in his voice as he mentally returns to Rwanda for the first time since he left a decade prior. Sometimes he can't speak at all and the silence is unbearable. This man is the picture of humility.

On the other hand, in the DVD commentary for *Hotel Rwanda*, Paul Rusesabagina says—and this is a direct quote—"The militia knew they had to kill me because I was the only person who was protecting the refugees. They had to kill the protector, who was myself."

In the film, the Rusesabagina character has conflicts with Hutu Power hotel workers who resented him and felt entitled to take up residence in large suites while eating and drinking like kings. The reality of the situation, as I and many other refugees saw it, was that the hotel workers who stayed on, be they Hutu or Tutsi, did no such thing.

To delve further into the representation that Paul fought constantly with hotel employees who were Hutu Power hard-liners, it would be more accurate to say that many Hotel des Mille Collines workers resented him simply because of his takeover of the hotel and his self-serving, autocratic manner. Indeed, some of the employees were Hutu, and some of those Hutu would consider themselves supporters of the Hutu Power movement. That being said, most "true" Hutu Power hard-liners were outside killing and stealing. It is a case of the action defining the person committing the action. If you were a real Hutu Power hard-liner, you would not have been working inside a hotel peacefully. Additionally, in this time of utter nationwide chaos, there was a lot more money to be made out in the streets pillaging and stealing than by staying inside the hotel working and not getting paid.

The misbehaving hotel employee composited in the movie— "Gregoire"—was most likely supposed to be Pasa, the man who was reluctant to hand the master keys over to Paul. Representing Pasa as a thug who took over a suite and was drunk all the time is completely inaccurate. Pasa shared his room with numerous others around his age. Moreover, he was an individual who was not afraid to stand up to Rusesabagina when he felt he was doing wrong, and for this, Rusesabagina got permanent revenge—through a movie that will live on forever.

The Rusesabagina character also receives and distributes corn and beans that he gets from the Red Cross as a quid pro quo for heroically taking in genocide orphans from the Red Cross.

None of this is true.

When this scene comes up early in the movie, Rusesabagina, in his commentary with Terry George, admits, "There were orphans," but stops short of saying he arranged with the Red Cross to take them in. To the best of anyone's knowledge, Rusesabagina did not work with the Red Cross to take in genocide orphans, nor did he accept provisions and hand them out freely. It was the refugee committee, led by Tatien Ndolimana, who worked with the Red Cross. Rusesabagina did not want the Red Cross food unless he could profit from it, which he eventually did when he had the hotel staff cook it in the kitchen before selling it to the refugees.

One scene that did expose some of the true horrors of the situation in our country during the Hundred Days was when the Rusesabagina character goes to visit Rutaganda, and militiamen are raping women outside his door. This sort of behavior went on throughout the genocide and it was as despicable as the slaughtering of innocents. And yes, it went on at Rutaganda's business. Rutaganda and the militias had moved their headquarters into a building bought by him at auction a few months before the genocide. In that building Interahamwe raped women, and all that the militias stole was kept there. In real life, Rusesabagina had never refused to go there and was not afraid for his life to go there. What I wonder is, did Paul tell anyone what he saw there before the movie was released?

In his commentary, Paul goes on to talk about his calling the king of Belgium, the White House, and so on. This lines up somewhat with his 1995 statements to Philip Gourevitch, but as Philip points out, what was once a "we" has now turned into an "I." Prior to Rusesabagina's arrival, such calls were, indeed, going out, from people—well-connected people—who had sought refuge inside the hotel. Even after Paul arrived, he often had those same well-connected and important people making such calls, or he allowed them to make such calls, rather than Paul himself calling.

The film then moves to a scene of a new swarm of refugees coming into the hotel, many of them beaten and bloody. Indeed, not everyone arrived on the same day; people stumbled on in throughout the Hundred Days. In his commentary, Rusesabagina talks about "giving out passes" so people could come into the hotel, and that he told the militias to let these people in because he, Paul Rusesabagina, had personally signed these passes.

I know of no passes. No one I know who waited out the genocide inside the hotel spoke of any passes. All of us had our own personal tales of sneaking in, being smuggled in, or bribing people to help us get in. None of those tales involved Rusesabagina-signed passes. What the film, and Rusesabagina's speeches after the film, have led people to believe is that he, personally, got nearly everyone into the hotel and he, personally, kept us all alive. This is simply not true.

There is a tension-filled scene in the movie where the Rusesabagina character is told by an army officer to evacuate all the hotel guests within thirty minutes. Instead, Paul is shown working the phones, calling General Bizimungu, and heroically getting the threat lifted. In the second edition of her marvelous book, *A People Betrayed: The Role of the West in Rwanda's Genocide*, author and journalist Linda Melvern states that it was the Tunisian UN peacekeepers who kept the army at bay, making the planned attack and invasion of the hotel moot, not Rusesabagina. Released in 2009, the second edition of this book is, perhaps, the very best chronicle of the entire genocide and its background. In it, she adds in her notes that "serious doubts have been raised about the role played by Rusesabagina."[19]

Major Brent Beardsley states, "General Dallaire's threats to General Bizimungu ensured that Bizimungu protected the hotel with his troops and did not risk a massacre which could be laid directly on his head. I have no knowledge of Paul Rusesabagina's role and how it worked with the general's actions."

Beardsley would have known of such a role. He was Dallaire's aide-de-camp. To speak to one was to speak to the other. Beardsley has no reason to lie. In the movie and in his book, Paul claims to have made several requests for protection to General Dallaire of the UN and UNAMIR. When I asked Beardsley directly whether Paul Rusesabagina asked him or any of the UNAMIR contingent to increase the UN military presence at the hotel, he replied, "I have no knowledge of his requests or actions. The hotel was one of several protected sites which included the Amahoro Stadium, the Méridien Hotel, the King Faisal Hospital, and several other locations which I cannot recall."

In the movie, there is a very dramatic scene where Paul Rusesabagina goes to the Hotel des Diplomates with General Bizimungu to offer him some liquor. Bizimungu informs Paul that at that very moment militias are attacking the Hotel des Mille Collines. This theatrical scene shows the character Rusesabagina confronting Bizimungu fearlessly, even causing Bizimungu to reach for his sidearm to shoot Paul, who bravely dares him to fire the weapon. This is followed by Rusesabagina spinning tales of American observers, satellite spies, and lists of *génocidaires* with the general's name prominently upon it. Bizimungu and Rusesabagina quickly return to the Mille Collines, and the general quells the impending slaughter by the Interahamwe.

---

[19] Linda Melvern, *A People Betrayed: The Role of the West in Rwanda's Genocide,* 2nd ed. (London: Zed Books, 2009), chapter 16, note 8.

In his commentary, Paul goes on to say that because of his "persuasiveness" with the general, Bizimungu told his sergeant that if any militiaman killed a refugee in the Mille Collines, Bizimungu would kill him. The date is June 17.

I specifically asked Major Beardsley about the June 17 Interahamwe attack on the hotel, when I and most of the other refugees had already been safely evacuated from the hotel—another important fact distorted in the movie. We were led to believe a high commander of the Rwandan interim government stopped the attack from killing those still in the hotel. What did Beardsley know of this and what role, if any, did UNAMIR play?

He responded by saying, "It does coincide with General Dallaire's threat to Bizimungu and to the stationing of a section of armed troops and an armored personnel carrier in addition to the MILOBs at the hotel." The Hollywood version is that a little, unarmed hotel manager screamed in the face of an armed and powerful Rwandan general, getting the general to back down from attacking the hotel. In reality, it was a UN general doing the screaming and threatening and getting the job done. Meanwhile, the timeline is completely off, as most of the refugees were already safe and long gone.

We are alive today because of the UN peacekeepers, the RPF, well-connected and generous fellow refugees, and the international community because of the various roles they played in our survival. Had Paul Rusesabagina never lived, every one of us who took refuge in that hotel and is still alive would *still* be alive.

> Had Paul Rusesabagina never lived, every one of us who took refuge in that hotel and is still alive would *still* be alive.

The best the movie has to offer is that it helped in bringing to the Western world the story of the Genocide Against the Tutsi. For this, I commend it, as do most of the survivors. And for all the controversy he sparked among the survivors for making a hero out of Rusesabagina, even director

Terry George got it right when he stated the following in his May 10, 2009 *Washington Post* op-ed piece:

> Last May I had the chance to meet Rwandan President Paul Kagame in Rwanda. I sat beside him as he and his wife and most of Rwanda's parliament watched the movie. Afterward he leaned over to me and said the film had done much good around the world in exposing the horrors of the genocide. The next evening, I screened the film at Amahoro Stadium for some 10,000 people. It was the most emotional screening I have ever been at. I spent close to an hour afterward accepting thanks and congratulations.[20]

I recently talked to Bernard Makuza, who is today the vice president of the Rwandan Senate but was also one of the refugees in the hotel. He told me that when he saw the film at that very showing Terry George talks about, he was beside himself with irritation and aggravation. When the media approached him that night (he was serving as Prime Minister at the time), he said, "The story is wrong. That is not what happened."

Most people in America, where I live today, are painfully uninformed about Rwanda and the entire African continent. I hear young people mentioning the atrocities in Darfur, but when I try to speak to them about it, I find most of them know few if any of the details of that conflict. They know killing and genocide are bad and I appreciate that, but beyond that, few appear to know who exactly is killing whom, where, and why. Most are not aware that Darfur is not a country itself, but a section of a country—Sudan. Most also cannot find Sudan, or Rwanda for that matter, on a world map. It is a sad commentary.

But the negatives caused by the film of Keir Pearson and Terry George continue to mount, and certain areas of dishonesty clearly

---

[20] George, "Smearing a Hero."

fall at their feet even more so than those of Paul Rusesabagina. In the same *Guardian* article cited earlier, journalist Linda Melvern states, "There is an inherent danger in repackaging recent history for Hollywood because distortion can creep into the accepted version of events, and fiction readily becomes established fact."[21]

While there is no credit at the beginning or the end of the film that indicates the movie is "*based* on a true story," leaving the viewer to believe the filmmakers stand behind it as an *absolutely* true story, there is one line that does appear in the closing credits: "Part of the profits from this film shall go to The Rwandese Survivors Fund." We survivors have attempted to track this money, but we have never been able to find any that has gone from the filmmakers to the victims of the Genocide Against the Tutsi. According to the Internet Movie Database, the film currently lists gross revenues of $33,882,243 on an original budget of $17,500,000. To paraphrase what Paul Rusesabagina incessantly said to us in the hotel, "Where is our money?"

There is no "Rwandese Survivors Fund." Odette Nyiramilimo, Paul's friend who is depicted in the film and who assisted the filmmakers when they were doing their mini-documentary in Rwanda, personally spoke with me on this issue. During our chat, she told me she had a contract with the filmmakers that 5 percent of *Hotel Rwanda* revenue would go to the Fund for Support to Genocide Survivors (FARG). She also said that when she followed up with Terry George and his people about the money, they told her the film didn't do well—it lost money. Despite this, they said they would try to raise funds for child survivors of the genocide. Then they told her they raised between $70,000 and $80,000. Odette told them to put the money in FARG or any other Rwandan survivors organization. They said they didn't want to put that money in FARG because it is controlled by the Rwandan government. Later still, they told her they put the money in the United Nations Development Programme (UNDP).

---

[21] Melvern, "Hotel Rwanda."

As an aside, Odette came to sincerely befriend Terry George and his family during the filming of *Hotel Rwanda*. Like so many of us refugees, Odette appreciated that the film awakened the West to the genocide story itself. Still, as we did, she had problems with certain fictions that were never admitted to be fictions, as well as with what Paul did with his newfound fame—something from which Terry George seemed to divorce himself.

In an April 23, 2006, e-mail she sent to Terry George, she asked him, "Have you heard of Paul's book? He also spoke on the radio yesterday and I was surprised on how he said that refugees came to him and said that if he leaves them there, they'll go to the top of the hotel and jump in the air! I do not know really when that happened! I am so scared to see our closest friend turn to a different way from what I expected him to do, just because of the film [sic] success! Please Terry, can't you help him put his feet on earth again?"

Odette also brought up the money George had promised from the film's profits. In his e-mail response later that day, George explained:

> With regard to the 5 percent of the net Producers Profits, I have explained to several people and will be more than happy to explain to anyone who wishes and to show them the financial statements from MGM. According to MGM, "Hotel Rwanda" is not in profit, indeed it is still millions in debt to MGM. Here is the rough breakdown of the figures for "Hotel Rwanda." The film cost approximately $20 million to make. MGM spent just over $20 million on releasing and publicizing the film and on the Oscar campaign. So far in the US the film has made $23 million in cinemas. So MGM are showing somewhere in the region of $17 millions [sic] in the red.
>
> With regard to the rest of the world, "Hotel Rwanda" was not very successful in the cinemas. The sum total of all this is that MGM and Sony, who now own MGM, will not be paying any producer profits for a long time. Indeed, Alex Ho and I

both put our producer salaries into the film and will probably never get those back. I will have the exact numbers set out on a balance sheet so that everyone can see what is going on.

The next day Odette replied, stating:

Now the big issue is that Paul has profited off the success of the film, *which is a fiction as you always said it was* [emphasis added], to try destroying politics going on in the country, while we all hoped it will help building! *People thank him on how he was taking care of orphans in the hotel, and he agrees! Terry, there has never been orphans!* [emphasis added] Who would have brought them? Some people even call me or send nice messages to me thanking me to have been taking care of the orphans at that tragic period. Of course I explain it did not happen like that! But it has happened maybe somewhere else. People cannot understand the difference between fiction and reality! But Paul does. So he should not maintain the confusion. On a talk show in the radio, I explained well how you wanted to tell the world what happened in Rwanda and you did it extremely well. Actually I'll always thank you for this and ask you to understand people who want to express their feelings about what they also think!

Finally, Terry George responded to this by saying:

Look, Paul is doing his own thing now, yes he is making a lot of money, and yes he is saying things about Pres. Kagame that I do not necessarily agree with, but he's in the US, which despite how it behaves abroad, claims to allow everyone to voice their democratic decision. So he has the right to earn and say what he wants. I can tell you that attacking his memory of what took place at the hotel is the wrong way to go about criticizing him because it forces me and many like me—Samantha Power, Gourevitch, Richard Holbrooke—to step in and say that what he said was basically right. He should be challenged on the facts as they exist today, on how much Rwanda has progressed, on the peace in the country and not on the small details of the past. Paul, as you know, has a very good memory. The details he has in the book are, I think, accurate, and if, in the debate over what happened in the hotel in 1994, he is proven mostly right, then it is going to appear that he is being persecuted, and then the debate will have shifted from whether Rwanda has made such great progress to why is such a celebrated son being attacked in this way. If Paul is left to say what he thinks, then his audience will only dwindle and fade away. If he continues to be attacked from Rwanda then it will become a big news item and this will throw gasoline on the flames. Trust me on this; I am an expert from previous films. Please tell all these people who attack him to leave him alone, his moments in the spotlight will be over in a few weeks when the book tour ends. If people in Rwanda create a martyr out of Paul, he and his publishers will exploit it to the maximum effect. The only people who will listen and print what [IBUKA][22] says are the *Kigali New Times*. If they give Paul another platform he will have the *New York Times*, CNN, the BBC—the whole world of media who just love stories like this. You and Jean Baptiste are among the most honorable, wonderful people I and my family have ever met. You as much, even more, than Paul were the inspiration for "Hotel Rwanda." I really want to stop this nonsense so please can you implore the people in Rwanda who are angry with Paul to say no more because his time is soon over.

---

[22] IBUKA, which comes from a Kinyarwanda word for "remember," is an umbrella organization connecting the groups that aid survivors of the 1994 Rwandan Genocide.

"His time is soon over." This was written in April 2006. It is now 2014 and Paul is larger, wealthier, more decorated, and more powerful than ever.

I believe that Terry George went into the *Hotel Rwanda* project with the purest of intentions. I would never imply otherwise. Had he not made his film, Hollywood might never have made *any* film about the genocide, and for this he deserves much credit. Not one criticism has been thrown his way by me or by any other hotel refugee I know regarding his accuracy concerning the genocide itself. That much he got right.

Where he is open to criticism, though, is clear. Samantha Power and the late Richard Holbrooke, America's current and former ambassadors to the UN, will never and would never have rushed in to defend Paul Rusesabagina as an individual, for they were not there and they likely couldn't care less about who exactly saved the refugees of the Mille Collines. I sympathize with many of Terry George's hurt feelings in these e-mails, such as when he expresses pain that organizations like IBUKA criticized his film. His film is his baby and no one wants to see their baby castigated. But as much as Odette attempts to reassure him and redirect him, he fails to see that the problem is not his vision of what happened during the genocide, but only what he has done by creating a fiction around Paul Rusesabagina, a fiction that has led to catastrophic results.

We refugees feel George's research, which deified the hotel manager, was slipshod. We feel it was a terrible creative decision not to make it clear the movie was merely inspired by true events. We believe he did not think through the possible outcome of creating a living saint—a very dangerous thing to do with any person. And when he agrees with Odette that yes, the movie was fictionalized, and that Paul has done bad things with the fame George is responsible for giving him, why does he not do anything about it?! He suggests simply ignoring Paul, thinking he will just go away, just as the West ignored the genocide, hoping it, too, would go away. Terry George, more than anyone, should have known better than to think such a strategy would work. I know from speaking with Odette that George bled and cried for the victims of the genocide. I would never accuse him of being a bad man. Instead, we feel he made reversible mistakes and did not make amends or apologies for them.

As to the money, I feel it would have been more prudent and humble of him not to have tacked his charity announcement onto the end of the film, given that he knew the ways of Hollywood accounting and that there was a strong possibility no money would make it from the film to the genocide survivors. It is like a man who shows up at a telethon, announces a large monetary gift to a charity, receives the audience's applause, and then never makes good on the pledge. Even if there is good reason for the money never being disbursed, the sin is one of vanity. Better to turn over a check in private and have your rewards given to you in heaven.

To return to the discussion of specific charities, the Survivors Fund (SURF) is based in London. Not only do they give direct support to Rwandan genocide survivors, they also work in partnership with all legitimate nonprofits doing similar work. In short, if you want to know who is truly helping Rwandans who suffered from 1994's genocide, or if you want to help as well, SURF is the place to go.

David Russell, director of SURF, told us his organization was approached by Oorlagh George, Terry George's daughter, initially in November 2004. She presented a wonderful wish list of things her father wanted to do to help Rwanda—health initiatives, education, development, and a particular endowment of a film center at a Rwandan university, all funded from the profits of the film *Hotel Rwanda*.

SURF responded, but then there was silence. SURF tried to restart the discussion in February 2005 by sending Ms. George an announcement regarding a £4.25 million grant SURF had obtained from the Department for International Development to save the lives of 2,500 women survivors raped and infected with HIV during the

Rwandan genocide. This was *real* assistance for Rwandans—exactly the sort of thing we needed, the inference being that, if the filmmakers hadn't spent their profits yet, why not get on board?

Oorlagh replied that the filmmakers would rather have something to call their own. She went on to describe a program they were developing to be called "The International Fund for Rwanda." In searching for a record of such an entity, search engines directed us to a website entitled "The International Fund for Rwanda—Hotel Rwanda Film." It included a five-point plan including the enigmatic "film school" Oorlagh had previously mentioned to SURF. The fund's website, which contained a logo for the UNDP, promised to link to specific PDFs to describe in detail each initiative, but when we attempted to access them, none opened. There was also a link to the private (non-UN) "International Fund for Rwanda" site Oorlagh mentioned, which used the exact same URL she gave to SURF. That site contains not a word about Rwanda save for its title, but has blog posts such as "Exactly What Is Happening through Calgary Real Estate Investment?" In short, it is nothing but a phony or inactive site.

A visit to the site of the Kigali Institute of Science and Technology, where the film school was alleged to be opened, shows no such facility. We contacted a college student currently studying film in Rwanda. "The only film school that I know in Rwanda is called Kwetu Film Institute located in Gacuriro," she said. "The founder is Eric Kabera. He is also the founder of the Rwanda Cinema Center. Another one is at the School of Finance and Banking, but I do not know as much about their program." Eric Kabera is a Rwandan filmmaker. In 2001 he co-produced *100 Days,* the first feature film about the 1994 Genocide Against the Tutsi, shot right in Rwanda in the exact locations where the genocide occurred. Despite being minuscule in budget, profits, and fame compared to Hollywood's *Hotel Rwanda* in 2004, Kabera and his film gave back generously to Rwanda and its film culture.

Finally, in October 2009, SURF's David Russell attempted one last time to see if the Georges were really interested in helping Rwandan genocide victims. This time, Oorlagh informed him that the film's profits had simply gone to UNICEF via the United Nations Foundation. UNICEF is a wonderful worldwide organization, but none of the film's promised funding was ever directed specifically to support survivors. If it went anywhere at all—and no official accounting to the public or dollar amount appears to be available—it just went into general UN programs.

S. (name withheld upon request) is a social affairs officer for the United Nations Economic Commission for Africa, specializing in human and social development issues in Africa, especially youth, aging, disability issues, HIV/AIDS, and health. When shown the "International Fund for Rwanda—Hotel Rwanda Film" website (http://www.unrwanda.org/undp/hotel_rwa.htm), this is what she told us:

> First off, we don't accept money in this way. The United Nations does not get funded this way. That is the number one red flag. The UNDP logo on this site is not real—it is copied and pasted from somewhere else. It is distorted and does not look authentic. There is no way they would allow the logo to be placed on a site in this manner. It implies endorsement. It is like inferring that the UN is a sponsor of the movie, or that the film is a sponsor of the UN. The UN is a noncommercial enterprise; it cannot operate in such a manner. We don't accept individual private monies from entities such as Microsoft or stuff like that. So how would money like that be raised from a film? Any contributions they receive would be from a general pool fund. Look at all authentic websites for the UN. There are no corporate logos, nor are logos of the UN allowed on the websites or materials of corporations. It is a violation of our rules and our charter.

The *parent* website is also false. UNRwanda.org is not a real website. The real UNDP website is undp.org. The country-specific site is rw.undp.org/Rwanda.

Also, as someone who works for the UN in Africa, I can tell you that the initiatives mentioned on this site [*which match up precisely with what Oorlagh George told SURF via e-mail*]— recruitment of new doctors and nurses and "The Gender HIV/AID Sensitive Income Generating Project"—are not real projects. They are not projects we have ever done in Rwanda.

There are a lot of UN scams—people making references to the UN in order to scam people. That's what this looks like.

As to the websites associated with "International Fund for Rwanda—Hotel Rwanda Film," Kerry Zukus received an e-mail July 19, 2013, from Auke Lootsma of UNDP of Rwanda that further confirmed that "none of them is affiliated with UNDP in Rwanda."

"The UN Foundation, on the other hand," added Sandra, which Oorlagh George mentioned in her 2009 email to SURF, "*does* raise money from private sources, but again, it is usually pooled together. Furthermore, whereas the real UN Foundation site lists a January 2005 announcement of a proposed endeavor by the makers of the film *Hotel Rwanda*, compare that to the many other programs listed by the foundation. All others give follow-up information, including amounts actually given, status of projects, and so forth. This announcement is merely that—an announcement of an intent. There is nothing to infer this ever happened, or that the filmmakers ever turned over a dime."

All attempts to interview Pearson and the Georges, either directly or via their personal managers, to address these and other important issues have been met with silence.

22

THE FREEDOM TO BECOME HIS REAL SELF

PAUL RUSESABAGINA NOW makes a very comfortable living as a public speaker all over the world. If this were the worst of it, that Hollywood had turned an undeserving man into a mogul, perhaps the refugees of the Mille Collines could sleep better at night. Still bitter, still appalled at fate's sardonic turn, but otherwise safe in our own beds, relatively unaffected. But when one has wealth, what else is there?

Power.

Money can buy many things, but the most unique among them is power. It cannot be seen by the naked eye, and yet some people have maintained a lifelong struggle to get it. Because of Hollywood, Paul Rusesabagina has been put in a position where power can be purchased...and he appears to be in a buying mood.

It is odd to me, this particular path on which he has allowed fame to take him—and yet, knowing Paul Rusesabagina as I do, not odd at all. He could have merely playacted at being the character he was portrayed to be in the film. That would have been the conventional route, not only to fame, but also to power. Uncontroversial, for how could anyone argue with, "Thou shall not kill"? Who would ever protest against him in *favor* of genocide? He could have been universally loved, leading a parade of people shouting, "Never again! No more genocide anywhere under any circumstances," and he would have gotten larger and wealthier and, in doing so, even more powerful. He could have stood on podiums next to Rwanda's President Paul Kagame, each holding the other's hand aloft, smiling and offering themselves up as the new future of Africa, for it was Kagame and his RPF army that ended the 1994 genocide...Kagame who as the nation's president has been attempting to lead Rwanda away from that genocide, its darkest hour. A Rusesabagina–Kagame partnership would seem symbolically perfect and completely in line with the message of the movie.

But no. That would not be in line with Paul's politics. His beliefs appear far too engrained, and that is what is frightening. Hollywood never really investigated who they were lionizing, and now he belongs to them, for better or for worse.

President Kagame of Rwanda was the leader of the RPF, the man who led other expatriates back into Rwanda, back to their homeland. The RPF ended the Genocide Against the Tutsi. This is not opinion but historical fact. But Paul Rusesabagina never supported the RPF or its goal for a Rwanda that shared power between the Hutu and the Tutsi and that, in the end, ended those ridiculous divisions once and for all. Rusesabagina's politics are the politics of division and Hutu Power. And now he has a world stage upon which to espouse those philosophies.

I have heard him speak in the United States, and while I am offended by his pure self-aggrandizement, he often lets some of those personal politics trickle in. Shortly after the release of his movie, it was usually only a bit. In more recent days, it has grown to the point where it completely overwhelms all else he speaks about.

Here in America, the wealthiest country in the world, he seems primarily concerned with raising money. He set up a foundation that originally claimed to assist Rwandan survivors of the 1994 genocide—orphans specifically—yet all calls for specifics as to the disbursement of those funds went unanswered. Where could this money be going? Paul has not been in Rwanda since 1996 except for one short visit, and then another when he was filming a short documentary that accompanied the DVD of *Hotel Rwanda*. How could he even *get* money to Rwandan orphans? Who was working for him in Rwanda, distributing the money? What other legitimate nonprofits was he partnering with? When pressed to name the orphans with whom he shared the money raised by his America-based nonprofit, *Paul admitted he only provided financially for his own relatives!* More recently, the confidence game of pretending to raise money for "genocide orphans" has been removed from his foundation's website, replaced with more generic wording indicating that contributions merely go to helping Paul "raise awareness." And personal profit.

This leads into what Rusesabagina really raises money for. His foundation is nothing more than a PAC, a political action committee. His only charity is himself. He raises support for his personal political career and his true political beliefs, which are completely antithetical to how he was portrayed in the movie. If you fell in love with the character that shared his name in *Hotel Rwanda*, the last place you should want to send your money is to the Hotel Rwanda Rusesabagina Foundation.

Paul Rusesabagina, a politically active man who tried to portray himself in a movie as being apolitical, makes political speeches all over the world and raises money for political causes that have nothing to do with peace and everything to do with revenge. In short, Paul Rusesabagina is beginning to sound a lot like RTLM hate radio prior to the Genocide Against the Tutsi, which only we Rwandans would know because we were forced to listen to it daily. But unlike his predecessors, he does it with a smiling face made famous in classrooms around the world touting him as a living saint—thanks to Hollywood.

Paul Rusesabagina was a political activist when he lived in Rwanda and he continues to be one today. But he is also an international celebrity now. This makes him a very valuable commodity to those whose ideology he shares and continues to support.

I asked Etienne Niyonzima, a former member of the MDR Party who became a member of the Rwandan parliament after the genocide and is now a commissioner on the National Commission for Human Rights of Rwanda, about Rusesabagina's political activity before the genocide. He said:

> I know Paul Rusesabagina because we come from the same prefecture, Gitarama. I knew him when he was working in Hotel des Diplomates before the genocide and after the genocide. I was an active member of MDR and Paul was also an active member. He held the position of secretary of the party in the region where he was born and he was a member of the political bureau of MDR nationwide. In MDR, we had two ideologies: those who were moderate and were behind Twagiramungu Faustin, who was president of MDR, and Hutu Power hard-liners who were behind Dismas Nsengiyaremye, vice president of MDR, Karamira Froduald, also vice president of MDR and president of MDR in Kigali City, and Murego Donat, executive secretary of MDR. Paul Rusesabagina had joined the extremist group that convened at Kabusunzu and excluded from the party those who were moderate. There they created MDR–Hutu Power, which joined MRND and CDR and ended by committing the genocide. Paul was aligned with Karamira and Nsengiyaremye especially, because they came from the same prefecture, Gitarama, and had the same ideology.

The words of Paul Rusesabagina today contradict much of his own book and destroy in part or in whole the movie alleged to portray a segment of his life. Does he stand on the truth? The question should be, "Which truth; which lie?" Because of his political agenda, Rusesabagina confuses his listeners. Personally, I have noticed that it depends on which public he addresses. In America, he goes about his personal fundraising as carefully as possible. He always misleads the public in his speeches by redefining the Genocide Against the Tutsi as a tribal conflict resulting from the injustices of the past, echoing the propaganda of Hutu extremist ideologues and the Rwandan hate media of the early 1990s. He explains that the Rwandan tragedy goes back many generations to when the Tutsi used the Hutu as slaves. Factually this is simply not true. If it were true, how can he explain how his father, whom he claims was a Hutu slave, could have married his mother, whom he claims to have been a Tutsi elitist from the ruling class?

When he addresses African Americans, to attract their sympathy and emotion, he compares slavery in the United States to the situation the Hutu were living in when the Tutsi had power more than fifty years ago. During that colonial period many, many decades ago, the system was not fair, not only for the Hutu, but also for the Tutsi. All Tutsi were not in the ruling class. Hutu and Tutsi speak the same language; they lived on the same hills, shared the same customs, and intermarried. Only the political elite, the minority within the minority of the Tutsi group, hand-picked by the Belgians, enjoyed the privileges of power. Ideologues of genocide manipulated that historical reality to inflame minds and justify the diabolical plans they were hatching.

When he speaks to self-exiled Hutu in Western countries, genocide denial and revenge are often on the agenda. To predominantly white North American audiences, he blames Tutsi for being friends of European colonial powers in the late 1950s, stating that the Tutsi left the country together with the Europeans after Hutu fought and won a war of independence against them, and that the successive killing of Tutsi in Rwanda was revenge influenced by Burundi. A predominantly white continental-European audience will be fed rhetoric of an Anglo-Saxon conspiracy to grab African resources using Tutsi as proxies.

In each case, Rusesabagina claims there was a *good reason* for Tutsi to have been slaughtered. Their deaths were *justified*. Can any person imagine a Gandhi, a Raoul Wallenberg, a Dalai Lama—people Paul Rusesabagina is being compared to today—ever justifying or explaining away murder and genocide? This alone speaks volumes.

As a speaker, Rusesabagina is more valuable as a living, breathing museum curio. You cannot go anywhere today and see Gandhi or Raoul Wallenberg in the flesh, but you *can* tell your friends that you met Paul Rusesabagina. This is what people pay to see.

I went to see him at Ohio State University April 26, 2006, and Dayton University February 20, 2007. I didn't ask any questions or draw his attention to me because I wanted to hear him for myself, uninterrupted and unprompted by my own need to interject perspective and correction. I was doing research for this book. Researchers are supposed to be neither seen nor heard.

When he first enters the conference room or auditorium, the moderator informs the participants that no one is allowed to record him. Thus, although he frequently contradicts himself and emits wild statements of mistruth, without actual recording devices, little that he says can be held against him except by hearsay.

As the featured speaker, he sets his own tone and says whatever he wants. After his speech, he accepts only five questions. Each time, exactly five. Most of the time he demands that the questions be placed in a written form and given to him for screening prior to his speaking. It is a waste of time for any audience member to challenge him on any of his rhetoric because the questioner is given exactly one minute to ask a question, and then Paul takes five to ten minutes to accuse the audience member of being an extremist or a Rwandan government supporter—a paid shill for President Kagame. There is no give and take, no debate. He gives the answer he wants, and he cannot be contradicted or argued with. Seeing Rusesabagina speak live is akin to a totalitarian experience.

When I went to hear Rusesabagina speak at the University of Dayton in Ohio, he went so far as to say that all hotel employees who went to Kabuga had been killed. I was there, as were most of the people who appear in this book. Many of them were hotel employees. We are all alive! Rusesabagina *himself* was spotted at Kabuga; *he* is alive! No houses were set on fire; people were not moved out of any of the houses there, as he claims—this I witnessed with my own eyes. We were the survivors who *escaped* the killing, who once had nothing to eat but, once in Kabuga, were now able to fetch food for ourselves in order to survive. But these are the tales he spins. Even when he is relatively placid and respectful, such as in his American appearances (as opposed to when he is revved up and spitting blood as he often does when he is in other countries, as many other survivors who live in Europe and Africa have informed me), he still paints a picture with words—erroneous words. Slipping in the ridiculous anecdote about Kabuga allows his listeners to leave his talks thinking, "This genocide must still be going on back there. It sounds like nothing's changed."

He has refused to debate the survivors of the Hotel des Mille Collines. In February 2006, a Rwandan challenged and disproved many of Rusesabagina's statements at a press conference in Montreal. Before a crowd, Rusesabagina was goaded into agreeing to appear on a radio talk show on Radio Contact in Kigali. Waiting to debate "the ordinary man" was his old friend Odette Nyiramilimo, as well as Wellars Gasamagera and Pasa Mwenenganucye, all quoted here in this book, along with François Xavier Ngarambe who at the time was the president of IBUKA, the genocide survivors' association, but who now serves as Rwanda's ambassador to China.

The radio broadcast aired on February 5, 2006. Rusesabagina switched off his telephone and let it go to voice mail, refusing to participate and avoiding contradiction and ridicule. Paul Rusesabagina does not argue in real time, nor does he validate his accusations and boasts. He runs. Occasionally, he has political speechwriters answer for him after the fact, but again, this is not dialogue, but monologue.

On Voice of America Radio on June 14, 2006, Rusesabagina stated, "Hutu killed Tutsi during the Hundred Days. Tutsi also killed Hutu before the Hundred Days, during the Hundred Days, and also after the Hundred Days, and they are still killing them, because there are many people who are getting lost—Hutu and Tutsi at the same time now."

In an interview with Reuters on January 11, 2007, Rusesabagina said this: "Since 1994, Tutsi have been killing Hutu, and even now there are many who are being killed, or who simply disappear."[23]

He is deliberately confusing people about the differences between crime, war crimes, and genocide. The truth is, Rwanda today is a country less than two decades removed from a genocide of epic proportions. *Génocidaires* live next door to those whose relatives they killed.

On May 15, 2008, a ninety-year-old Tutsi woman, Genevieve Mukanyonga, a survivor of the 1994 genocide, was set on fire in her own house in Muhanga in southern Rwanda. The old woman had lost all her children during the genocide and lived alone. According to a Hirondelle News report, six villagers who were identified as her neighbors, "between the ages of twenty-four and seventy-seven, confessed to the crime, which they justified through their fear of being accused [by Mrs. Mukanyonga in a court of law] for looting goods belonging to victims during the genocide."[24]

---

[23] John Chiahemen, "'Hotel Rwanda' Hero Fears New Hutu-Tutsi Killings," *Reuters*, January 11, 2007, http://www.reuters.com/article/2007/01/11/us-rwanda-rusesabagina-idUSL1192073920070111.

[24] "Woman (90) Set on Fire by Her Neighbours for Fear of Facing Gacaca," *Hirondelle News Agency*, May 15, 2008, http://www.hirondellenews.com/ictr-rwanda/412-rwanda-political-and-social-issues/21898-en-en-150508-rwandasurvivor-woman-90-set-on-fire-by-her-neighbours-for-fear-of-facing-gacaca1094910949.

The heinous murder of this ninety-year-old woman is not genocide, by definition. There are also tales of Tutsi exacting revenge on Hutu who wronged them during the Hundred Days. All these acts are despicable, but they do not fit the accepted definition of genocide. Individuals, not governments, committed them against other individuals. Genocide is a *coordinated plan* to annihilate a *group*. Rwanda's current government has gone to great lengths to prevent revenge killings.

Rusesabagina wrote in his book, "Tutsi wives went to sleep next to their Hutu husbands and awoke to find the blade of machete sawing into their neck, and above them, the grimacing face of the man who had sworn to love and cherish them for life. And Tutsi wives also killed their husbands."[25] Does he have at least *one example* of a Tutsi woman who killed her Hutu husband during the genocide? One real example? But Paul does not deal in fact, merely imagery that supports his own biases. In discussing genocide, he creates false equivalencies—imaginary Tutsi women murdering Hutu men.

Rusesabagina has also become an apologist for the architects of the genocide, confusing the primary message contained in the film that made him famous. On Voice of America's broadcast of June 14, 2006, he said, "I would not blame the genocide on General Bizimungu. General Bizimungu was a general commander of the army; General Kagame was also a general commander of another army. Both armies killed innocent civilians. I never saw General Bizimungu kill people; I rather saw him saving people. To me, both were responsible for people who both killed."

Rusesabagina shared a lot with Bizimungu, Georges Rutaganda, and Colonel Bagosora during the entire period of the genocide. They drank and got drunk together. General Bizimungu led the troops and militia that committed the genocide. Bizimungu said in a BBC

---

[25] Paul Rusesabagina, *An Ordinary Man: An Autobiography* (New York: Penguin, 2006), 134.

broadcast on September 15, 2002, that "the Tutsi would be wiped out and the Rwandese Patriotic Front would rule over desert." To Paul Rusesabagina, this man is an innocent.

Rusesabagina also justifies the killing of Tutsi in 1973 for what happened in Burundi by saying, "We have a saying: Whatever happens in Burundi eventually spills over into Rwanda, and whatever happens in Rwanda will also spill into Burundi, and that was certainly the case in 1973. The government in Rwanda was sympathetic and began killing reprisals against Tutsi as kind of revenge." As a footnote, the international community reports two genocides occurring in nearby Burundi in the twentieth century: one in 1972, laid primarily at the feet of the Tutsi there, and one in 1993, blamed primarily on Burundi Hutu. Neither action, however, justifies the slaughter of innocents in a completely different country. All genocide is wrong and ever shall be.

Rusesabagina does not ignore what happened in Rwanda in 1973, but it is his way of misleading his listeners and allowing him to grotesquely justify why the Hutu killed the Tutsi. The truth is that the Tutsi had been killed in Rwanda in 1959, in 1963, and in 1967, as a way to maintain Hutu power. In 1973, Rwandan President Habyarimana had to find a way to take power. The Hutu leaders pushed Tutsi out of their jobs, as well as out of schools and universities. They killed them, and the survivors fled the country.

On page 199 of *An Ordinary Man*, speaking of Rwanda today, Rusesabagina makes the claim that "those few Hutu who have been elevated to high-ranking posts are usually empty suits without any real authority of their own." Rusesabagina remains in a world of Hutu versus Tutsi, where any coalition between the two insults his sensibilities, just as the Arusha Accords did. I can only wonder how much of this is tattooed irreversibly upon his soul, refusing to fade since he left Rwanda shortly after the genocide, not to return for any length of time, and how much is a product of his being used as a front for Hutu Power remnants in Brussels, Canada, the DRC, and the United States. I do believe he has the right to exercise his political and civil rights of free speech, but it is unfortunate when he uses those rights to deny the Genocide Against the Tutsi, which made him famous.

Yes, I said genocide denial. If you asked the survivors to sum up what Paul Rusesabagina tells audiences around the world, it is that what happened in Rwanda in 1994 was not *really* genocide. Why would he do this? Why would this man contradict his own film, a film *about* the Genocide Against the Tutsi, by claiming there was no Genocide Against the Tutsi? Why? Because how else could he garner the support of the same people who committed that genocide? How else could be become their leader, their spokesperson, their Trojan Horse?

As the 2004 release of *Hotel Rwanda* fades further and further from sight in the rear-view mirror of Paul Rusesabagina's life, the more caustic his speech gets. Whereas in 2004 and 2005 he only occasionally slipped from the character Keir Pearson and Terry George made for him, as time goes by, the real Paul comes more into view.

> Why would he do this? Why would this man contradict his own film, a film *about* the Genocide Against the Tutsi, by claiming there was no Genocide Against the Tutsi?

Keith Harmon Snow is a freelance American journalist quite out of the mainstream. For example, in a response to a comment on one of his own articles in *Dissident Voice*, a self-proclaimed "radical newsletter," dated February 9, 2008, he compares movie director Steven Spielberg to Adolf Eichmann, the Nazi architect of the Holocaust.[26] Based on his body of published work, this sort of outrageous rhetoric is Mr. Snow's stock in trade.

---

[26] "Steven Speilberg [sic] is Eichman [sic], but lives in a world (his own mind is merely an extension of the greater 'international community' he is part of) where he believes he is more like Anne Frank." Keith Harmon Snow, commenting on his article "Gertler's Bling Blang Torah Gang: Israel and the Ongoing Holocaust in Congo (Part I)," *Dissident Voice*, February 9, 2008, http://dissidentvoice.org/2008/02/gertlers-bling-bang-torah-gang/.

Perhaps it took a provocateur like Snow to bring out the beast in Paul Rusesabagina, for while Rusesabagina does indeed tip his hand somewhat in more mainstream interviews, it was when Snow interviewed him for progressive website *Toward Freedom* (April 20, 2007) that Rusesabagina's entire ideology seemed to pour out once he appeared to have found an audience hungry for it.

For instance, Snow mentions the movie and talks about the ending, with RPF rebels ending the genocide.

"No. No one stopped the genocide," says Rusesabagina.

This is a large part of what he preaches today, that unbeknownst to the entire world, genocide is still going on in Rwanda as we speak. You cannot see it; you cannot hear it; you see no blood on the streets. In reality, Hutu and Tutsi live side by side, work together, love together, but Paul—again, who has only spent a few days in Rwanda since the late 1990s—claims there is a massive genocide still going on there, with Tutsi killing Hutu. He just can't prove it. But you must believe him because a movie claims he is a hero who "single-handedly saved 1,200 people." And this makes him an expert. Do not believe the UN, NGOs, worldwide heads of state, and all the humanitarian organizations in the world. Only believe Paul. The real genocide is referred to, even by Paul between 1994 and 2006, as "the Hundred Days." Because that is how long it lasted. But that fact no longer suits Paul's politics.

In the interview, Snow says, "The Interahamwe, according to the common portrayals of genocide in Rwanda, were a bunch of murderous Hutu with machetes…"

But Rusesabagina cuts him off by saying, "How could that be? That is a problem. Because Kagame had infiltrated the [Hutu Power] army…, and the militias, everywhere; he [Kagame] had his own militia within a militia."

From here, Rusesabagina spins even more wildly out of control, explaining how Tutsi Paul Kagame had his own Tutsi on the dreaded roadblocks in order to kill other Tutsi. Why? According to Rusesabagina, the entire Genocide Against the Tutsi was a massive and devious plan by Paul Kagame to gain power by getting the world to pity him and the Tutsi. I wish I were making this up, but I am not—the full interview was readily available for months on Snow's website.[27]

Taken another way, this is like someone saying the Jews ran the Nazi concentration camps during World War II and marched each other into gas chambers as a publicity stunt to gain world sympathy for this "Holocaust" they themselves "invented." According to Paul Rusesabagina, everything is "Tutsi, Tutsi, Tutsi," and that the Tutsi killed everyone, including and especially themselves, in order to gain power. But how can anyone expect to gain political power if they are not alive?

This devolves into a concept popular among the sort of people Paul Rusesabagina fronts for today: dual genocide. In short, even after someone like Paul has tied himself in knots trying to claim that the Tutsi planned and executed the Genocide Against the Tutsi, they fall back to a position of claiming that both sides committed genocide. But this is patently untrue. It is, again, a false equivalency. So what exactly is genocide and what is not? I hold to the definition accepted by all the world scholars on the subject. The international legal definition of the crime of genocide is found in Articles II and III of the 1948 Convention on the Prevention and Punishment of Genocide. Article II describes two elements of the crime of genocide:

1) The *mental element,* meaning the "intent to destroy, in whole or in part, a national, ethnical, racial or religious group, as such," and

2) The *physical element* which includes five acts described in sections a, b, c, d, and e. A crime must include *both elements* to be called "genocide."[28]

---

[27] Keith Harmon Snow, "The Grinding Machine: Terror and Genocide in Rwanda," April 20, 2007, *All Things Pass,* http://www.allthingspass.com/uploads/html-191The%20 Grinding%20Machine%20interview%20with%20Paul%20Rusesabagina%20FINAL.htm.
[28] Prevent Genocide International, "The Legal Definition of Genocide," accessed October 17, 2013, http://www.preventgenocide.org/genocide/officialtext-printerfriendly.htm.

And to repeat what was stated in Chapter 7, those five acts are:

(a) Killing members of the group;
(b) Causing serious bodily or mental harm to members of the group;
(c) Deliberately inflicting on the group conditions of life calculated to bring about its physical destruction in whole or in part;
(d) Imposing measures intended to prevent births within the group;
(e) Forcibly transferring children of the group to another group.

Another important reference on the topic concerns how genocide develops, as it indeed does develop over time rather than instantly, in the passion of the moment. This is a major point, as genocide deniers such as Rusesabagina claim that the killing of the unarmed was a crime of passion with no premeditation.

The Eight Stages of Genocide, by Gregory H. Stanton, president of Genocide Watch, are:

1. Classification
2. Symbolization
3. Dehumanization
4. Organization
5. Polarization
6. Preparation
7. Extermination
8. Denial[29]

---

[29] Gregory H. Stanton, "The 8 Stages of Genocide," 1996, accessed October 17, 2013, http://www.genocidewatch.org/images/8StagesBriefingpaper.pdf.

Denial is the last stage of genocide. Denial is what we can read from the present-day words of Paul Rusesabagina. According to Stanton, it is among the surest predictors of future genocidal massacres. The perpetrators of genocide dig up the mass graves, burn the bodies, try to cover up the evidence, and intimidate the witnesses. They deny they committed any crimes and often blame what happened on the victims. That is the kind of message Rusesabagina espouses when he addresses the public and gives the sort of interviews he gives to people like Keith Harmon Snow and others.

During my lifetime and Paul's, Hutu in Rwanda were not the subjects of the eight stages of genocide. They were never, as an ethnic group, singled out and ostracized. They were never, as a group, treated as second-class citizens. The majority of the nation never treated them as subhuman and beneath the law. There was never any organized plan to completely exterminate them as a people. No thinking Hutu who lives in Rwanda, either now or in our days, could look at these definitions and disagree with my conclusions. This is, quite plainly, the definition of what happened to the *Tutsi* in Rwanda, not the Hutu. Only one Rwandan genocide occurred in our lifetime—the Genocide Against the Tutsi. Crimes against all people of Rwanda occurred and continue to occur, but crime itself is not genocide. There is a stark difference, and the great thinkers of the world have defined it.

"Genocide denial" is a phrase bantered about quite often when talk turns to Rwanda today. Some most certainly overreach when they use it. But in his 2007 interview with Snow, Rusesabagina does not imply it, does not dance around it, but espouses it directly. When Snow debates semantics with Rusesabagina, Paul responds by saying, "Well, we can call it, let's say, we have to call it genocide, *because we can never change it* [emphasis added]. This genocide designation has been decided by the [UN] Security Council...on November 8, 1994, this was the date of the Security Council resolution made to call it a genocide. We have to maybe wait for another resolution, maybe calling it…," and as Paul pauses, Snow offers the term "politicide" to signify both parties are responsible. Paul then goes on to state what he really wants is a UN resolution calling what the *Tutsi* did to the *Hutu* in 1994 "genocide."

This is genocide denial. He wishes for a UN resolution saying the Genocide Against the Tutsi never occurred, and even more insanely, for a new resolution to be drafted stating the complete opposite.

To any and all who wish to endlessly debate the semantics of what began in April of 1994, I ask, what of the lists? Why did people come to *my* house, looking for *me*? Because my name was on a list to be killed! Rusesabagina ignores or denies this. *There were lists!* There were lists just as there were lists of Jews during the Holocaust. It is the *lists* that give definition to the word "genocide." The lists indicate premeditation for the government-sponsored killing of a specifically identified group. I was part of that identified group. The government trained the militias, armed them, imported tons of machetes for use in killing Tutsi, and then went around the country encouraging the populace to kill. Rusesabagina ignores or denies all of this, and he does so in the most preposterous and offensive manner. This is why survivors challenge him to debates and protest his speeches.

In his April 2006 book, *An Ordinary Man* (most likely written in early to mid-2005), Rusesabagina writes, "The current president, Paul Kagame, was the General of the Rwandan Patriotic Front army that toppled the *génocidaire* regime and ended the slaughter, and for this he deserves credit."[30] Rusesabagina now refutes his own written words—or those written for him. Or supplants them with those being written for him *today*; take your pick.

In the introduction of his book, he writes, "It was a failure of the United States for not calling a genocide by its right name."[31] Today, Rusesabagina himself wishes to not call genocide, "genocide."

---

[30] Rusesabagina, *An Ordinary Man*, 198–9.

[31] Rusesabagina, xv.

Additionally, he wrote, "RPF leader Paul Kagame had fewer troops but while in exile he had instilled an impressive level of discipline and commitment into his army. Not for nothing was the international press calling him 'the Napoleon of Africa.'"[32] Now that it suits him, Rusesabagina calls Kagame a war criminal.[33]

Rwandan President Kagame, like me and other survivors, appreciates director Terry George's efforts to teach the West at least something about our struggles in 1994. Kagame, a military man, helped lead the RPF soldiers into Rwanda to end the Genocide Against the Tutsi and their stateless diaspora. Today, he lives as a lightning rod for much love and much hate from those who survived the conflict.

The reentry into Rwanda of the RPF was indeed a war of liberation; this is true. Tutsi needed to fight their way back into the country of their birth, and Kagame was an inspirational and tactical leader. To listen to testimonies of the architects of the genocide as well as Paul Rusesabagina, though, is to hear people try to make it sound as if Kagame is the entire reason for the genocide—had the RPF not reentered Rwanda, the genocide would not have occurred. This is like blaming US President Abraham Lincoln for the lynching of African Americans by hate groups like the Ku Klux Klan, because had Lincoln not emancipated the slaves, groups like the KKK would not have sprung up thereafter and done their dastardly deeds.

When faced with conflict and differing opinions, people make conscious choices. The RPF had already negotiated a peaceful sharing of power at Arusha. There had indeed been military skirmishes, but there was no need for a continued war from the signing of the Accords forward. Instead, the signing of the Accords was akin to

---

[32] Rusesabagina, 145.

[33] Snow, "The Grinding Machine." Rusesabagina says, "Well, to the best of my knowledge, I have never been one [a friend of Paul Kagame]. I've never been his friend, because, myself I knew Kagame from the beginning as a war criminal. Why a war criminal? Because, since Kagame came over from Uganda—on his way from Byumba and Ruhengeri in the northeast—what he did was to kill innocent civilians, innocent *Hutu* civilians."

Lincoln's Emancipation Proclamation. It was a wonderful thing for those who had been oppressed, but it brought out the worst in those filled with ignorance and hate. In Rwanda, those people fought back against it by a planned, systematic genocide of unarmed civilians based solely upon their ethnicity. These killers made choices, and in making the wrong choices, they earned the right to be regarded as belonging to a hate group. Little children cried, "I promise not to be Tutsi anymore," as machetes cut them open.

Having lived through the Genocide Against the Tutsi, I got to look into the eyes and the souls of *génocidaires*. It was an enlightening as well as a frightening experience. They justified their actions in their own hearts and minds. Regrets were few. Much of the regret is similar to that of any criminal: "I regret that I got caught." Had the RPF been repelled and driven back into Uganda and the entire Tutsi civilian population been eliminated, I can only wonder what sort of guilt, if any, would remain inside the souls of the killers. Would they have continued to feel their actions were justified? I can only shudder at the thought and wonder.

What none of us wishes to live through is another genocide. We only wish for peace and prosperity for our native Rwanda, a lasting peace between the Hutu and the Tutsi until eventually, maybe within our lifetime, there is little talk of there even being these ethnic differences, that we might only speak of ourselves as Rwandans and nothing more.

The Snow interview in its entirety is the single most enlightening look into the psyche of the real Paul Rusesabagina. He denounces the findings of respected and intellectually balanced scholars such as Alex de Waal of African Rights, London, and the late Alison Des Forges of Human Rights Watch. He criticizes Philip Gourevitch's book as well, without which nobody likely ever would have heard of him. He claims "the West" was "on the side of the Tutsi rebels," which explains how they won the war, forgetting all of director Terry George's screeds against American President Bill Clinton for doing nothing to stop the genocide. If the West had gotten involved, one million Rwandans would not have been slaughtered. The only true involvement of the West came in the form of the French, who trained, armed, and even fought alongside the Hutu Power extremists.[34] No Western power did likewise for the Tutsi, despite what Rusesabagina claims.

He disparages Gen. Roméo Dallaire, questioning why he stayed, peppering him with accusations, and wondering aloud who he was *really* working for. When shown the piece, Dallaire grimaced in restrained anger and said, "Someone needs to get their facts straight."

The facts, the facts. Who is Paul talking to, when, and why? Paul Rusesabagina changes his story whenever it suits him. Back in the December 20, 2004, edition of the *New York Times*, when he was in New York City promoting his movie, he talked about the withdrawal of the majority of the UN peacekeepers: "'You can imagine the situation,' he said, describing a scene of dead bodies piling up in the streets outside the hotel. 'The majority of the population is now killing systematically the minority, and no one just raises a finger to say this is wrong. And even the United Nations is pulling out.'

"'Everyone was listening to radios so we all knew what was going on in the Security Council. When other countries wanted to maintain their soldiers the U.S. said no. Of course I was angry against each and everybody. I was bitter. It's because it was Rwanda. It was Africa. What else can you conclude?'"[35]

As it suited the message of his movie, Rusesabagina stated that "the majority of the population is now systematically killing the minority." The Hutu were and always will be the majority. They were

---

[34] Kinzer, *A Thousand Hills*, 78, 105.

[35] "Revisiting Rwanda's Horrors with an Ex-National Security Adviser," *New York Times*, December 20, 2004, http://www.nytimes.com/2004/12/20/movies/20rwan.html?pagewanted=all&_r=0.

killing the Tutsi, a minority. But that was Paul Rusesabagina *promoting the movie;* talking about April 1994. By 2007, he was saying a minority was killing the majority *and* a minority. Furthermore, in the 2004 *New York Times* he correctly defined genocide as systematic killing. Today, he denies it was ever systematic, despite the lists of those to be killed.

The 2006–2007 period marked a major turning point for the public tone and tenor of Paul Rusesabagina. Prior to the deeply inflammatory Snow interview, he gave an interview to William Church, the director of the Great Lakes Centre for Strategic Studies, and a man who spends most of his time in Rwanda and its neighboring regions—unlike Rusesabagina, who left Rwanda and Africa in 1996. Mr. Church, after personally interviewing Paul, had this to say in an editorial in the *Conservative Voice*, which he wrote on January 16, 2007:

> Rusesabagina's claims of continued government killings have been refuted by three different Rwandan human rights organizations: National Human Rights Commission (NRC), League for Promotion and Defense of Human Rights (LIPRODHOR), and the Federation of Leagues and Associations for the Defense of Human Rights in Rwanda (CLADHO).
>
> The Reuters article [of January 11, 2007, which I quoted earlier; see note 23 on page 186] negates the reality in Rwanda. The diplomatic community and numerous national and international human rights organizations monitor the human rights situation in Rwanda. The United States recently awarded Rwanda Millennium Challenge Account Threshold status, which requires a country to meet human rights and political freedom standards. The United States ambassador recently commented on the positive human rights and political freedom trend in Rwanda.

These positive views of Rwanda come from people and organizations that live and work in Rwanda. This contrasts Rusesabagina, who has been in self-imposed exile for a decade and rarely visits Rwanda. His information comes to him from the diaspora political parties, many of them based in Brussels and some of them linked to extremist elements dedicated to the violent overthrow of the Rwandan government.[36]

---

[36] William Church, "Rwanda: Rusesabagina, Genocide, and Identity Politics," *Conservative Voice,* January 31, 2007, http://allafrica.com/stories/200701190573.html.

23

PRESIDENT RUSESABAGINA?

TODAY, PAUL RUSESABAGINA is the perfect front man or spokesperson. He officially lists his occupation as "humanitarian." For him, it is a no-show job that pays quite well. Hollywood has canonized him, yet those same genuflectors are asleep as he peddles his archaic hate speech.

Paul launched a political party, PDR-Ihumure, largely composed of Hutu Power extremists, in a meeting held in Washington, DC, in June 2006. He appeared at rallies and fundraisers for this group of Rwandan expatriates. They have praised his name as they would that of a saint. Yet when confronted with the relationship between Rusesabagina and this new political party, PDR-Ihumure denied that Paul was even a member, let alone their star. Meanwhile, virtually no communiqué has emanated from this organization without mention of his name, always in hallowed, fawning terms. Furthermore, he rarely missed its public conclaves, and little to nothing they did was done without his consultation and approval.

When those of us who knew of his true actions and political leanings when he lived in Rwanda criticized Rusesabagina, his responses were swift and often not even produced by him directly, but by political parties like PDR-Ihumure acting in his defense. When he does produce a written response under his own name, the verbiage and writing style are strangely identical to those coming directly from such highly articulate and politically savvy groups. One might gather that they are currently acting as his official ghostwriters, and he as their celebrity talking head.

Unlike in America, where there are only two major political parties, Rwanda—and many other nations, for that matter—has innumerable small political parties. To attain power, they often group together to form coalitions. Thus, while climbing to the top of, say, the Republican Party in the United States would take many years, requiring anyone able to do so to spend many years in the public spotlight and become a household word along the way, no other spokesperson for this PDR-Ihumure group has had any major public profile at all. So what do you do when you have no star power? You hire a star—Rwanda's only Hollywood star.

On September 8, 2007, the "ordinary man" called for the launching of what he called a "Truth and Reconciliation Commission in Rwanda." Judging by his description of this group's mission, its not-so-hidden agenda is to preach amnesty for those who committed the genocide and to institutionalize the theory of double genocide.

On November 24, 2007, Rusesabagina called a "Conference on Truth and Reconciliation," but it was really a conference of genocide denials. The question that immediately comes to mind is how someone can reconcile and explore truth while one is telling lies. Rusesabagina's character in *Hotel Rwanda* embodied many lies. Now, he himself lies by saying that whatever *truths* there were in the movie were the real lies.

To recap his changing views, the movie portrays the Genocide Against the Tutsi. Paul's book, for the most part, acknowledges the Genocide Against the Tutsi. When he speaks today, though, as clearly demonstrated through interviews such as those he gave to journalists like Keith Harmon Snow, he indicates that he now be····res there was no such thing as the Genocide Against the Tutsi, mere is genocide denial; there is no other term for it. Like claimed that the Holocaust was simply an "act of conflict," "a tribal skirmish," "sectarian violence," one would call that person a genocide or Holocaust denier. By his own words, there is simply no denying that Rusesabagina, now that it suits him financially and in terms of potential power, is a denier of the Genocide Against the Tutsi.

Upon reading his hate-filled rhetoric (which is far more openly vile in Europe than in the Americas), the Catholic University of Louvain-la-Neuve and other institutes of higher learning in Brussels denied him a conference room for his planned gathering. He was forced to rent a private room. He also took strict security measures: Three roadblocks were set up to prevent entrance to anyone who did not share this group's narrow, specific view of "Tutsi bad, Hutu good; there was no Tutsi genocide."

PDR-Ihumure and Rusesabagina created lists of "undesirable" persons from the Rwandan community of Brussels,[37] mainly Tutsi, so they could be denied entrance to the conference. Those manning the roadblocks either knew for sure that certain people were Tutsi or they used morphologic criteria—the way they looked or spoke. They also asked for IDs. If you had a chance to pass through the first roadblock, you proceeded to a second and then a third. Some made it as far as the third before being turned away.

Irony abounds. This was exactly the same criterion used during the genocide, when Hutu Power militias set up roadblocks to prevent the Tutsi from escaping. The only difference was that no one in Brussels was killed. They were only prevented from entering a conference room.

Without any sort of ideological balance or eyewitness accounting of past and recent Rwandan history, the conference was a plethora of propaganda. Furthermore, Rwanda already *has* a Commission on Truth and Reconciliation, instituted by the Arusha Accords. But it

---

[37] I hesitate to use the phrase "Rwandan community of Brussels." In one of their written tirades, PDR-Ihumure fired away at the concept that someone could claim that an official organization named the "Rwandan Community of Brussels" exists. Of course there is not; nor did anyone claim there was. There are, however, Rwandans living in Brussels, period.
　hing more.

does not feature Paul Rusesabagina, nor does it reserve seats for leaders of the 1994 Genocide Against the Tutsi.

Rusesabagina's philosophical cohorts in these ventures include debunked radical journalists regularly sued for libel, French nationalists, lawyers who perpetually represent defendants accused of genocide before the International Criminal Tribunal for Rwanda, and conspiracy theorists of all stripes.

At the November 2007 conference, PDR-Ihumure called police to take further action if Tutsi turned away from the conference resisted leaving this public place. How can you book a hall for a public conference, encourage people to register to attend, and then turn away any attendees who "appeared" as though they might disagree with the one-sided presentation of the speakers? If some people were excluded based on ethnic criteria, how can Rusesabagina talk truth and reconciliation among Rwandans?

On March 28, 2008, a similar conference in Montreal, Canada, called "The Media and Rwanda: The Difficult Search for Truth," ended in chaos after hundreds of protesters overwhelmed the genocide-denying speakers. Some protestors at the failed conference were quoted in the media as saying that the revisionist conference was against Canadian law. Canada already had a law that makes it an offense to deny the Holocaust, and the Canadian Jewish Congress (CJC) has been advocating for the same to be applied to the Genocide Against the Tutsi. The aborted conference was to be addressed by Pierre Péan and Robin Philpot, two of Paul Rusesabagina's most frequent fellow panelists and apologists. Péan's main cause is to deny all French involvement in the genocide, and Philpot is a vehement French Canadian separatist and avowed political enemy of fellow Canadian, General Roméo Dallaire.

According to the *Canadian Jewish News* of April 3, 2008, the CJC joined local Rwandan leaders to condemn this conference because it questioned the historical accuracy of the 1994 genocide against Rwanda's Tutsi and moderate Hutu. The CJC claimed that the event featured panelists who have "'used their voices in the media, politics, and law to launch an unacceptable historical debate and framing the Tutsi victims as perpetrators,' CJC said. It joined the groups PAGE-Rwanda [Association of Parents and Friends of Genocide Victims in Rwanda] and Humura [an Ottawa group of survivors of the Tutsi genocide] to unveil a slate of events marking 14 years since the massacre of some 800,000 people. 'The questioning of whether genocide actually took place in Rwanda is absurd, bordering on hateful,' CJC executive member Adam Atlas said."[38]

If there was ever a central principle to PDR-Ihumure, it is that there was no Genocide Against the Tutsi and that, if there are any *génocidaires* at all, they are the elected officials running Rwanda today. And if PDR-Ihumure relocated to Rwanda itself and ran a candidate for president, that candidate likely might be Paul Rusesabagina, whom Hollywood has made the most famous man in the nation.

Rusesabagina is alleged to have conducted numerous meetings with members of the FDLR, the remnants of the group that conducted the genocide, which the UN has designated a terrorist group. While he has mostly stayed away from Rwanda, tales abound that Rusesabagina has visited with FDLR soldiers in the DRC and South Africa.

Put in most simplistic terms, FDLR is an army. It sprung from a previous army known as the Army for the Liberation of Rwanda. Whereas political parties such as PDR-Ihumure are merely that—parties—FDLR is much more. It is armed. Put a philosophical movement like PDR-Ihumure together with an army and you've got something quite dangerous.

Chris McGreal is a world-renowned journalist for the *Guardian*, one of Britain's foremost newspapers, read all over the globe. In a column published May 15, 2008, McGreal visited the army camps

---

[38] "Revisionism Rapped," *Canadian Jewish News,* April 3, 2008, http://www.cjnews.com/node/80848.

of the FDLR, which are located primarily in the DRC, along the Rwandan border.

McGreal interviewed Jerubaal Kayiranga, an FDLR leader who was responsible for recruiting children, beginning at age ten, into its military ranks, many of them forcibly, before he fled back to Rwanda last year.

"[The young ones] are worse than the older ones because they don't even know how Rwanda is," said Kayiranga. "They don't know any Tutsis. They just hate them as the enemy. It's the same as they [extreme Hutu leaders] were telling us during the genocide. They told us what we should do is kill all the Tutsis in the country."[39]

A young Hutu boy under the influence of FDLR genocide ideology stated, "The Tutsi stole our country and they are killing the Hutu or making them slaves. We have to kill them wherever they are. It is the only way to get our country back. When they are defeated I can go home. It's not hard to kill. You shoot."[40]

This is a boy who has never even lived in Rwanda. I am reminded of the famous song lyric from Rodgers and Hammerstein's *South Pacific*: "You've got to be taught to hate and fear." Bigotry like this is learned. One is not born with it. It must be taught, over and over again, until it is accepted without question. Those taught to think this way must be quarantined against all opposing thought so the philosophy is never challenged. This is the definition of fanaticism.

FDLR's website is nearly identical in its message as PDR-Ihumure's. Both describe the present government in Rwanda, led by Paul Kagame, as fascist, bloodthirsty, arrogant, and barbaric. In an interesting about-face from reality, it also says the Tutsi are seeking to exterminate the Hutu. Their own mission, they say, is merely to seek democracy and justice. But do these children with guns sound like pacifists? Do they

---

[39] Chris McGreal, "'We Have to Kill Tutsis Wherever They Are,'" *Guardian*, May 15, 2008, http://www.theguardian.com/world/2008/may/16/congo.rwanda.
[40] Ibid.

sound like the educated leaders of a new nation, built upon morals and peace?

The present Rwandan government seeks a peaceful resolution with the Hutu who have taken up residence in the Congo, choosing to accommodate their re-acclimation to their homeland rather than continue to fight border skirmishes with child soldiers such as these. Yet as McGreal describes, the reality is this:

> Others have been killed trying to escape the FDLR's clutches… "If our chiefs thought we were going back to Rwanda, they would take you and kill you," says Kayiranga. "I saw Colonel Haguma killed because he wanted to come back. They beat him and he died. I know a sergeant who was hanged from a tree because he had the idea to come back. They call a meeting and they point at you and say you want to go back to the Tutsi government and then they kill you. Sometimes they kill you by hitting your head with a hammer. They have many ways."[41]

Strangely, PDR-Ihumure had always countered that not only is Paul Rusesabagina not its leader, he is not even one of its members. But on December 8, 2008, an official press release stated that PDR-Ihumure had decided to form a coalition with another anti-government group, RUD/RPR (Rally for Unity and Democracy/Rally for the Rwandan People), to act as the main political opposition group to the RPF and all other political parties participating peacefully and democratically within Rwanda. The new group would be named Democratic Opposition Rwandan, or ODR. ODR's general secretary is Félicien Kanyamibwa, the founder of the FDLR, and one of its Council of Presidents is Dr. Jean Marie Vianney Higiro, who was once the first vice president of the FDLR. Another of its

---

[41] Ibid.

officers: Paul Rusesabagina, listed as being in charge of "diplomacy." It seems that if you wish to take over a nation by force, it is good to have an army in place (the FDLR), experienced organizers (Higiro and Kanyamibwa), and most importantly, a world-famous "humanitarian" to give you diplomatic cover.

On February 15, 2011, Rusesabagina finally made the mistake of appearing in a public forum in America without his "five questions" rule and its accompanying censorship. Or perhaps the venue itself refused to allow his artist rider to be enforced or just neglected to do so. Addressing some five hundred students in the student union at the University of Central Florida in Orlando, as well as members of the public including native Rwandans, Rusesabagina, when pressed by the retorts of the Rwandans present, repeatedly called the FDLR a "Rwandese liberation movement" seeking to bring about change in Rwanda. To him, FDLR is not a terrorist group, even after being listed as such by both the United States and the United Nations.[42]

The RPF also began as a rebel force, of course. But it did not indoctrinate and utilize child soldiers, a concept nearly as repugnant as genocide itself. Child soldiers are the rank and file of the FDLR army, whether its leadership likes it publicized or not. Nor was the charter of the RPF to "take over" Rwanda and give it Tutsi leadership. RPF's goals were met in Arusha, with the Accords. It simply wanted a situation where Tutsi who were born in Rwanda and then driven out could return and be treated like equal citizens, and that civil rights be likewise given equally to all Rwandans.

And what exactly do Rusesabagina and his friends in the FDLR want to liberate people from? Rwanda is still a Hutu-majority country. It always will be, so long as anyone continues to insist on chronicling the ethnicities of all its citizens, a concept that peace lovers are trying desperately to move away from. Rwanda's Hutu have full

[42] Willis Shalita, "Rwanda: Rusesabagina Admits Connections to FDLR and Gang of Four," *New Times Rwanda*, via *AllAfrica*, February 19, 2011, http://allafrica.com/stories/201102211387.html.

voting rights, full rights of every sort. Today's Rwanda makes no ethnic designation in any form. No more national ID cards. Hutu and Tutsi are treated the same in every way. Even FDLR soldiers are welcomed back as a matter of official state policy. Only the leaders, the real *génocidaires* from 1994, are put on trial for the crimes they committed, and no death penalty awaits them if convicted. Others, such as the young people who could not have possibly committed any crimes of genocide, or who merely supported the ideals of Hutu Power but took no murderous actions, face no trials and are given full citizenship after taking a class in civil education. Those who wish to serve in the army are reintegrated into the army, others into society.

On November 15, 2012, journalist Linda Melvern, who is also an honorary professor at the University of Wales, Aberystwyth, in the Department of International Politics, prepared a document for the British Parliament as evidence that the United Kingdom should continue to provide aid to Rwanda, a heavily debated topic due to the sort of speech exercised by people such as Rusesabagina. In it, she states, "The Hutu Power ideology which underpinned the 1994 genocide of the Tutsi never went away: to this day its supporters remain organised and well-financed. They live among us. Inspired by racism they are determined to oust the current government by violent means if necessary in order to claim power in the name of the 'majority Hutu people.' Whilst this opposition advocates a violent overthrow of the current government, it has offered no programme for the advancement of the Rwandan people who continue to be cursed by rumours, lies and racist propaganda."[43]

Additionally, Melvern says of the FDLR, "A major splinter group of the FDLR, known as the Ralliement pour l'Unité et la Démocratie-Urunana (RUD-Urunana), is currently under investigation by a US law enforcement agency and a criminal case against them is being

---

[43] Linda Melvern, "Unravelling International Conspiracies Against Rwanda," *New Times Rwanda*, accessed October 17, 2013, http://www.newtimes.co.rw/news/index.php?a=65784&i=15322.

prepared. There is detailed evidence on the RUD-Urunana recently provided to US investigators including documents on the group's communication networks and money transfers. The leadership of this group, which is more efficient than that of the FDLR, resides in North America and it has considerable skills in lobbying operations."[44]

Melvern then quotes from a report written by Belgian FDLR specialist Raymond Debelle that states, "The FDLR 15-member Executive Committee is comprised entirely of those involved in the Genocide against the Tutsi of 1994; while this group publically supports justice and reconciliation it continues to destabilise and try to destroy the current government by promoting disorder and uncertainty in Rwanda. This group is suspected of being behind deadly grenade attacks in Kigali which have targeted the civilian population."[45]

Yes, lobbying. Where he was once pleased to simply have his picture taken with world leaders, Rusesabagina now lobbies them quite publically. On January 14, 2013, he posted and had reposted a public letter he had written to former UK Prime Minister Tony Blair, acknowledging Blair's "special relationship" with President Kagame, and essentially calling upon him to denounce it as well as Kagame himself and to remove his support for the present regime.[46] On July 18, 2012, Rusesabagina did likewise with a letter to former President Bill Clinton.[47] In January 2009, President Obama, with whom he'd done a photo op during Obama's 2008 presidential campaign, got a similar public/private letter from Paul.[48]

---

[44] Ibid.

[45] Ibid.

[46] PRLog, "Hotel Rwanda's Rusesabagina Asks Tony Blair to Denounce Paul Kagame's Activities in the Congo," January 14, 2013, http://www.prlog.org/12058471-hotel-rwandas-rusesabagina-asks-tony-blair-to-denounce-paul-kagames-activities-in-the-congo.html.

[47] Paul Rusesabagina, "Letter from Paul Rusesabagina to President Clinton," Hotel Rwanda Rusesabagina Foundation, July 18, 2012, http://hrrfoundation.org/letters-from-paul.

[48] Hotel Rwanda Rusesabagina Foundation, "Paul Urges President Barack Obama to Action in the Congo," February 2009, http://archive.constantcontact.com/fs045/1102372137713/archive/1102442499391.html.

Rusesabagina's PR firm is Kurth Lampe out of Chicago. Run by married couple Kitty Kurth and Kevin Lampe, through its actions it has become one of the most highly connected firms serving the US Democratic Party. Lampe has worked in some capacity for every Democratic presidential candidate from Dukakis to Obama. He handles all the speakers at the Democratic National Convention, even working with President Obama on his keynote address. Kurth's resume is equally impressive, with similar roles in recent Democratic presidential campaigns as well as numerous international endeavors. These are Paul's image makers, speechwriters, and damage-control experts. And they are both one degree of separation from President Obama and other prominent Democrats, particularly those in the greater Chicago area, where Rusesabagina does much of his speaking, quite often at the behest of Democratic politicians. On June 2, 2011, for example, Paul was the guest of honor at a fundraising event for his Hotel Rwanda Rusesabagina Foundation at Matt Lamb Studios, Chicago. Prestigious guests included Illinois's governor, Democrat Patrick Quinn.

Rusesabagina took his political aspirations to a new level when he personally filed a criminal complaint against Rwandan President Kagame at the International Criminal Tribunal for Rwanda, set up by the UN as a postscript for dealing with leaders of the Genocide Against the Tutsi. Rusesabagina accused Kagame of war crimes, crimes against humanity, and crimes of genocide. He even offered himself up as a witness. This is perplexing. To the best of anyone's knowledge, mine included, Rusesabagina never even *saw* Kagame during the Hundred Days. There is even the strong likelihood the two have never met in person, and if they did meet sometime after the Hundred Days, there is no possibility Rusesabagina would have been a witness to Kagame himself personally committing acts of genocide. This would be like me filing criminal charges against, say, the president of Latvia, despite the fact I have never been to Latvia, nor have I ever personally witnessed any crimes committed by said president.

What would be Rusesabagina's legal standing to bring charges against a man whom he never saw commit a single crime, perhaps has never even met in person, in his entire life?

Fame. Fame and power. It may have been Rusesabagina's own idea, hatched amid his runaway egomania, or he may have been put up to it by some of the numerous *génocidaires* he volunteered to defend personally in testimony before the same court as well as other smaller international venues. If someone with true legal standing had filed charges or given testimony, it would be back-page news. But if it were a Hollywood hero...

In 2008 he testified on behalf of four Rwandans held on genocide charges in the United Kingdom. Under questioning, he revealed he only knew one of the four defendants, and that his testimony was not in regard to the man's guilt or innocence, but to put himself forth as an expert on present-day Rwanda in hopes of keeping all four men from being deported for trial. After intense questioning, where Rusesabagina revealed he had not even lived in Rwanda since September 6, 1996, Judge Anthony Evans savaged his testimony. The judge stated he had made "a number of wild and general allegations about human rights in Rwanda which are made without any supporting proof." Judge Evans specifically noted Rusesabagina's rants about "prisoners [being] used as, effectively, slave labour in the Congo; and, strangest of all, that there are secret jails located in unidentified areas unknown to humanitarians, human rights activists, and journalists. He produces no supporting evidence for any of these allegations."[49]

As to Rusesabagina's retelling of the same conspiracy theories he espoused to Keith Harmon Snow, such as that the RPF manned the dreaded roadblocks during the genocide and that there was no systematic government-led genocide, Evans found Rusesabagina's tales "so contrary to all evidence and facts placed before this court as to

---

[49] The Government of the Republic of Rwanda v. Bajinya, Munyaneza, Nteziryayo and Ugirashebuja, (2008), http://www.trial-ch.org/fileadmin/user_upload/documents/trialwatch/Rwandan4Decision.pdf, para. 388–429.

212 | INSIDE THE HOTEL RWANDA

be worthless…He is clearly a very strong opponent of the present regime, even going so far as to suggest that it was responsible for the genocide, and making other wild and exaggerated claims." Evans thanked the lawyers who cross-examined Rusesabagina, demonstrating to the court that "the evidence was not that of an independent expert, but rather that of *a man with a background strongly allied to the extremist Hutu faction* [emphasis added], and as such cannot be considered as independent and reasoned. In the light of the bias displayed, I am satisfied that no weight can be attached to this evidence."

When President Paul Kagame visited the United States on April 30, 2011, lawyers for Madame Habyarimana, the widow of former Rwandan President Juvénal Habyarimana, attempted to serve Kagame in Oklahoma City with a civil suit in the US District Court for the Western District of Oklahoma, charging him in the death of her husband.[50] Part of the filing included "a summary of some of the crimes committed by Defendant Kagame and co-conspirators in the furtherance of the conspiracy…prepared by Paul Rusesabagina, the main figure depicted in the award winning film, *Hotel Rwanda*."[51] The case was dismissed with the support of President Obama. Kagame's lawyer, Pierre-Richard Prosper, former ambassador-at-large for War Crimes Issues under President George W. Bush as well as a war crimes prosecutor for the United Nations International Criminal Tribunal for Rwanda, stated, "We are pleased that we were able to win this matter on the long-standing doctrine of head of state immunity. We are confident, however, that had we been forced to address this matter on the merits we would have prevailed."[52]

---

[50] "Rwanda President Paul Kagame Sends Off Oklahoma Christian Grads amid Controversy (VIDEO)," *Huffington Post College,* last modified May 25, 2011, http://www.huffingtonpost.com/2010/05/01/rwanda-president-sued-ami_n_559705.html.

[51] *Madame Habyarimana and Madame Ntaryamira v. General Paul Kagame etc.,* US District Court for the Western District of Oklahoma, Case No. CIV-10-437-W.

[52] "US Court Dismisses Lawsuit Against Rwanda's Kagame," *Reuters,* October 29, 2011, http://www.reuters.com/article/2011/10/29/ozatp-rwanda-usa-kagame-idAFJOE79S00T20111029.

In late 2010, French judge Marc Trévidic ordered an inquiry into exactly how President Habyarimana's plane was downed, and if it was shot down by some sort of missile, who likely fired it. (The French crew on the plane also died, thus explaining the country's official interest in the matter.) Unofficially, scuttlebutt had been brewing for years that France was determined to use every opportunity possible to wash the blood from its own hands regarding the genocide and its support of the *génocidaires*, perhaps hoping that placing the blame for Habyarimana's crash on Paul Kagame could focus more negative attention on him and the RPF and less on France.

This inquiry, the first by an international team of legal as well as technical experts that physically went into Rwanda to the actual crash site and personally interviewed suspects, witnesses, and others, released an official report on January 10, 2012. Their conclusion was that the president's plane was shot down by elite presidential troops of the Rwandan army loyal to the Hutu Power movement.[53] This conclusion supported what most Rwandans had suspected for years—that extremists impatient with Habyarimana, convinced he was too moderate because of his support of the Arusha Accords, decided to murder him in a manner that might be blamed on the RPF and/or the Tutsi and provide an excuse to call on the militias and the citizenry to begin the genocide.

This issue aside, one must ask, where does Paul Rusesabagina fit into all of this? He has never touted any firsthand personal knowledge of how the president's plane was brought down. He has never claimed to be a witness to that event. He has been deemed in courts of law as not being an expert on present-day Rwanda. But he is a celebrity; a celebrity in search of the ultimate celebrity prize: his own country.

Paul continues to tour the world, especially targeting gullible media groups, as well as universities and colleges where people are starstruck, open to suggestion, and not conversant with Rwandan

---

[53] CNN Wire Staff, "Report: Rebels Cleared in Plane Crash That Sparked Rwandan Genocide," January 11, 2012, http://www.cnn.com/2012/01/11/world/africa/rwanda-president-plane/index.html.

history. His message is intended to reverse the history of the 1994 genocide. His mission to become a major political player in Rwanda directs his actions toward classic negative campaigning. His target: President Paul Kagame. He publically claims President Kagame is planning a new genocide or continuing the 1994 one—in such conditions of secrecy that only Paul Rusesabagina, even though he has not been to Rwanda in years, is aware of it. But Rwanda as it stands today is not moving in that direction at all. If you do not believe it, go visit the country. George W. Bush has. Bill Clinton has. Tony Blair has. Why have none of these world leaders seen what Rusesabagina is talking about? Why have the NGOs not seen it, either? Rusesabagina is shouting "Fire!" in a crowded movie theater, but worse, he himself is not even in the theater. His is more like a bomb scare, phoned in to whomever will listen that "There is a genocide going on!" or "There will be a new genocide!" even though he has spent, at best, less than a week or two in Rwanda during the past decade or so—and only then under the escort of the Rwandan Army as a courtesy from the man he so despises, President Paul Kagame.

There is simply no sense or logic to Rusesabagina's cries of "wolf!" except that he wishes to use his celebrity to affect the internal politics of Rwanda by calling the Hutu majority to follow his message of a return to the ways of the divisive dictator Habyarimana. If he wanted to go into politics, which is his civil right to do, why didn't he move back to Rwanda to challenge the current government's policies and show how he can improve the lives of Rwandans, instead of inciting the Hutu by using the same scare tactics used in 1994?

> If he wanted to go into politics, which is his civil right to do, why didn't he move back to Rwanda to challenge the current government's policies and show how he can improve the lives of Rwandans, instead of inciting the Hutu by using the same scare tactics used in 1994?

Most of the supporters he targets are nostalgic for Habyarimana's regime, which committed genocide and whose members do not recognize the current Rwandan government. To win their trust and support, Rusesabagina has to champion their ideology. That is why he builds on ethnic divisions.

In all of his diatribes—or shall I say, those likely written for him by the people he represents, those who wish to overthrow the present government—he talks derisively of the "Tutsi elite" who "control the nation." Those are fighting words. Those are hateful words. Those are divisive words. Those are polarizing words. Those are words meant to stir up armed conflict. Those are the same words we heard before and during the Hundred Days. These are now Paul Rusesabagina's words. They are identical to the catcalls of "rich Jews" who "run everything" when Hitler's supporters were attempting to bring the Nazi Party to power in post–World War I Germany. And yet Rusesabagina continues to sign as his occupation, "humanitarian."

Listen to the words.

As a new decade arrived, Rusesabagina's words took on added hatred and deceit and his personal political ambitions became more transparent. His ties to armed terrorists such as the FDLR attracted suspicions, as fundraising for and arming such groups can be illegal.

In October 2010, Martin Ngoga, Rwanda's prosecutor general, said, "We have evidence that Paul Rusesabagina is…financing the same genocidal rebels of the FDLR."[54] According to the *Guardian* of October 28, 2010, the prosecutor general told Rwandan public radio that the case against Rusesabagina was solid. Ngoga said that in Rusesabagina's case, money was transferred via Western Union to two FDLR commanders. "We have the dates of transactions made. Money was sent from San Antonio, Texas [one of Rusesabagina's many homes is in Texas], and received in different banks in Bujumbura [Burundi]

---

[54] Xan Rice, "Hotel Rwanda Manager Accused of Funding Terrorism," *Guardian*, October 28, 2010, http://www.theguardian.com/world/2010/oct/28/hotel-rwanda-manager-terror-funding-charges.

and Dar es Salaam [Tanzania]. The people who received this money told us what the money was for."[55]

Rusesabagina, as expected, denied the charges. But according to the *Guardian* in June of 2011, the Belgian police arrested and interrogated Rusesabagina for more than three hours based on the charges, concluding the allegations made in Rwanda and the accompanying evidence were worthy of review.[56] Two prosecutors from Rwanda witnessed the interrogation as required by international law. Rusesabagina could be extradited to Rwanda to face charges of assisting terrorism and threatening state security.

Even when Rusesabagina defends himself against charges such as this, he tends to reveal other lies he has told in the past. In a June 2, 2011, blog entry, genocide scholar Tom Ndahiro noted that in a press release on October 28, 2010, the Hotel Rwanda Rusesabagina Foundation (HRRF) claimed that "Rusesabagina Combats Fiction with Facts." In the release, Rusesabagina noted that "the last time I sent money to Rwanda was in 2002 or 2003, I think 2002, to my younger brother for a brain operation. It was about 500 or 1000 Euros."[57]

The press release, written by his Chicago PR titan Kitty Kurth, refuted allegations that he has been sending money to the *génocidaire* organization FDLR. But the revelation that he hasn't been sending money to Rwanda was even more important.

On November 1, 2009, Chido Nwangwu, the founder and publisher of Houston-based USAfricaonline.com, the first US-based, African-owned newspaper on the Web, reported that Rusesabagina "founded the Hotel Rwanda Rusesabagina Foundation (HRRF), an organization which has been providing psychological care and material assistance to children who were orphaned by the genocidal

---

[55] Ibid.

[56] As reported in IPP Media, "Hotel Rwanda Movie Hero 'Arrested,'" June 26, 2011, http://www.ippmedia.com/frontend/?l=30545.

[57] Tom Ndahiro, "Rusesabagina: A Humanitarian or Conman?," *Friends of Evil,* June 2, 2011, http://friendsofevil.wordpress.com/2011/06/02/rusesabagina-a-humanitarian-or-conman/.

killings in Rwanda. HRRF also supports thousands of women who were abused during and after the Rwanda genocide."[58]

It was Ndahiro who put two and two together. "I have made inquiries into whether HRRF has a branch in Rwanda, and the answers have all been: 'NO.' It is not possible to assist thousands of people without some sort of presence. I asked the genocide survivors organization, IBUKA, if it has ever received money from Rusesabagina, and it affirmatively denied knowledge of any such assistance."[59] London-based SURF reports the same exact thing.

Rusesabagina places himself upon a humanitarian pedestal by stating his foundation helps "thousands" of Rwandans devastated by the genocide and that he uses these philanthropic claims to continue to raise money for his nonprofit "foundation." Yet in the next breath he says he has not sent any money to Rwanda since before his movie came out and his foundation was created—and even then it was to his brother, for his own personal use! Misappropriation of the funds of a nonprofit corporation is a form of money laundering, a crime punishable in many countries by severe fines as well as a prison sentence.

Amid all of this, he continued to be rewarded by underinformed yet seemingly well-meaning organizations. For instance, the Lantos Foundation for Human Rights and Justice, based in Concord, New Hampshire, decided to award Rusesabagina its annual Lantos Human Rights Prize at a large soiree in Washington, DC, on November 16, 2011, only five months after his arrest in Belgium. The foundation is named after Tom Lantos, the only Holocaust survivor to serve as a US congressman.

This was the tipping point for those of us who have gnashed our teeth for years as Paul Rusesabagina found venue after venue

---

[58] Chido Nwangwu, "Rwanda's Anti-Genocide Activist Speaks in U.S. This Week; Clinton Apologizes Again," USAfricaonline.com, November 1, 2009, http://usafricaonline .com/2009/11/01/rwandan-anti-genocide-activist-paul-speaks-in-us-nov4/.

[59] Ndahiro, "Rusesabagina: A Humanitarian or Conman?"

to aggrandize and legitimize himself and his hate-filled politics. I personally helped organize protests at the Lantos offices in New Hampshire, turning over a petition signed by six thousand survivors and their supporters, as well as letters from genocide survivors' associations that had previously been sent to members of the Lantos Foundation, calling upon them to reconsider their decision to honor Rusesabagina.

Professor Jean Pierre Dusingizemungu, president of IBUKA (National Association of Genocide Survivors Organizations), and Chantal Kabasinga, president of AVEGA Agahozo (Association of Widows of the Genocide), wrote:

> We request the immediate withdrawal of this nomination as it is an unforgivable insult to the honour of the victims of the genocide of the Tutsis, and an affront to the memory and dignity of survivors.
>
> The survivors of the Hotel des Mille Collines ("Hotel Rwanda" in the film) have repeatedly testified that Rusesabagina did nothing to save their lives...Rusesabagina did not selflessly offer a safe refuge for refugees fleeing the genocide but demanded payment for rooms at the hotel.
>
> Rusesabagina has and continues to enjoy the success of the film *Hotel Rwanda* to enrich himself and his family. He claims to have established a support fund for widows and orphans of the genocide in Rwanda, but neither IBUKA nor AVEGA are aware of a single beneficiary of this fund in Rwanda.[60]

SURF, the Survivors Fund, mentioned on its website that the campaign to protest Rusesabagina's Lantos Prize was being backed with an online petition launched by GAERG (National Survivors

---

[60] SURF Survivors Fund, "Lantos Prize," October 27, 2011, http://survivors-fund.org.uk/news/lantos-prize/.

Association of Graduate Students), also adding that "The Hotel Rwanda Rusesabagina Foundation, of which Paul Rusesabagina is President, has never made any grant to support survivors of the genocide. For an individual that purports to have been driven in his actions by the interests of survivors this raises serious questions. And such actions (or lack of actions) speak louder than words."[61]

Our message seemed at first to be greeted respectfully. Our hopes were high that we had provided ample evidence that Rusesabagina was completely undeserving of any human rights prize. It was time to turn the tide and stop all this nonsense caused by a Hollywood movie. Give the prize to Roméo Dallaire, give it to Bernard Kouchner, give it numerous other people, but do not give it to a complete and utter fraud.

I wish I had been behind the closed doors of the Lantos Foundation when they decided to ignore us all and award him the prize anyway. Perhaps it was something as simple as public embarrassment—to announce that a prize was going to one person and then give it to another. The foundation had always been so uncontroversial in the past. Its previous recipients had been the Dalai Lama and Elie Wiesel—truly wonderful people. Perhaps Rusesabagina's powerful American PR firm intervened. Who knows? But the end result was too much to bear. Another prize. Another layer of legitimacy. No accountability. No truth. No one wanting to listen to the real refugees. It reminds one of the American Western film *The Man Who Shot Liberty Valance*, with its famous line, "When the legend becomes fact, print the legend."

> It was time to turn the tide and stop all this nonsense caused by a Hollywood movie. Give the prize to Roméo Dallaire, give it to Bernard Kouchner, give it numerous other people, but do not give it to a complete and utter fraud.

---

[61] Ibid.

Instead of being conciliatory in her official response to the protesters, Katrina Lantos Swett, president of the foundation, attacked, suddenly praising Rusesabagina not for his alleged actions in 1994, but for his actions of today, spreading erroneous propaganda about the current nongenocidal Rwanda government.[62] This, more than anything, leads me to believe, although I cannot prove it, that Rusesabagina's hardball-playing Chicago PR firm was driving the message.

Blogger Wandia Njoya, PhD (Penn State University), senior lecturer and head of the Department of Language and Performing Arts, Daystar University, Kenya, perhaps put it best:

> Katrina Lantos Swett issued a rude response to the protests against the award of her human rights prize to Paul Rusesabagina, the hero created by a Hollywood movie.
>
> [Her] response essentially says, "If you did not say anything before, you should shut up now." According to Swett, those protesting her pick of Rusesabagina are not credible because they did not say anything when the movie *Hotel Rwanda* was released, or when Rusesabagina was awarded a presidential medal by George [W.] Bush.
>
> However, the fact that she did not hear any protests does not mean they didn't exist. And there is such a thing as research to confirm that there were no protests. But research? On Africans? Why bother? Just like their skin, the surface tells it all.
>
> Besides, Swett didn't hear anything probably because the release of *Hotel Rwanda* marked the first time a larger American public heard about the genocide. Clinton had done a mighty good job of preventing the UN from declaring the slaughter genocide.

---

[62] Karen Langley, "Award Recipient Isn't Everyone's Hero," *Concord Monitor,* November 10, 2011, http://www.concordmonitor.com/news/4482159-95/katrinaswett-lantosfoundation-paulrusesabagina.

Even if there were no protests then, that does not invalidate the protests now. The voices of victims are validated not by the length of time it takes for them to speak out, but by the victims' experience and the victims' humanity. That is why the world recognized the Armenian genocide and the Herero genocide a century later. And that's why priests are convicted for sexual abuse of children who speak out as adults.[63]

Shortly before the Lantos debacle, Paul received yet another award. I wonder aloud whether he has simply become the designated "African humanitarian award recipient" for organizations who know of no other Africans, now that a great man like Nelson Mandela has died, and the equally deserving Bishop Tutu has already received so many.

This time it was in Boston, for the Armenian Heritage Foundation, on October 20, 2011, in remembrance of the horrible and underrecognized 1915 Armenian genocide. Blogger Willis Shalita, a Rwandan born in diaspora in Uganda who later moved to the United States and worked for years as a special investigator for the State Bar of California in the chief trial counsel's office, was there. According to Willis, "In his one hour speech, the man did not use the word GENOCIDE, not once. Zilch. 1994 was 'a civil war.'

"And when you have heard it all, Rusesabagina surprises you. He said, 'What happened in 1994 all started in my house.' Really? The man is a legend in his own mind...[H]e gives credit to Gen. Bizimungu for saving the people that were at the Hotel Mille Collines. Yes, Bizimungu, the man now serving a life sentence for genocide and crimes against humanity."[64]

---

[63] Wandia Njoya, "The Lantos Prize: There's No Controversy; Just Cowardice," *Umuvugizi* (blog), November 18, 2011, http://umuvugizi.wordpress.com/2011/11/18/the-lantos-prize-theres-no-controversy-just-cowardice/.

[64] Willis Shalita, "RUSESABAGINA SPEAKS IN BOSTON: Same Tired Story, Lies and Pomposity," October 21, 2011, http://willisshalita.wordpress.com/2011/10/21/ruseabagina-speaks-in-boston-same-tired-story-lies-and-pomposity/.

Louis Gakumba of Bulawayo 24 News, Zimbabwe, caught his act on May 14, 2013, at Lyman High School in Lebanon, Connecticut. According to Gakumba, "His roar if amplified could shatter your eardrum. On the podium Rusesabagina calls himself an 'Ordinary Man who does Extraordinary things.' For those of you who don't know the meaning of my name, R U S E S A B A G I N A means one who disperses enemies."[65]

Gakumba goes on to infer that after the blowsy puffery of attempting to build himself up as some sort of superman, Rusesabagina spoke not of the *Hotel Rwanda*, but instead went into what has become his post-2010 political stump speech of painting everything in Rwanda after 1994 as evil incarnate, focusing naturally on President Kagame. No balance, no context, a terrifying lack of factual data, and no firsthand information whatsoever.

On January 11, 2013, the political newsletter *Counterpunch* featured an interview with him conducted by Daniel Kovalik. Kovalik is a labor and human rights lawyer who also teaches at the University of Pittsburgh School of Law. In this interview, Kovalik reports being "stunned" when Rusesabagina states, "the governing elite has a special program of sterilizing men so that they don't produce…Yes, sterilizing Hutu men. Yes, and what did you call this? Is this not a genocide? This is not the people's choice; it is the government's choice."[66]

Rusesabagina repeats this new accusation every opportunity he gets. But what is its basis?

It seems that the Hotel Rwanda Rusesabagina Foundation has posted the source material: an academic paper written by someone named Jordan Moore while she was an MPA (master of public administration) candidate at the University of Memphis. This

---

[65] Louis Gakumba, "Why Is the Hero of *Hotel Rwanda* Controversial?," *In2EastAfrica*, May 28, 2013, http://in2eastafrica.net/why-is-the-hero-of-hotel-rwanda-controversial/.

[66] Daniel Kovalik, "Hotel Rwanda Revisited: An Interview with Paul Rusesabagina," *Counterpunch*, January 11–13, 2013, http://www.counterpunch.org/2013/01/11/hotel-rwanda-revisited-an-interview-with-paul-rusesabagina/.

fifteen-page paper does indeed state, "A chilling example of Rwandan discriminatory health care policy is President Kagame's program to slow population growth by implementing a plan to sterilize 700,000 Rwandan men between 2011 and 2013. While Rwandan officials claim involvement is voluntary, the program has been widely criticized by human rights organizations for targeting poor Hutu citizens for coerced participation (Kambanda, 2011)."[67]

It also states, "This mass vasectomy policy has further been accused of being a form of genocide with the primary aim being to limit the number of Hutu births. The law further calls for sterilization of those with developmental disabilities…This program's gross disregard for human rights echoes back to Nazi Germany and the quest for the perfect race (Survivors Network, 2009)."

This is upsetting stuff, essentially accusing the current government of using certain despicable tactics once developed by the Nazis…

…until one reads more carefully.

The author, Jordan Moore, is a former employee of the Hotel Rwanda Rusesabagina Foundation! But this is not the worst part. The citations? "Kambanda, 2011" is not a piece of peer-reviewed academic research. Its full title and location is "Rwanda: Why Sterilize the Poor?", retrieved July 17, 2012, from http://groups.yahoo.com/group/Umusoto/message/27137.

It is from a Yahoo! chat group! A group that no longer exists!

This intellectual exercise is not merely lazy; it is academically illegitimate. A real academic paper cannot cite scuttlebutt in chat rooms, and one wonders if the University of Memphis even accepted this paper and graded it as acceptable. If so, it is a mark of shame against that university.

To provide a more acceptable academic citation, we made the effort to find out whether some paper on this topic even exists by

---

[67] Hotel Rwanda Rusesabagina Foundation in collaboration with Jordan Moore, "Rwandan Health Care Corruption and Inequality," n.d., http://hrrfoundation.org/wp-content/uploads/2012/08/Health-Care-Issues-in-Rwanda-2.pdf.

someone named Kambanda, and we actually found one. It is a short article written by Charles KM Kambanda, PhD, a public policy analyst and international human rights lawyer at St. John's University School of Law in New York.[68] Kambanda is a frequent critic of President Kagame and that is his God-given right. In Kambanda's actual article, a commercial opinion piece and not a peer-reviewed academic work written in 2011, he debates the merits of a family planning proposal by the Rwandan minister of health that involved voluntary male sterilization (he comes out against it, which is again his right). But he never states in that article that "the program has been widely criticized by human rights organizations for targeting poor Hutu citizens for coerced participation." That part Moore appears to have made up for her former employer.

Next comes the "Survivors Network, 2009" citation. This appears to be someone's personal website for a biased, violently anti-Tutsi political discussion forum. No author even accepts credit for it. Again, not a real academic citation, just yammering on the Internet, where everyone has an outrageous opinion for which no one is responsible. Not truly citable by any respectable professor of higher academia.

Stanley N. Katz, PhD, lecturer with the rank of professor in Public and International Affairs; director, Center for Arts and Cultural Policy Studies, Woodrow Wilson School, Princeton University; and recipient of the National Humanities Medal by President Barack Obama, read the Moore paper Rusesabagina cites and had this to say:

> This appears to be a fairly typical paper by a graduate student who has stronger views on a policy subject than the evidence he or she cites can support or sustain. Nothing that the author says or cites would lead me to believe that he or she has an evidentiary case for the existence of such a program. The references are difficult (and in one case impossible) to

---

[68] Charles Kambanda, "Rwanda: Why Sterilize the Poor?," *Proxy Lake,* accessed October 17, 2013, http://www.theproxylake.com/2011/02/rwanda-why-sterilize-the-poor/.

track down, and this text gives no evidence that the author can back up his or her very damaging assertion. This is not, in my judgment, a paper that any social science school would take seriously as policy evidence.

We also quickly Googled family planning in Rwanda in general and all that came up were technical reports of how it's been successful. The paper by Rusesabagina's former employee does cite one fact correctly: President Kagame was, in fact, featured as the keynote speaker at the London Summit on Family Planning July 11, 2012. So much for international uproar over his family planning policies.

There are no forced sterilizations going on today in Rwanda. No plan is in action to eliminate the Hutu population. These are researchable facts. But no one cares. Why? Because Hollywood did not make a movie saying that Paul's detractors single-handedly saved 1,200 people during a genocide. If they did, the world would listen, just as they listen to him. This is the intellectual tragedy.

But it all culminated when, in a formal statement on December 15, 2012, Paul Rusesabagina said, "On today's date, I am proud to declare solemnly that I assume the full rights and responsibilities as President of the Party for Democracy in Rwanda, the PDR-Ihumure who elected me to this position when the Ordinary Congress [met] in the month of June in the United States."[69]

Paul Rusesabagina is now the president of the major coalition party opposing Paul Kagame for the presidency of Rwanda. Because of an error-filled movie.

After a nine-page diatribe listing his entire platform—basically a continuation of his slander against everything going on in present-day Rwanda—he lays out this quite literal call to arms: "But, dear compatriots and friends of Rwanda, we are not naïve. We know very well that

---

[69] "Allocution de M. Paul Rusesabagina a l'occasion des assises d'evaluation du PDR-Ihumure," paragraph 5, December 15, 2012, accessed October 17, 2013, http://pdrihumure.com/documents/alllocution15122012.pdf.

the only language understood and highlighted by this power is that of arms. If the RPF has not yet understood that the Rwandan people [have had] enough [of being] persecuted and oppressed, [they] will be responsible for the suffering and tragedy of the Rwandan people and the sub-region and primarily responsible for the consequences that might result. *We say loud and clear that a military solution is not our first choice. But it should also be understood that our arsenal of peaceful solutions is not inexhaustible. Enough is enough* [emphasis added]."

He threatens armed war. Another civil war. And African civil wars have an historical tendency to be quite bloody, often involving genocide or genocidal actions against the unarmed.

I have to wonder, do director/screenwriter Terry George and screenwriter Keir Pearson realize what they have done? Do they realize they have plucked a man from obscurity and given him delusions of becoming the leader of an entire nation? Do they realize this man is now the front for every group that wishes to overthrow the current elected Rwandan government? That this overthrow is, like most overthrows, likely to involve great amounts of bloodshed? How do they feel about this? Do they dream of directing a sequel to the first movie? Do they, Lionsgate Films, MGM, or United Artists, the distributors of the film, feel any sense of responsibility at all for what may happen in the future? Never before in world history has such a thing happened—Hollywood potentially causing a genocide and the overthrow of a country by propping up an imposter—and yet it is unraveling directly before us.

All it would have taken was some fact checking—corroboration of Rusesabagina's story wherein he claimed to have personally saved us all. The official press releases for all of Paul's speaking engagements read almost identically, as is common practice for those managed, as he is, by a speakers' bureau:

"The real-life hero portrayed by Don Cheadle in the film 'Hotel Rwanda' will bring his story to *[fill in the blank]*. *Paul Rusesabagina single-handedly prevented the slaughter of more than 1,200 refugees at the*

Mille Collines Hotel [emphasis added] for one hundred days during the Tutsi genocide from April to July 1994."

This is exactly how he insists on being introduced. When a man's introduction itself is a complete falsehood, does that not completely void and bring into question the integrity of whatever it is he has to say? The introduction is a declaration of a right to a large audience, yet the introduction is untrue.

As journalists are required to check their facts and corroborate their claims, doesn't Hollywood need to do the same when they produce and distribute a movie and publicly claim it to be fact rather than fiction? Particularly so when, in this case, Hollywood may end up being responsible, yes responsible, for a new genocide yet to come? Do his speaking agents have any moral responsibility to fact-check the introduction they prepare for those who book his appearances through them?

Back in 1980, a woman by the name of Rosie Ruiz was declared the winner in the women's category of the Boston Marathon. Because fellow runners developed suspicions, an investigation followed that revealed Ruiz, who did run part of the race, spent most of it riding trains, got off only a short distance before the finish, then jumped back into the race, acting as if she had run the entire twenty-six miles. Her title was stripped after it was discovered she had not run the entire course. If Ruiz went to this same speakers' bureau claiming to have won the Boston Marathon, would it not be prudent for the agency to fact-check the claim before representing her? And as to the film, would it not have been good business for Lionsgate, MGM, and United Artists to have done the same rather than take what Rusesabagina, Pearson, and George said at face value?

My American co-author, Kerry Zukus, said to me during the writing of this book, "You know what this reminds me of? A book entitled *The Plot Against America* by Philip Roth."

Indeed, as he told me of this book, the similarities are eerily relevant. Roth's book is a reimagining of history—historical fiction. He explores what might have happened had Charles A. Lindbergh, an American hero, run against Franklin Delano Roosevelt in 1940, on the singular platform of nonintervention against Hitler and the Nazis regardless of their threat to American allies. The truth is, in 1940 this was one of the major campaign issues used against Roosevelt, but the Republicans had no candidate charismatic and famous enough to run with it and unseat the popular president. But Lindbergh was popular—very popular. He was also a Nazi sympathizer. In Roth's reimagining, Lindbergh wins and America begins pogroms similar to those of Hitler, ostracizing Jews in much the same manner Tutsi were ostracized in my country in the buildup to the 1994 genocide. Eventually, Lindbergh institutes martial law and opponents like FDR are arrested as enemies of the state.

Lindbergh really was a popular hero, lionized in a Hollywood film starring James Stewart. His claim to fame was being the first man to make a nonstop solo airplane flight from New York to Paris. One could argue, as many have, that this was a rather flimsy reason to regard someone as a hero. He saved no lives; he cured no disease; he led no great armies. He was simply a daredevil. Others imitated his aviation exploits shortly thereafter, but no one remembers their names. But this "heroism" granted "Lindy" a world stage from which to speak, as he did in support of Hitler, touting him as the answer to the world's real problem as he saw it: Soviet Russia and communism.

There is one major and unmistakable difference, though, between Lindbergh and Paul Rusesabagina: Lindbergh really did fly solo between New York and Paris.

Paul Rusesabagina did not "single-handedly prevent the slaughter of more than 1,200 refugees at the Mille Collines Hotel," period. This is 1,000 percent indisputable. But its repetition—the legend—makes it so, regardless of its complete factual inaccuracy.

Take away a film putting forth a multitude of inaccuracies, and who is Paul Rusesabagina? Nothing more than one of 1,200 people who lived in a hotel in Kigali, Rwanda, in April, May, and June of

1994. Why does Zozo, the hotel's porter, not run for president of Rwanda? Or Pasa, the desk clerk? Why are they not being flown around the world, given medals from world leaders and called "hero"?

Because of a movie. A poorly researched movie its creator told one of us was fiction, not a documentary. Take away the movie *Hotel Rwanda* and Paul Rusesabagina has no platform from which to speak. Others may, and certainly do, provide verbal opposition to President Kagame, and that is how democracy should work. But none of them has a Hollywood movie claiming they are a singular hero of epic proportions. None of them has that bully pulpit from which to speak. They would instead have to be judged on their ideas alone and not on their false reputation.

Charles A. Lindbergh had every right to run for president of the United States, touting his well-documented and undisputed daredevilry. Paul Rusesabagina can only tout a heroism that *never ever* happened. This living lie undercuts every word out of his mouth.

There is something else that baffles me. Some very good and sincere people who listen to our tale still say, "Yes, but didn't he display heroism by plying the bad men with liquor and getting them to not kill the refugees?"

Here is a key question: Did the "bad men" ever say this is the reason they did not slaughter the hotel inhabitants? The people in question—Bagosora, Bizimungu, Karamira, Rutaganda—all stood trial for their crimes. I prosecuted Karamira myself. Did he or a single other one of them say under oath that their friendship with Paul Rusesabagina was the reason the refugees in the hotel were not killed?

No.

If Paul had lobbied the leaders of the genocide to stay our execution, they would have said so during their trials as a way to moderate their sentences or belie their guilt. They could have called him as a witness. Georges Rutaganda talked a lot about Rusesabagina during his appeal, but never once did he say that Paul requested his help to keep the hotel refugees from being killed. For who was Paul anyway, to negotiate for our protection? Most Hutu who negotiated to protect Tutsi were killed where they stood, and then the Tutsi in question was killed immediately thereafter, for any Hutu who made such a request was considered a moderate who did not share the *génocidaire* ideology.

To buy into the central conceit of the film and the central story of Paul Rusesabagina's heroism is to believe the word of only one person—Paul himself. Even with certain supportive statements from people like Thomas Kamilindi, Odette, and others, none could possibly say with certainty that Paul's socializing saved lives. The only people who could really support such a contention would be the *génocidaires*, and not a single one of them ever made such a claim.

Allow me to approach this another way. Let's say I confessed that on September 11, 2001, I was sipping scotch with Osama bin Laden. I live in Columbus, Ohio, and Columbus was not attacked on 9/11. Would I be heralded as a hero if, without bin Laden to corroborate my story, I claimed my socializing with the al-Qaeda leader had convinced him not to attack Columbus? Or would your first thought be, "What was he doing cavorting with bin Laden? What sort of terrorist is this?"

The point is not whether Columbus, Ohio, was *ever* a target of al-Qaeda, but that Bagosora, Bizimungu, Karamira, and Rutaganda were horrible men who were responsible for hundreds of thousands of murders. The hotel *was* a target, but then again, anywhere any Tutsi could possibly be was also a target. Every nook and cranny of our nation was a target, and in Rwanda, those four men were as terrifying as America ever considered bin Laden.

The only thing Kamilindi, Odette, Zozo, or anyone else can claim is that Paul partied with the leaders of the genocide and later, perhaps, bragged to them that he got the *génocidaires* to leave us all alone. But none of these supposed witnesses actually heard the original conversations. They probably saw the partying, as I myself did, and then heard Paul's descriptions of it. But without that particular corroboration, which could only be gotten from the *génocidaires*, Paul's main claim of heroism flies out the window.

Paul's calls and faxes to foreign leaders and diplomats? The work of people in the hotel who actually knew such important people.

Paul's calls to UNAMIR? Denied by UNAMIR.

Working with the Red Cross and personally taking in genocide orphans? The work of the refugee committee, which Paul was not on. Some orphans were brought in by UN peacekeepers, whereas still others simply showed up at the hotel as we all did. Paul did nothing in regard to any of this.

Purging the computers and changing the room numbers to protect targeted refugees? UNAMIR. And why did UNAMIR say they did it? Because Paul Rusesabagina's collaboration with and support of the leaders of the genocide put our lives in danger.

The heroic scenes from the movie where Paul allegedly called Hutu Power generals for help, or confronted them fearlessly and with threats? No witnesses at all except for the generals themselves, none of whom ever spoke of such conversations.

What heroism?

What heroism?

24

RWANDA TODAY

URING MY LIFETIME, before the genocide, no one ever had been punished for killing a Tutsi. It simply was not considered a crime. This was the legacy of the First Republic of President Grégoire Kayibanda, which began in 1962, and the Second Republic of 1973 under President Habyarimana. Amnesty was granted to any Hutu accused of bringing harm to a Tutsi.

Justice is the cornerstone of unity and reconciliation in Rwanda. If there is no judicial truth, there will not be any conciliation. Reconciliation will follow the path of justice. Without justice, there is no hope of reconciliation. Today, survivors are living on the same hills with the murderers.

It is difficult perhaps to imagine that, just twenty years after the 1994 genocide that killed a million people over one hundred days, Rwanda could be on the cusp of the most promising economic changes in its history. Its poverty levels declined from 70 percent in 1994 to 57 percent in 2006 to 45 percent in 2011. The country had a consistent real economic growth record of more than 5 percent per year between 1994 and 2004, the second highest in Africa, and an 8.2 percent real GDP growth in 2010–2011.

Apart from foreign aid, Rwanda's principal sources of income are mining, coffee, and tourism—$200 million per year combined. According to the Brenthurst Foundation, a South African strategic adviser to the president of Rwanda, the coffee industry has changed hugely over four decades. Today it is focused on top-end Bourbon coffees, with Starbucks buying heavily from Rwandan coffee plantations. Rwandan tourism is concentrated in the luxury, high-yield gorilla watching and international conference markets. Many wealthy Americans and Europeans travel to Rwanda to see its amazing gorillas in the wild, going on photo safaris while preserving and respecting the animals themselves.

Would Starbucks, a publicity-sensitive, "new age" American company, invest millions in a country currently undergoing a genocide against the enemies of its "ruling ethnic elite"? Of course not; they would never tolerate the public embarrassment. One would have to imagine that Starbucks executives have spent extensive amounts of time in the country itself—not simply in the metropolitan areas, but in the hills where the coffee is grown. The same goes for Macy's and Costco, which also do business with the "new Rwanda," as well as celebrity visitors such as Christina Aguilera, NFL star Larry Fitzgerald, Jr., Quincy Jones, Ben Affleck, and Bill Gates. According to the July 17, 2013, *New York Times*, Grace Hightower De Niro, wife of Academy Award–winner Robert De Niro, recently began

> Grace Hightower and Coffees of Rwanda, a Fair Trade coffee sold at Whole Foods, Union Market, and other upscale grocers...She took Eugène-Richard Gasana, the permanent representative of Rwanda to the United Nations, and his wife, Agnes, to breakfast at the Plaza Hotel [in New York City]. "I asked them what I could do to help," Ms. Hightower said. "Agnes said, 'We need trade, not aid.'"[70]

Have these people seen the "Hutu genocide" Paul Rusesabagina speaks of, the people "disappearing" in those hills? No. The wealthy

---

[70] Joshua David Stein, "Grace Hightower De Niro: The TriBeCa-Rwanda Connection," *New York Times,* July 17, 2013, http://www.nytimes.com/2013/07/18/fashion/grace-hightower-de-niro-the-tribeca-rwanda-connection.html?_r=0.

ecotourists, have they seen the murders and slaughters of the unarmed by the "forces of the RPF"? No; they would have reported such things to the world, for they have no allegiance to anything but the truth. These are people who have actually spent time in Rwanda over the past eighteen years, unlike Paul.

Regarding business and the economy in today's Rwanda, in his interview with Keith Harmon Snow, Rusesabagina stated, "Today, people support no one; businesses have stopped. No one is allowed to sell even beans. Even if you cultivate your beans you are no more allowed to go and sell your own beans on the market. The RPF has taken over everything—even all the markets. They have appointed people who go and buy everything and sell them at their own prices. The RPF controls each and everything."[71]

Untrue, yet stated from a very large soapbox no other Rwandan is given.

Not to belabor the situation, but when it comes to business, Paul Rusesabagina harbors a rather personal vendetta against the current government. After the genocide, Rusesabagina went back to the Hotel des Diplomates. Because the government was not yet functioning properly, he was managing the hotel on his own. We called it *kubohoza*—the taking over of unknown property. It happened throughout the nation, and not just with hotels. If this rather anarchic system had not taken place, there would have been no services, as well as rampant and unnecessary homelessness in the wake of the genocide and after the war. But as things began to improve, civilization and its laws began once more to put things in proper order.

When the government began to work properly, it decided to privatize the Hotel des Diplomates and the Hotel Kiyovu. The managers of those hotels, because they were running them as if they owned them (despite having never bought them), claimed the government owed them reparations to compensate them for money they said they had

---

[71] Snow, "The Grinding Machine."

used to repair the hotels. Enormous bills were presented. Meanwhile, not a word was said about the money those "squatter hoteliers" had been taking in. In any business, there are expenses, but there is also income. Rusesabagina felt entitled to the income, but felt the expenses were the government's responsibility. When it was suspected that the bills for reparations were grossly overblown, a criminal investigation was opened on the owners of the Hotel des Diplomates and the Hotel Kiyovu. When the hotels were sold to the highest bidder in a proper auction, neither of the caretaker hoteliers managed to win owner-ship—understandable with the stain of criminal investigation color-ing their reputations. Those who served in the justice system and knew of this situation believe this is why Rusesabagina fled the coun-try. He would come back a few years later to make the short docu-mentary that accompanied his movie. If he had left Rwanda because he was persecuted (as he claims) and the government wanted to kill him (which he also claims), why did he get a proper military escort, arranged by the government, when he made his return?

In the 2008 Global Peace Index rankings released by Vision of Humanity, Rwanda's position was just below halfway, at 66th, in a table of 138 countries. Unsurprisingly, Afghanistan, Sudan, Somalia, and Iraq came last in that list, while Iceland, New Zealand, Japan, Switzerland, and Denmark, respectively, proudly topped the table.[72]

Rwanda ranked higher—better—than the United States, Mexico, India, Thailand, Israel, and the Philippines. Most significantly, Rwanda was thirteenth out of thirty-two African countries ana-lyzed. It was far more peaceful than South Africa (#94), Cameroon, and Algeria. In its specific geographic area, the only country above Rwanda in the entire Great Lakes region was Tanzania (#56).[73]

The 2008 index, which was derived from twenty-four qualitative and quantitative indicators from highly respectable sources, lumps together internal and external factors. These scores are then assessed

[72] Vision of Humanity, "Global Peace Index, 2008," accessed September 23, 2013, http://www.visionofhumanity.org/#page/indexes/global-peace-index/2008.
[73] Ibid.

through applied mathematics rather than pure speculative opinion. The indicators include:

- Number of external and internal conflicts fought
- Estimated number of deaths from organized conflict (external)
- Number of deaths from organized conflict (internal)
- Level of organized conflict (internal)
- Relations with neighboring countries
- Level of distrust in other citizens
- Political instability
- Level of disrespect for human rights (Political Terror Scale)
- Potential for terrorist acts
- Number of homicides per 100,000 people
- Level of violent crime
- Likelihood of violent demonstrations
- Number of jailed population per 100,000 people
- Number of internal security officers and police per 100,000 people
- Military expenditure as a percentage of GDP[74]

But things have changed. According to the 2013 Global Peace Index, Rwanda has dropped precipitously in rank to 135 out of 162. To quote the report:

> Rwanda's western border with the DRC has been a source of tension and conflict with both governments often accusing each other of supporting armed rebels. The tension between the two countries goes back to the Rwandan genocide. Rwandan civil society has also suffered with a clampdown on independent media and attacks on political opponents. The

---

[74] Institute for Economics & Peace, *Global Peace Index 2013*, http://www.visionofhumanity.org/pdf/gpi/2013_Global_Peace_Index_Report.pdf.

destabilizing effect means that Rwanda has seen an increase in its *Political Terror Scale*, the number of people jailed per 100,000 people, *political instability*, level of organised internal conflict, availability of small arms and light weapons, homicide rate, and terrorist activity. These factors have contributed to Rwanda experiencing the third largest fall in the GPI since 2008.[75]

As the report indicates, conflicts along its border with the DRC have been perpetual since at least 1994. And while both countries do, in fact, blame each other, both acknowledge the primary player in all such conflicts is the FDLR, whom Paul Rusesabagina publically defends and is accused of monetarily supporting. No border conflict fails to include their participation or agitation.

The report cites "political instability, level of organized internal conflict, availability of small arms and light weapons, homicide rate, and terrorist activity." What changed between 2008 and 2013? Rwanda's government had the exact same leadership in 2008 as it does in 2013, and most all of its laws and official policies remain unchanged.

It would be solipsistic for me to blame it all on Paul Rusesabagina, but then again, let's examine the quote from the report more closely. I truly believe Rusesabagina is not the "brains" behind his own political machine, but simply its face, its spokesperson. But the coming together of Paul and those he fronts for corresponds with the timeline of political instability, an increased level of organized internal conflict, greater availability of small arms and light weapons, a higher homicide rate, and an increase in terrorist activity in Rwanda. Political instability is what they openly call for—loudly and often. And how is political instability achieved? Through organized internal conflict, citizen access to weaponry, and terrorism, just as what

---

[75] Ibid.

happened in the run-up to the 1994 genocide (i.e., the Hutu Power militias and constant negative messaging on RTLM hate radio). What Hutu Power leaders did not have in 1994, though, was an international Hollywood hero as their focal point.

A rubric by which one could measure the *government's* part in internal violence is the Economic Impact of Violence Containment Rankings. What percentage of a nation's GDP is spent containing violence? Here, even in 2013, Rwanda is near the bottom (which is a good thing), spending only 5 percent of its GDP on violence containment. This may be far behind Iceland, which only spends 1 percent, but is far better than leading countries like North Korea at 27 percent and Syria at 24 percent. But on this measure, Rwanda is less of a police state than such countries as the United States at 11 percent, Israel at 10 percent, South Africa at 8 percent, Mexico at 7 percent, and the United Kingdom at 6 percent.[76]

Recent stories that illustrate Rwanda's efforts to improve the rights and safety of its citizens and the quality of its governance include the following:

> We are the only country in the world—and in the history of the modern world—where there has been a female legislative majority.

• According to Professor Gerald DeGroot in the *Christian Science Monitor*, April 28, 2008, "About 83 percent of the Tutsi population was murdered in a Hutu version of the Final Solution. The survivors carry terrible scars—physical and mental. Thousands of women still cope with the trauma of rape. Many were intentionally infected with HIV, itself a weapon of genocide...After the genocide, the constitution was rewritten...One prominent component of reform is the share of authority given to women. At present, women

---

[76] Ibid.

constitute 47 percent of the legislature—the highest proportion of any country in the world."[77] We are pleased to say this is something that has *improved* since 2008, because as of this writing, *64 percent* of our parliament is women. We are the only country in the world—and in the history of the modern world—where there has been a female legislative majority.

- The Mines Awareness Trust, a three-year program funded by the United Kingdom, announced that Rwanda made history by becoming the first country in the world to be officially declared free from landmines—no easy task considering how many were planted during the time of hostilities between the Hutu and Tutsi.[78] To reach this historic designation, not only does a country have to ensure its land is free of mines, but also that it destroyed its landmine stockpiles. The United States, on the other hand, will not even *sign* the Mine Ban Treaty, also known as the Ottawa Treaty.

- Citing President Paul Kagame's zero tolerance for corruption, and his willingness to listen and learn from people who oppose him, Reverend Rick Warren, the famous American clergyman who gave the invocation at the inauguration of President Barack Obama in 2009, nominated Kagame in April 2009 as his personal choice to be included in *Time* magazine's list of the 100 World's Most Influential People.[79]

---

[77] DeGroot, "Rwanda's Comeback."

[78] Tom Parry, "Rwanda First Country Officially Landmine-Free," *Daily Mirror,* December 4, 2009, http://blogs.mirror.co.uk/developing-world-stories/tag/Mines%20Awareness%20Trust.

[79] Rick Warren, "Paul Kagame," *Time,* April 30, 2009, http://content.time.com/time/specials/packages/article/0,28804,1894410_1893847_1893843,00.html.

One of the most prominent challenges facing Rwanda today is finding ways to prevent future genocides, such as what may be bubbling under the surface of the efforts of such groups as PDR-Ihumure. As a template, many of the efforts by the world's Jewish community to attack Holocaust denial have been taken to heart. Rwanda has put six measures in place to fight what we call "genocide ideology": programs to change mind-set, build community spirit, teach conflict resolution, fight poverty, improve law enforcement, and facilitate coordination between various levels of government.

To quote Rwanda's former minister of local government, Protais Musoni, in 2008: "The genocide ideology takes time to entrench in society and in many forms: culturally, politically, and economically. That is why we should see to it that all aspects of human life are improved."[80] To this I add that as long as it takes for such ideology to become entrenched within a society, it takes nearly as long if not longer to be eradicated.

Genocide ideology is a cancer within a society, and cancer is not quickly or easily cured. When the Holocaust was unleashed upon Jews in Germany, their population was reduced from well over half a million to about fifteen thousand after the war.[81] In 1990, at the time of German unification, there were approximately thirty thousand Jews residing in the merged country, only double the meager immediate postwar figure. Germany's population as a whole today is just over 81 million.[82] In other words, within Germany, in purely numerical terms, the Jewish community is completely insignificant.

---

[80] James Karuhanga, "Parliament Quizzes Minaloc over Genocide Ideology in Schools," *New Times Rwanda*, July 10, 2008, http://www.newtimes.co.rw/news/index.php/index.php?i=13587&a=7756.

[81] "History of the Jews in Germany: Jews in Germany from 1945 to the Reunification," *Wikipedia*, last modified October 13, 2013, en.wikipedia.org/wiki/History_of_the_Jews_in_Germany#Jews_in_Germany_from_1945_to_the_reunification; "German Jews During the Holocaust, 1939–1945," United States Holocaust Memorial Museum, last modified June 10, 2013, http://www.ushmm.org/wlc/en/article.php?ModuleId=10005469.

[82] CIA World Factbook, "Germany," last modified September 10, 2013, https://www.cia.gov/library/publications/the-world-factbook/geos/gm.html.

Right after the World War II, few people could imagine that a Jewish population would ever again settle on German soil, establish roots, and survive. And yet, from 1990 to today, the German Jewish population has almost quadrupled in size to nearly 119,000. This remains a pittance when compared to the population of Germany as a whole. But it has been almost seventy years since the Jewish genocide in Nazi Germany. Why did it take the Jews so long before they felt it was safe for them to return? A significant percentage of the modern world Jewish community has its roots in Germany,[83] and Yiddish, once so prominently spoken within that community, has its roots in the German language, too.

The Tutsi remain a minority in Rwanda today, although their numbers comprise a much higher percentage of the total Rwandan population than Jews living in Germany today. But unlike with a religion or religious group, every effort is being made to remove these designations for good, to remove the words "Tutsi" and "Hutu" from the national dialogue. Today, the ID cards, thrust upon us by the Belgians in 1933, are gone. Rwandans are now only Rwandans. Using the words "Hutu" and "Tutsi" is unacceptable in post-genocide Rwanda. Suggesting one group is favored over another is illegal. And yet this is still Paul Rusesabagina's stock in trade. This is still how everything coming from him or his political comrades is referenced.

According to Leana Wen of the *New York Times*, June 15, 2007, "Rwanda shows significant signs of growth. There is an effort to achieve universal primary education. There are functional hospitals and even a plan to provide universal healthcare. Paved roads run through the country. Rwanda is among the safest places to walk around in Africa."[84] None of this has regressed in recent years, but has instead increased and improved.

---

[83] "History of the Jews in Germany: Cultural and Religious Centre of European Jewry," *Wikipedia*, last modified October 13, 2013, http://en.wikipedia.org/wiki/History_of_the_Jews_in_Germany#Cultural_and_religious_centre_of_European_Jewry.

[84] Leana Wen, "Rwanda, Past and Present," *New York Times*, June 15, 2007, http://twofortheroad.blogs.nytimes.com/2007/06/15/rwanda-past-and-present/.

Unlike the leaders of most other emerging nations, President Kagame publicly expresses disappointment that Rwanda receives graciously offered foreign aid from wealthier nations, and instead lobbies those nations to *invest* in Rwanda, not give it a handout, much like the advice given to Robert De Niro's wife.

When I was a child, in many cases you could not go to secondary school if you were a Tutsi. This means you had to automatically forget about university and international scholarships. Now, Rwandan children receive a universal primary education without regard to their ethnicity because they all must have an education. They all go to secondary schools. If their performance merits it, they go to the universities of their choice, which have proliferated in the country since the genocide. Some are even selected to represent our nation at prestigious American universities and colleges.

Whereas most Rwandan children were only taught French—a holdover from the colonial period—in addition to our native Kinyarwanda, English is now taught to all Rwandan schoolchildren, and other languages are also encouraged, just as they are in Western public schools. Even adult education is blooming and being offered readily to whoever desires it.

While Paul Rusesabagina talks of a deteriorating public health system where Nazi-style forced sterilizations occur, the United Nations Department of Economic and Social Affairs Report on Population Estimates and Projections, released July 18, 2013, states that Rwandans now have a life expectancy of sixty-two years—ten years longer than in 2003.[85] Data released from the UN's World Health Organization on July 26, 2013, reported that Rwanda spends 23.7 percent of its annual budget on healthcare, the highest in Africa.[86]

---

[85] United Nations, Department of Economic and Social Affairs, Population Division, Population Estimated and Projections Section, "World Population Prospects: The 2012 Revision," accessed October 17, 2013, http://esa.un.org/unpd/wpp/unpp/panel_indicators .htm.

[86] "Rwanda: The Highest Spender on Healthcare by Percentage in Africa," *RwandaPost,* July 26, 2013, http://www.rwandapost.org/2013/07/26/rwanda-the-highest-percentage-spender-on-healthcare-in-africa/.

It would be disingenuous of me to ignore the statement from the UN report mentioning that "Rwandan civil society has also suffered with a clampdown on independent media and attacks on political opponents," but it is worth discussing.

The concept of legislating against "genocide ideology" is in place, and in my opinion it is a good thing for Rwanda. It has its roots in the laws of many other countries. Seventeen nations, along with the European Union, outlaw Holocaust denial. But there can be a downside. It violates free speech principles such as the First Amendment to the US Constitution. But Rwanda is not America. No other country is America. And no other country is Rwanda.

Rwanda is only twenty years past one of the worst genocides in recorded history. As one who was there at its end, I woke up most days imagining we would never have a real country again. The predictions that, at the end of the genocide, one side or the other would rule over desert seemed prophetic. We had nothing, and yet somehow we were supposed to make a nation out of it.

Now, living in America, I try to learn what I can about American history and attempt to make some sort of comparison, but none exists. At the end of America's Revolutionary War, there was already a new government in place to lead: the Continental Congress. Civilian casualties were extraordinarily light in comparison to Rwanda's. But even then, in the twenty years after the end of that war, problems arose, problems that were not always solved by traditional or historically perfect means. According to *The Age of Federalism* by Stanley Elkins and Eric McKitrick, President George Washington, elected unanimously by the Electoral College, was not a member of a political party; he hoped they would not be formed, fearing they would undermine republicanism. He faced the Whiskey Rebellion—protests caused by Congress's decision to raise money by taxing liquor—and sent in armed militias against the citizenry. His successor, John Adams, signed the Alien and Sedition Acts, which allowed the federal government to imprison or deport immigrants it deemed a threat. The Sedition Act actually made it a crime to criticize the government—a complete repudiation of the First Amendment's free-speech clause. Adams's successor, Thomas Jefferson, had his former vice president, Aaron Burr, arrested for treason—yet did not have him arrested for the murder by duel of former Treasury Secretary Alexander Hamilton, whom he personally disliked even more than he did Burr. Jefferson broke treaties with Native American tribes and forcibly removed them from their lands, and personally owned hundreds of slaves.[87]

None of these facts takes away from the greatness that is the American Experiment. But they illustrate that nations are built as omelets are—with the cracking of more than a few eggs along the way—and that history looks back and judges even the most heroic men, men such as Washington, Adams, and Jefferson, as fully capable of making errors of judgment, though at the time these patriots believed these decisions were in the nation's best interest.

I find a better parallel for Americans by drawing the comparison not with the nascent stages of the United States after its revolution, but after its civil war. American schoolchildren know that the Civil War was fought over slavery, and that the abolitionist Northern states overpowered the seceding, slave-owning Southern states. But I ask you to imagine: What if that war had been fought by the slaves themselves—that it had been the African slaves fighting all the white people of America? And the vastly outnumbered slaves won? *That* is more akin to what Rwanda woke up to in the late summer of 1994.

Imagine, then, an American President Frederick Douglass attempting to put together a new nation. Like Paul Kagame, he would need to build coalitions, for he and his party would be a significant numerical minority. He might have to think creatively to maintain order and a peaceful march forward for his war-torn nation.

---

[87] Stanley Elkins and Eric McKitrick, *The Age of Federalism: The Early American Republic, 1788–1800* (New York: Oxford University Press, 1993).

And as honorable a man as Douglass was, he might still have to break a few eggs along the way.

As you consider this mind-boggling proposition, use that same filter to analyze the accusations heaped upon the presidency of Paul Kagame. Don't just focus on the criticisms, for every leader of every nation throughout history has been criticized, but offset them with the accomplishments. Hate speech destroyed my country prior to and during 1994. Kagame feels one of his greatest responsibilities is making sure that never happens again. And yes, other great nations, nations such as postwar Germany, likewise felt the need at a certain point in their histories to put some common-sense restrictions on hate speech. And for a period, even the United States had its Alien and Sedition Acts, which were far more overreaching than anything going on in Rwanda today.

People ask me about Kagame's recent reelection with 93 percent of the vote. Yes, such things are strange to Americans used to presidential victories of 51 percent or even less. There is no question some of the hate speech laws can constrain public debate and opposition-party formation and development, particularly those with sectarian ideology. I have an opinion—and it is only that, one man's opinion. I believe Kagame feels the weight of the world on his shoulders. While every nation's president feels this way, with Kagame it is far more acute. The president of Italy need not fear that if he lost power, the entire nation might go on a domestic killing spree. So, too, the prime minister of Japan. Neither nation faced such a thing in its postwar leadership. Yes, both nations were deeply involved in a world war nearly seventy years ago, but not an internal genocide. The Genocide Against the Tutsi not only happened during Kagame's lifetime, but he was the military leader who stopped it. He may live each day of his life feeling that same responsibility—to keep genocide from happening again no matter what.

I do not know the man personally, but I believe Kagame feels if Rwanda can just make it through one generation of peace, one generation without divisionism and ethnic hatred fueled by the central government, such as it experienced with the colonial powers in the first half of the twentieth century and the Hutu leadership of the postcolonial period, the nation might have a chance. That is his charge—to just hold it together long enough for the young people of the nation to grow in an environment free of such hatred of neighbor versus neighbor that a bright future might actually have half a chance.

Democracy is a system of government always in search of improvement, and Rwanda is a democracy in that sincerest sense of the word. On July 31, 2013, Agence France-Presse reported that Rwanda's Upper House unanimously passed a bill amending its law against "genocide ideology," which had been criticized as muzzling free speech and suppressing opposition. According to Deputy Attorney-General Jean Pierre Kayitare, "This means that as soon as it is published, the old law will be repealed and all cases in court related to genocide ideology will immediately start using the new law."[88]

According to the story, "rights groups had criticized the original law as too vague and said it was being used to crack down on opposition to the regime of President Kagame. Under the amended law, criminal intent must be proved, and an act of inciting genocide must be carried out in front of more than one person. The bill punishes only 'an intentional act' in public, whether in a speech, writing, video, or other medium. The action must be 'characterised by thoughts based on ethnicity, religion, nationality, or race to foment genocide and/or support genocide,' it reads. Prison sentences are also reduced from twenty-five years to a maximum of nine, in line with a new penal code that has reduced sentence lengths in general."

It is cliché to say that a nation is "at a crossroads." Nations are perpetually at crossroads. On September 10, 2001, the United States was a nation at peace, enjoying economic prosperity and a balanced

---

[88] "Rwandan Senate Approves New Genocide Law," *Africa Review,* July 31, 2013, http://www.africareview.com/News/Rwandan-senate-approves-amended-anti-genocide-law/-/979180/1932950/-/ddevp9z/-/index.html.

federal budget, and was purchasing oil at $27.66 a barrel.[89] Today, all of that has changed.

There are those within Rwanda today who are attempting to move forward, while others, like the leaders of the FDLR and their supporting political parties, plot to overthrow these people through any means necessary, throwing us back into the days of Hutu versus Tutsi—not one nation but two, or one nation by virtue of having eliminated all other ethnic groups.

Rwanda needs heroes today, as every nation does. I speak today not simply for myself, but as one of hundreds, perhaps more than a thousand, who survived the Genocide Against the Tutsi within the walls of the "Hotel Rwanda." We were there. We lived to tell the story, the truth. Ours is a tale of many small heroes, many more ferocious villains, and a few petty irritants.

As a Tutsi in Rwanda, I was raised as one who felt lucky simply to be alive each and every day, not just during the Hundred Days. I belonged to a people who were discriminated against and marginalized by the society around me. That affects people deeply. It causes them to spend their lives looking over their shoulders, afraid, reluctant to speak up and let their opinions be known for fear of violent or even lethal reprisal.

When April of 1994 began, I was running for my life. As much as I thought I could find nothing to surprise me, given my upbringing, nothing I had experienced before this could have prepared me or my brethren for what transpired during those next few months. But today I live in America. It is a new day, just as it is a new day in Rwanda. There, it is a new day for both the Tutsi as well as the Hutu. A phrase now gaining favor in my native land is, "I am not Tutsi; I am not Hutu; I am Rwandan."

---

[89] John Miley, "The Economy Before and After 9/11," *Kiplinger's Personal Finance*, September 7, 2011, http://money.msn.com/investment-advice/article.aspx?post=7be1200a-e79a-4b35-a974-031570ce1a28.

I pray for my country, the land of my birth. I listen to the voices of negationism and genocide denial and all I can hear in them is a return to the bad days, the bad days of such a short time ago. The world is still capable of allowing this all to happen again. The world has watched the atrocities in Sudan, Syria, and Sri Lanka and does little or nothing. Genocide is reacted to, not prevented. The world waits until after a conflict, after the deaths of hundreds of thousands, and then it sorts through the rubble. If those most victimized somehow prevail, trials are held and justice is finally served, but it is served too late. Tell me, if you could prevent the deaths of thousands of innocents, would you do it? Or is it safer to wait until afterward and then hold trials for the killers? And if the evildoers win, do you simply bite your lip and do business with them, making them your trade partners in a world where commerce overrides morality?

> A phrase now gaining favor in my native land is, "I am not Tutsi; I am not Hutu; I am Rwandan."

Like the Jews who survived the Holocaust, we Rwandans look to examples of strength and resolve in people like Elie Wiesel and Simon Wiesenthal, who did not accept their freedom from atrocity as a ticket to selfish hedonism, but as a call from God to give back, to vigilantly assure that such atrocities would "never again" happen anywhere in this world, especially to their own people. Today, we Rwandans speak out. We argue. We expose. We debate. We hold liars accountable. We shine a light. We speak and we make sure the entire world is listening so that maybe, if things begin to turn again, the world can act positively before it is too late.

In doing so, we become like heroes, heroes a billion strong. Like our experience in the hotel, it is not necessary that the world know our names or even that we all know one another's names, but that we act heroically each and every day. Acting together, we all can be heroes.

ACKNOWLEDGMENTS

I OWE A TREMENDOUS debt of gratitude to all the people who trusted me and supported me during the research and writing of this book. In particular, I would like to thank my coauthor, Kerry Zukus, without whom this book would never have found its way to publication.

I would like to thank all the survivors of the Hotel des Mille Collines, especially those who agreed to collaborate on this book, particularly Bernard Makuza, Odette Nyiramilimo, Wellars Gasamagera, Egide Karuranga, Augustin Karera, Tatien Ndolimana, Denney Bucyana, Isdore Munyakazi, Jean Marie Vianney Rudasingwa, Jean Marie Mutesa, Eugene Kitatire, Christophe Shamukiga, Alexis Vuningoma, Jean Pierre Nkurunziza, Wycliff Kajuga, Pasa Mwenenganucye, and Serge Rusagara. Without your assistance and testimony, the true story behind the movie *Hotel Rwanda* would still be a mystery to the world.

To former UN peacekeepers General Romeo Dallaire and Major Brent Beardsley of Canada for reading our manuscript, giving testimony, and selflessly helping to save our lives when the world turned its back.

We must also thank Gerard Prunier, Philip Gourevitch, Linda Melvern, David Russell, Mara Drogan, Gerise Herndon, and Stanley Katz for their academic expertise and assistance, and express our gratitude for the resources of Princeton University.

To Ethienne Niyonzima, Theodore Ntarindwa, Honore Karera, and Aline Mukashyaka—your contributions to this book were invaluable.

I would like to thank the Stichter family. My family will always treasure your love, friendship, and support.

My sincerest gratitude is extended to my literary agent, Linda Konner, for believing in this project and advocating for it when others gave up hope.

To our editor, Brian Nicol—a joy to work with, who never lost his enthusiasm and always went the extra mile. So, too, our copyeditor James Fraleigh. To the entire BenBella family: Glenn Yeffeth, Adrienne Lang, Debbie Harmsen, Jessika Rieck, Vy Tran, Jennifer Canzoneri, Alicia Kania, Sarah Dombrowsky, Lindsay Marshall, Monica Lowry, and Cortney Strube. It was an enormous pleasure to feel part of such a large team that always pulled together in the same positive direction.

To my nieces Honorine Kayitengerwa and Elise Kwizera, and my nephews Remey Nshuti and Olivier Butera, thank you for all you have done in supporting me and my family during the time I was writing this book.

I would like to thank Father Jean Baptiste Mazarati and Mama Emmanuel for your prayers and support.

Above all, my deepest appreciation is reserved for my beautiful wife Marie I. Uwamariya, my son Arnauld, and my daughter Leora. Without your love and patience, in spite of all the time it took me away from you, this book would not be possible. It was a long and difficult journey for all of us.

I beg the forgiveness of all those who have been with me over the course of the years and whose names I have failed to mention.

ABOUT THE AUTHORS

EDOUARD KAYIHURA is a human rights activist and survivor of the Genocide Against the Tutsi in Rwanda, during which he was a refugee in the Hotel des Mille Collines, a.k.a. "Hotel Rwanda." Before he moved to the United States, he was the first deputy prosecutor in charge of the department of prosecutions of the crime of genocide and crimes against humanity before the Tribunal of the First Instance of Kigali. He was also an executive secretary and legal representative of Kanyarwanda Human Rights. He speaks at different schools and universities in the States about his experience, transitional justice and reconciliation, and genocide denial. He is a member of the International Association of Genocide Scholars and an International Consultant on Rule of Law and Access to Justice.

KERRY ZUKUS's debut novel, *The Fourth House*, was named a finalist for the prestigious James Jones Award, annually given to the best first novel by an American author. An alumnus of the renowned Berklee College of Music in Boston, he has authored, coauthored, or ghostwritten over forty-five fiction and nonfiction books.

INDEX